TRUE WEALTH

Paul Hwoschinsky

*with photographs by
the author*

TEN SPEED PRESS

Berkeley, California

PHOTOGRAPHS:

page v, magnolia blossoms
page xiv, Dixie National Forest, Utah
page 6, aspens, Telluride, Colorado
page 10, Poipu area of Kawai, Hawaii
page 18, Tam Serku and Kantega, Khumbu, Nepal
page 22, dandelion
page 29, Zion National Park
page 35, Death Valley National Monument
page 42, Ama Dablam, Khumbu, Nepal
page 48, lone skier, Carson Pass area, California
page 54, Precipice Lake, Mineral King, Sequoia National Park
page 61, reflection, Tuolumne Meadows area, Yosemite National
    Park
page 71, grasses at Mono Lake, California
page 78, Rolwaling Himal, Nepal
page 82, Tesi Laptsa La, Nepal
page 87, Point Reyes National Seashore, California
page 92, eyes of the Buddha, the Great Stupa at Bodhnath, Nepal
page 95, prayer flags at the Great Stupa, Nepal
page 101, great oak tree, Hornitas, California in the Sierra
    Nevada foothills
page 104, hieroglyph, Nepal
page 108, Ohmstead Point, Yosemite National Park
page 118, Icelandic poppy
page 122, Antelope Canyon, Page, Arizona
page 126, skyscraper, Oakland, California
page 137, dunes, Death Valley National Monument
page 140, river bank flowers, Grand Canyon National Park near
    Phantom Ranch
page 142, Manang, Annapurna area, Nepal
page 148, stream-driven prayer wheel, Khumbu region, Nepal
page 151, shooting stars
page 164, garden path, Denmark
page 168, fence, Ranchos de Taos, New Mexico
page 173, natural bonsai tree, high Sierra Nevada, California

☯

TEN SPEED PRESS
P.O. Box 7123
Berkeley, California 94707

Cover photograph by Paul Hwoschinsky,
    Tam Serku, Khumbu, Nepal
Cover and book design by Nancy Austin
Composition by Wilsted & Taylor

Library of Congress Cataloging-in-Publication Data

Hwoschinsky, Paul.
True wealth / Paul Hwoschinsky.
p. cm.
ISBN 0-89815-361-1
1. Finance, Personal.   2. Wealth.   3. Quality of Life.   I. Title.
HG179.H89   1990
332.024—dc20   90-31267
                                                              CIP

Printed in the United States of America

1   2   3   4   5   —   94   93   92   91   90

ACKNOWLEDGMENTS

A great many people have contributed to this book. There was the Sherpa whose question started it all. There were the ten individuals who took the first workshop that so helped me develop the concepts and make them practical. And as the book took manuscript form, there were the readers who offered constructive thoughts, among them Bob Teresi, David deWeese, Jan Boggia-Puthoff, Pat Janes, Ross Popkey, and Michael Ray. I especially want to thank Bill Howdon, who read and reread numerous versions. A financial expert, he critiqued the financial information, and his agreement with the non-financial aspects of the overall process was important confirmation of my ideas.

I wish to recognize both Carol Henderson, who was essential as an editor, and Nancy Austin, who showed great creativity with the graphics and book layout. I want to thank George Young of Ten Speed Press, who believed enough in the manuscript to want to see it as a book.

I also wish to acknowledge the importance of my exposure to, and experience of, Psychosynthesis as well as the many mentors who have helped me see life in new ways.

Finally, I want to especially thank Carol, my wife, who joined me in leading the workshops and who was so supportive during those times when I wondered if the whole thing was really worth it.

To Carol
who is my life partner, teacher, and friend
&
to our relationship, from which has come
trust, joy,
learning, and meaning.

Contents

1.   An Introduction to the True Wealth Process   1

True Wealth happens when you develop an awareness that allows you to connect who you are with what you do every day. This simply means building a bridge between your dreams and your day-to-day realities. You have the ability to attain what you want, provided you hold onto your own power and take charge of managing your financial and nonfinancial assets. The end of the True Wealth process is *empowerment*.

2.   Connections   11

Connections are the "stuff" of wealth. They are the conduit through which True Wealth flows. Everyone and everything is connected. Abundance and well-being start with the notion that financial and nonfinancial resources are meant to be joined rather than separated. Being conscious of this relationship creates a whole new bunch of options.

3.   VISION AND PURPOSE   19

But *how* do you link who you are with what you do? By becoming aware. Developing awareness is nothing more than connecting the inner and outer aspects of your life. The first step is to identify your particular vision of life—those values you feel most strongly about. Then discover whether what you do—your purpose—links with who you really are. Connecting the two gives a feeling of rightness that creates True Wealth.

4. GOALS 43

Goals represent the task list that connects vision and purpose. They are an expression of how what you do gets done. Because they are specific, have time frames for completion, and are measurable, they are of the outer world. Because they reflect who you are, completing them gives you the experience of connection.

5. RESOURCES 55

You have more than you think! Money is only one of your resources. In addition to your material belongings, you possess all of the intangible aspects of who you are—your education, health, good nature, friends, creativity, etc. These nonfinancial resources often drive the financial ones, creating whole new life options. So it is doubly important to identify them and consciously make use of them.

6. RISKS AND RISK TAKING　79

The dictionary calls risk "undefined danger," but it is just as appropriate to see it as undefined opportunity. Without risking, there is no change or growth. What you feel about something governs what you *do* about it. Many people feel fear around money matters because they separate the financial from the rest of their life and from who they are. In taking—or not taking—risks, you are again linking who you are and what you do. By becoming aware of how you feel about risk taking, you learn to connect risk with who you are, which in turn enables you to accommodate risk with less fear.

7. ADVISORS　93

Advisors can be positive if used to fill the gap in areas where you or I feel unsure. They can be disastrous if selected haphazardly and without goals and resources in mind. Both financial and nonfinancial advisors are available to offer you support. Ultimately, though, you are fully responsible for who you hire and for the rightness of their advice—which means that you must clarify your vision, purpose, and goals before you delegate tasks to someone else.

8. INVESTMENT TOOLS   109

Building anything requires tools—building a life is no exception. Tools are your means of making your dreams visible in the world. To be used to best advantage, financial and nonfinancial tools must be linked. In fact, nonfinancial tools—time, networking, awareness, information, to name just a few—may be more powerful than financial ones.

9. FINANCIAL AND NONFINANCIAL ENVIRONMENTS   123

Like everyone else, you live a connected life. You are affected by happenings near and far—in the relationships and work that make up your personal environment as well as in the politics, economics, even the weather, that shape the national and global environment. Environmental factors are often beyond an individual's control. Even when patterns seem to be emerging, random events can occur to shatter expectations. Yet in the midst of chaos there is order. The whole world is organic and, as with any organism, it reaches for balance, healing, correction. You must tune your awareness to signs of change. It isn't as hard as you might think, as long as you hold to your goals.

The Question That Began It All . . .

Late one afternoon in the Nepali Himalayas, I had a most remarkable experience. I was high up within the Annapurna Sanctuary. A true marvel of nature, it has the imposing scale of the Grand Canyon of the Colorado. Entering this place is like coming into a hidden kingdom. As one follows the glacier in and stands among the brown grasses, one sees a ring of peaks stretching twenty to twenty-five thousand feet above. It is like standing in the bottom of a giant bowl.

We had made camp at eighteen thousand feet and were relaxing in preparation for a climb the next day. The sun was setting and I was photographing the late light as it ignited the white ice into flaming colors. The views were remarkable, the peaks full of majesty. Clouds, drifting in and out, lent a soft mystery to the already mystical mountains. Every now and then there would be the crack and subsequent roar of a distant avalanche. Then, awesome quiet.

For me, the seeming emptiness of high-altitude ice offers an opportunity for introspection. When the color had gone and the peaks turned a chalk white, my Sherpa companion and guide came over to me and asked with clear intensity:

"Paul, are you rich ?"

There was something very powerful and thought-provoking in that question, for here was an inner-directed Buddhist asking a very "outer" question. In a split second, I seemed to revisit all the values I held. I was also aware that the average annual income in Nepal was $100. Then the answer came to me:

"No, I am not rich, but I am wealthy."

Suddenly I had seen the artificial separation we often create between money and the rest of our lives. Puzzlement came over the Sherpa's face at my response. Compelled by a need to explain to him—and to myself—I began to articulate the ideas and feelings that were coming to me. In a candle-lit tent in below-zero temperatures, we talked into the night. As he listened to me, I listened also, for I found that I was dealing with the core values of my life.

Disquieted by his question, I began to doubt my own wealth. Was I really wealthy, after all? How would I know?

As a result of this experience I began to assemble thoughts and feelings about money and about how money connects with wealth. I am a venture capitalist and use money as one component in creating new companies. Although many in this business feel that money is THE key, I have long known that people—and how they work with one another—are pivotal and that nonfinancial factors drive the financial ones. As I worked with these thoughts, I made a number of discoveries that are at the core of this book.

1. I learned that financial assets are often nonfinancially driven. When this insight is really experienced a whole new set of life options opens up.

2. I found that wealth has more to do with experiencing than having. "Having" is not at all bad; it simply is not "it."

3. I discovered that to have a shot at being wealthy, it is first necessary to become fully aware of who one is, in order to connect that experience with what one does. Making this connection between one's being and one's everyday activities brings a deep sense of rightness to a life. That is why people who truly love what they do seem so happy. They have made the essential connection. As this book will show, we are all capable of making this connection.

Although from my outer perch I will be offering a lot of advice in this book, I will really be asking you to go within to discover the truths lodged in yourself. In this sense, True Wealth is a thought form, as that Sherpa in Nepal helped me realize. The proof, however, is in the practice of it. This book is about the process of developing awareness in order to connect who you are with what you do, so that the more appropriate life options will emerge and your life will be more meaningful for you. The inner and the outer must be joined. All of us need to be whole, and it takes wholeness to be fully alive.

This process will be empowering. It will also be nuts and bolts practical because to work, it must address not only the joys of life but also how to exist in the nitty-gritty world of bills, illness, and stress. In effect, you will learn how to "be in this world without being of it."

*True Wealth is a continuing process of
consciously becoming who we already are.*

1

AN INTRODUCTION
TO THE
TRUE WEALTH PROCESS

We live in a time of great uncertainty and rapid change. Earlier it was possible to feel secure about job and family, to quietly save for a home, invest in education, and work hard to enjoy some of the material things that are a part of the American dream.

Today everything is different. Jobs are no longer secure as whole industries come and go in the face of international competition. Many of us will have five or six jobs before we retire. Layoffs, inflation, deflation, recession, boom, and large fluctuations in interest rates can all take place in a matter of a few years. Moreover, parts of our country can be in boom while others are in depression. Debt levels are frighteningly high. We are also beginning to feel the effects of diminishing natural resources and of the damage to the environment caused by air, water, and waste pollution.

In our personal lives, too, the picture has changed. Due in part to inflation, in many families both spouses work just to meet expenses and perhaps save for a home. Increasingly, uncertainties and hardships result from divorce and single parenting. Relationships tend to be successive rather than enduring. As more women enter the work force, they find new freedoms as well as job-related stress. As children move away to find work, the comfort and ties of the extended family are disappearing.

In the midst of all this, value systems vary widely. While some people purchase consumer goods at increasing rates, others are starting to seek a higher quality of life. With so many changes affecting us personally, we ask many questions:

- How can I make ends meet?
- How can I plan in times such as these?
- What do I really want from life? What values are important to me?
- How do I reconcile these values with the demands of earning a living?
- How can I save anymore?

- How can I make investment choices when I look out there and it is all a blur?

A New Path to Well-Being

Since some of the old answers don't seem to work anymore, I want to offer a new tool, one that I've called True Wealth. It is based on connecting who you are with what you do. Making this connection means finding ways to integrate your fondest vision of what your life could be like and all the hard issues people face every day: paying bills, doing a job, raising children, working through relationships.

In this book I ask you to think of money in a new light. All too often we experience a separation between money and the rest of our lives. In the True Wealth philosophy, money is just one part of the total system that produces a feeling of well-being. **The challenge is earning money to live life rather than living to earn money.**

The starting point in the True Wealth process is to connect inner hopes and dreams with the outer world. Abundance and well-being begin with the recognition that financial and nonfinancial resources are meant to be combined rather than unnaturally separated. Seeing the links between these two realms is the key that unlocks new options.

This book is about finding your own path to True Wealth. In this way, what you discover will be fully appropriate. My aim is to help you to determine what your life is about and to connect this information with your everyday activities. In fact, it is only after you have linked who you are with what you do—connected your vision and values with specific life goals—that you will have a proper context for choosing appropriate financial and nonfinancial investments that generate well-being. In a real sense, bringing all of the facets of your life together is probably the most important "investment process" you will ever embark on.

During the first part of this process you will be striving for awareness—of who you are (what I call vision) and whether this finds expression in what you do (your purpose). You will discover all the many resources—financial and nonfinancial—at your disposal to enable you to act in harmony with who you are. This is the inner-looking part of the process.

The rest of the process takes place in the outer world. You will identify advisors who can help you progress toward goals you have selected. You will explore financial and nonfinancial tools and learn about factors that have to be considered in deciding among various actions.

Finally, you will integrate all of the knowledge you have gained into a life plan.

You can see the whole system approach in the accompanying Investment Process map. All through the book I will be referring to this map. It will help keep the connections clear. Most important, though, is for you to use the map in whatever way you see fit. Just plug into the system at any point, but know that the way to optimize well-being is to work with the process from start to finish.

How True Wealth Concepts Can Change Lives— A Few Examples

A LONG-TIME SCHOOLTEACHER MAKING A CAREER CHANGE

A single woman, she taught in a public high school for over thirty-five years. During this time her job became more and more demanding. Few students would really study, and parents expected teachers to parent and impose discipline as well as teach. Her own highest value, learning, was

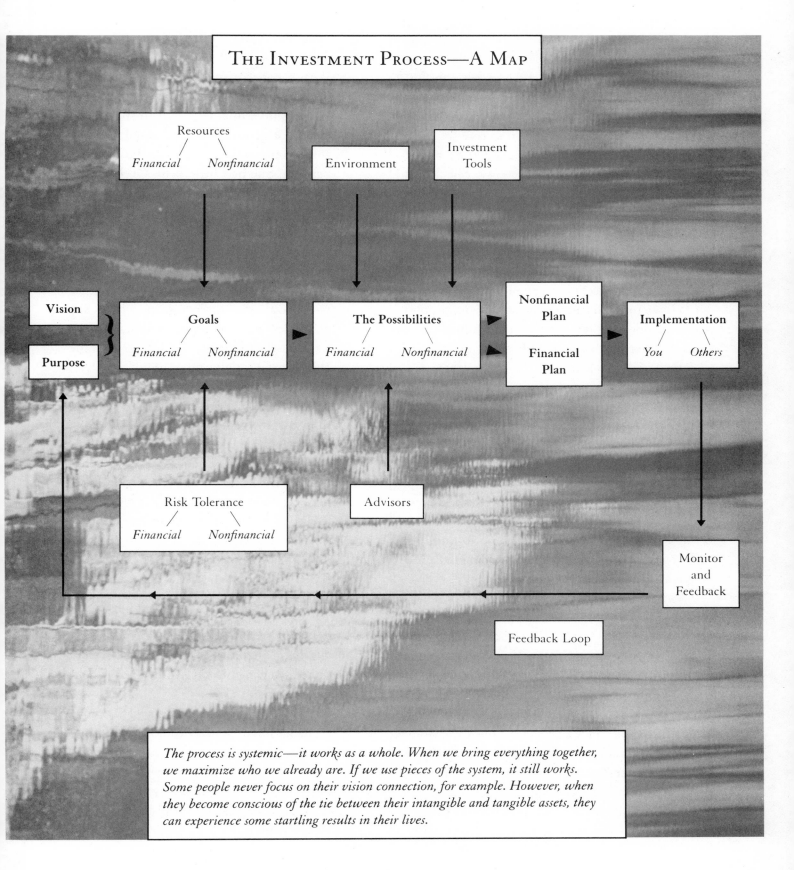

THE INVESTMENT PROCESS—A MAP

Resources

Financial / *Nonfinancial*

Environment

Investment
Tools

Vision

Purpose

Goals

Financial / *Nonfinancial*

The Possibilities

Financial / *Nonfinancial*

Nonfinancial
Plan

Financial
Plan

Implementation

You / *Others*

Risk Tolerance

Financial / *Nonfinancial*

Advisors

Monitor
and
Feedback

Feedback Loop

The process is systemic—it works as a whole. When we bring everything together, we maximize who we already are. If we use pieces of the system, it still works. Some people never focus on their vision connection, for example. However, when they become conscious of the tie between their intangible and tangible assets, they can experience some startling results in their lives.

not valued by the community or the students. Typically, when one's values are in conflict with one's work, stress results, and she felt constant stress. Eventually she experienced burnout.

She did not have independent wealth. On the other hand, she had no children to care for or to put through school. Still, meeting bills on a public schoolteacher's salary was not easy. She knew nothing about financial planning and little about investing.

At the same time, she was finding great satisfaction in doing volunteer work for a local foundation that organized people-to-people trips to the USSR. The idea was to ease international tensions by helping the American and Soviet peoples to know one another. She saw the positive effect these exchanges had on both sides, as barriers dropped and people began to communicate.

In effect, she saw special meaning in this "peace work." It represented values and a vision she held as important. But above all, it represented a way to connect who she was with what she did—a True Wealth concept. Teaching no longer fulfilled that role.

Thus her question was, "How can someone like me, without independent income, make a job switch from one that earns income to one that offers no financial return but that does offer me a way to fully express who I am?"

This is how she did it.

1. She began by acknowledging that her peace work truly validated her value system. She noted that when she was active in this work, she became more alive. In connecting who she was with what she did, she was following the first True Wealth principle, on which all the others are based.

2. She set about really looking at *all* of the resources immediately available to her, nonfinancial as well as financial. This meant drawing up a nonfinancial balance sheet as well as the usual financial one. The insight that most of our financial assets are nonfinancially derived is another True Wealth concept that she put to good use. On the financial side, she had a house, a car, and investments on which she earned a modest return. She discovered that she could retire early and start to draw on her pension. She had little debt. On her nonfinancial balance sheet, she listed health, personal motivation to do something about changing her life, and a great many friends who acted as a support group. She also noted education, a successful teaching career, and the sure knowledge that peace work was the direction in which she wanted to go. It was these nonfinancial assets that were to make the difference in the changes she sought in her life.

3. She examined the level of risk she was willing to take. She did this by becoming fully aware of how comfortable, or uncomfortable, she felt with various options. In other words, she concentrated on what risking feels like versus what it "thinks" like. Exploring risk at this gut level helps to diffuse the fear that can make it impossible to act. Again, she was following the True Wealth approach.

4. Based on the qualities of peace and love that most expressed who she was, she made a list of financial and nonfinancial goals, the *doing* of which would be an expression of these qualities for her. They were linked. It was this conscious tie that held the excitement.

5. She then sought out the financial and nonfinancial advisors who could help her assess the options open to her. From her nonfinancial balance sheet, she saw that she had resources—friends and contacts through friends—who could be immediately useful.

6. From these sources she got an understanding of the financial tools available to her. She looked at what early retirement would yield. She also saw her house as an earning asset that could be leased to one or two boarders. She plugged all of this into a financial plan, and . . .

7. She found that she could generate enough income to start working full-time with the foundation. Not long after that, she became a group leader and thus her trips abroad were paid.

The bottom line?

She is now **doing something that ties who she is with what she does.** Although she works hard, she experiences much less stress. Her values are manifested in her work and she is supporting herself to boot. She has financial and nonfinancial plans that are appropriate to her needs. She knows where she is and where she is going.

In line with the Investment Process map on page 3, this teacher related her life vision (peace) to what she does (work with the foundation) by bringing all of her resources, including the nonfinancial ones, to bear upon goals she had selected to help her realize her vision. By linking all of these parts in a system, she was able to develop a plan that expressed how she could do what she wanted, even with a modest financial net worth. When she saw this, she made the move, confident of the rightness of it.

AN ENTREPRENEUR WHO RETIRED FOR A WHILE

A middle-aged businessman who had started his own company had done very well. He drove good cars and lived in a nice neighborhood. He was not outrageously rich, but he woke up one day and realized he had enough to retire on. He did just that. He hired a manager to run his business and became, in his words, a house husband.

At the outset his new life seemed fine. He got up late, had breakfast with his wife and children, and did all the chores he had not had time for when he worked all day. Soon, however, boredom set in. He had free time to do things, but his friends, all of whom were still working, did not. He began to feel anxious. He missed the routine, the challenges, the deadlines, the human contacts that he had taken for granted.

When I met him, he was looking for a business start-up in which to invest and work. He had come to realize that his money was only a medium. It wasn't money he was seeking, since he already had enough to live comfortably. Rather, he sought well-being through work—the intangible part of wealth. Although he was not sure exactly what qualities he was seeking, he knew that work brought him in close proximity to them and consequently he felt better when he worked. His solution was to return to work for "more of the same."

What might he have done to make his experience more meaningful?

Had he spent time identifying the qualities his work brought to him—creativity, challenge, connection to people—he might have been more directed in his search for a new business. Probably he would not have retired in the first place. Having done so, however, he could have used the time to become conscious of what it was he missed when he wasn't working. This would have been a True Wealth approach, enabling him to link who he was with what he did. The awareness of that single connection makes all the difference.

A YOUNG FAMILY LOOKING AT THE PRESENT AND THE FUTURE

Recently married, both partners have master's degrees and are interns working toward getting counseling licenses. Neither has independent wealth, although the wife has a small amount of savings.

Their chosen field is not a lucrative one, and their wages as interns are so low that they spend about what they earn. Many of their friends in business drive BMWs, own homes, and take luxury vacations. From their rented apartment, the two of them look over the fence and often the grass does look "money greener" on the other side. Still, they have many interests and, when they think about it, some assets too. Their health is good, and they maintain a high level of physical function by exercising regularly. On wilderness treks they have backpacked several hundred miles together. At home they save money by doing repairs themselves and performing routine maintenance on their old cars. They have a lot of fun on very little.

They have been thinking about the future lately because they are expecting their first child. Also, their licensing exams come up soon, and the husband is busy completing his second master's degree.

How can True Wealth ideas help them?

Both share the goal of being supportive to others through their work as therapists. Their life vision therefore has to do with service. In addition, both want a sense of freedom, something they find on their walks in the wilderness. As counselors in private practice they are independent business people and thus experience freedom and self-determination in their work as well. They have consciously chosen work that connects who they are (service and freedom) with what they do (counseling). As a result, they enjoy a sense of rightness about their work that helps confirm their direction and provides a quality of calm in a world that is often frantic. This calm, in turn, helps their clients.

When they review their situation, they can count good health, education, their love for each

other, friends, and contacts in the business world among their intangible resources. But where is the tie to money in all this? It is in their access to financial advice. They have a source who advised them what stock fund to buy and when to sell it. Their money rode the bull market up to more than two and a half times its original value in the mid-eighties. Then in August 1987 they were advised to sell. As it turned out, they hit the very top of the market rise and were in government reserves when the Dow dropped over 500 points in October of that same year. While others lost, this couple held on to all their gains.

Each of them has an individual retirement plan. When they married, however, their advisor asked them to consider not investing further in these restricted tax shelters but instead to save in fully taxable—and thus fully flexible—instruments that could be drawn on to buy a home at an appropriate time.

For this young family, then, the relationship with a financial advisor—a clearly nonfinancial resource—has paid off handsomely, even though their financial balance sheet may not be impressive at the moment. Using the True Wealth system approach, they are starting to develop a life plan in which the interconnected elements work much more powerfully together than they would as discrete parts. It is the old idea of $1 + 1 = 3$, where the whole is greater than the sum of the parts.

A RETIRED COUPLE REEXAMINING LIFE VALUES AND LOOKING FOR NEW ACTIVITIES

This is a couple in their late sixties with two children and three grandchildren. They own a home in the suburbs. He is retired from a middle-management position and she is a retired hospital administrator. Both receive pensions plus social security. For the moment their income is sufficient to meet their requirements. They have few needs, their children are well on their own, the cars are paid for, and they are in reasonable health.

How should they apply the True Wealth process?

Like anyone else, they will start by identifying their vision, purpose, and goals. Once they are clear on these, the task will be to gather their financial and nonfinancial resources and bring them to bear on achieving their goals.

Retirement represents a major life transition. It is an ideal time to reexamine vision and purpose and get in touch with the values that seem to matter at this stage. The wonderful part of retirement is that it provides a chance to express one's personal qualities in totally new forms. A retired counselor no longer needs to counsel to be of service. This can now be done through volunteer

work. Or something can be chosen that one always wanted to do but never had time for, such as expressing beauty through flower arranging, art, photography, or some other form. The point is that it is possible to look again at purpose and to select an activity in the light of who one is at this stage in life, without the constraints of also having to earn a living in the "doing" part.

In this couple, the wife is looking for a new way to continue to show her quality of service. She is considering starting a company to teach preschoolers how to learn through play. This move would represent a whole new career, one in which her husband could join by contributing his business expertise. He may choose instead, though, to bring his skills to bear on helping ghetto businesses through some difficult times.

Now, where do they go from here?

Having clarified their vision, purpose, and goals, this retired couple should consider the resources available to them with which they can act. Financially, all of their core needs are taken care of. They have no debt, and in addition to their retirement income they receive a modest amount from an investment account. Nonfinancially, they have education, many friends, and no major health concerns. Neither smokes anymore. Both, however, have occasional back trouble and are a mite overweight. They talk about the need to exercise beyond the odd game of golf. These are nonfinancial liabilities that they will want to keep an eye on, with the goal of eventually turning them into something positive.

Each has developed hobbies over the past twenty years, which means they have healthy interests and are creative. But what about their relationship with one another and others? We do not know the answer to this vital nonfinancial question, but they do. It is an important resource or liability. If it is the latter, and if they both want to do something about it, they have the other resources (money, time, and drive) to act on their desire for change.

What they decide to do doesn't really matter. The important thing is to do something specific that symbolizes who they are. This is what limits stress and brings peace.

What is really happening in all of these cases?

The individuals in these examples have experienced the knowledge that **nothing really happens that is not in relation to the whole**. All of the pieces in a life, a business, or whatever, work together as a system, as the Investment Process map suggests. Because each of us emphasizes some elements more than others, our individual cases appear to be unique. In fact, we all belong to the very same system, which is constantly reaching to unite all pieces into an organized whole.

The Purpose of the True Wealth Approach

The aim of this book is to create opportunities for those who want to participate in a systems view of their situation. All of us waste a lot of our assets because either we fail to recognize them as valuable or we don't see a link between two or more assets that could create wealth. Individual assets may have little value, but when connected to one another they can create forward motion and be catalysts for change. For example, you may have a friend whom you enjoy meeting for coffee occasionally. One day you realize that the friend has a skill that relates to a business need of yours. The friend helps you turn a problem into an option.

By relating your assets and liabilities to your visions and goals, you start the process of creating options. Look again at the Investment Process map on page 3 and start to think about your own situation within this context. You will begin to see both assets and liabilities as resources. I recall the young woman who suddenly saw her bad back as an asset. Instead of a liability it became a stimulus for focusing on health generally, encouraging her to learn a lot about diet, exercise, vitamins, and the like. Without the back pain, she would not have found that emphasis. As we all discover at one time or another, we can learn a lot about health within a context of illness. Similarly, we can discover a lot about financial assets within the context of our financial liabilities. There is just no apparent limit to the creativity within each of us once we link *all* of who we are with what we really want to do.

How to Get the Most Out of the Process

This book is a guide. It points out a new way to view life. However, it works best if you participate. To actively bring yourself to the process, you will need to create an awareness about yourself. This is the purpose of the exercises—to help you become aware so that you can link all the scattered bits and pieces of your life. You can learn by just reading the text, but you stand to gain much more if you invest the time and thought to complete the exercises.

Wonderful things happen when people connect seemingly unrelated aspects of their lives. It is like organizing a garage or storeroom. Suddenly you can find things you need and chuck the rest. The organization allows you to tap resources you could not put your hands on before.

You will come to see that miracles are not so miraculous. What seems miraculous is simply the association of who you are with what you do.

This linkage creates the insights that will allow you to take off. It is like finding the yeast that "grows" the bread.

I am reminded of the metaphor of the woven piece of cloth. Although each thread is not necessarily touching all the others, the threads are so interwoven that a real connection exists. Tug on any single thread and the whole piece of cloth is affected.

These same linkages exist in our lives. We, too, are like the woven fabric. Our health affects our work and vice versa. A boring, unfulfilling job can create illness. A rewarding job, connected to who we are, can be energizing and can draw out creativity we hardly knew we had. This, in turn, brings success. As John Muir observed, "Every time I pull up a wild flower, I find it connected to the universe."

The connections between who we are
and what we do
are the conduits through which
True Wealth flows.

2

CONNECTIONS

Real empowerment begins with awareness—of both self and the surrounding world. It comes from knowing who you already are and then acting on that knowledge. Your awareness is the basis for being able to experience the links that create power.

Empowerment has more to do with feeling than understanding. It is an inner force—the engine within. Being aware of all the inner and outer connections in a life creates the conduits through which True Wealth can flow.

Making Connections Leads to Change—Two Examples

For years Anne referred to her back as "bad." It caused her pain and prevented her from doing many active things like backpacking, running, and skydiving. Although she was only in her forties, she felt very fragile. Then she had an insight: she realized that we get most in touch with health in the context of illness. Both conditions are a part of the whole. To fully experience either one of them requires an acknowledgment of the other. It is like the dark shadows in a black and white photograph; without the shadows, light cannot even be seen.

Having become aware of the essential connection between illness and health, Anne knew there was a bridge back to health. She sought people who could help with physical therapy. She began doing yoga, meditation to reduce stress, and lots of exploring of her own awareness of herself. She now backpacks, and she refers to her back as "good" because its pain led her to new health.

A friend of mine provides the second example. He came to me looking for a job. He had been fired and was feeling low. I suggested that we explore his nonfinancial resources and asked him to list all his intangible assets as a way to determine how we might proceed. He was puzzled but agreed. Together we were able to note a number of well-placed friends whose contacts allowed him to get several consulting jobs. Those first few assignments developed into a thriving consulting business in his engineering area of interest.

In effect, he used a connection between his intangible, or nonfinancial, resources and his financial need. Previously he had treated money issues as unconnected to the rest of who he was or what he intangibly had.

We Are a Part of, NOT Apart From

We are already a whole. We have only to experience it. Like a piece of woven cloth, each of our lives is made up of many threads. Money is just one of the threads. Others can be love, education, family, friends/enemies, health/illness, hobbies, skills, creativity, pain, an up or down disposition, etc. The list is endless. While each thread may not touch every other thread, all the threads are inextricably associated in a very integrative way. Tug on any thread, and the others feel it and are affected by it. So it is with our lives. We tend to see money as separate and to ignore its connection to health, love, and creativity, when actually all of these aspects are linked as a part of who we are. When we experience this connection, we can become who we are—which is the basis for True Wealth.

Because our lives are woven of many threads, the connections are varied and exist at many different levels. Our jobs are linked to who we are. Our relationships obviously are. Moreover, our financial assets are really nonfinancially derived and thus are closely connected to who we are. This insight alone can spawn many new life options.

Since action follows thought (what we envision tends to be what happens), our very thoughts are directly linked to what happens to us. Our fears can actually bring upon us that which we fear most. Those who are afraid to drive often tend to have accidents.

The essential thing is to become aware of the wholeness that is with us right now. Become fully conscious, and stay with every fiber of this awareness.

When I teach photography, I have participants gather at the outdoor site where we go to take pictures. I ask them to sit comfortably and close their eyes. I then ask them to become aware of their breath, and thus of their living process. This enables them to really listen to the sounds they are conscious of hearing—cars, the ocean, birds, their own breathing, someone's cough, wind in the trees. Next I ask them to become aware of what they are feeling—their fannies against the ground, a twitch on their face, a tickle on their foot. I then switch to what they smell— a salt sea breeze, newly cut grass, or the fragrance of flowers.

After a level of awareness has been redeveloped, we all open our eyes and consider the photographic options around us. We find many more than we had imagined at first. We can now photograph the "smell" of a sea breeze or the fury and strength of wind. We create great images because we first created fine inner imagery. After all, photography is nothing more than linking the inner and outer anyway. A photograph of a grandchild, for example, is an "outer" expression of one's "inner" feelings for the child.

My point is that we must **connect our inner awareness of ourselves with the outer world in which we act and work.** When we accomplish this, we have a sense of doing the thing most appropriate for us. It is automatically correct because it is linked to who we really are.

Multilevel connecting is nothing more than a process of becoming.

A metaphor from the computer industry will help demonstrate the value of connection. Until very recently, individual computer companies worked separately to develop increasingly powerful machines, each one operating according to software instructions peculiar to that brand of computer. Now the computer buying market is seeing the value (and thus vendors are facing the task) of connecting different brands of computers in order to achieve a more powerful level of communication and integration. The growing awareness of the usefulness of computers in the work place has taught that those designed competitively to be incompatible with one another must now be linked in order to be competitive! When connection is achieved, when all the machines can talk to one another, a tremendous surge in productive power will result.

Similarly, True Wealth suggests that a new level of awareness will link parts of our lives inwardly and outwardly to trigger a similar surge in productivity and well-being—inwardly by connecting who we are with what we do, and outwardly by linking our financial and nonfinancial resources with other people and activities as a way to achieve our vision, purpose, and goals.

In a way, this process can be conceptualized as a linkup between humans analogous to the one between computers. However, because we are dealing with human beings, with all the depth and power of human intuition and spirit, the energy release will be infinitely more powerful.

The Ultimate Connection— Linking Who We Are with What We Do

To connect who you are with what you do, you must first explore who you are. But what does this really mean?

It means identifying with something that you feel particularly strongly about. I call these "somethings" life qualities. Examples are love,

beauty, wisdom, order, faith, freedom, and light—all superior characteristics of life. The qualities that are important to you help define your "vision" of life, that is, who you are. In the next chapter we will explore life qualities and vision at length, and find ways to uncover the qualities with which you feel a real tie. The key word is *feel*. This is not something you think about. It is something you already know and need only rediscover.

Suppose that a friend wants to reflect the quality of beauty in his life in such a way that his life vision might eventually be summarized by a single line on his tombstone reading "He Was Beauty." How might he do this?

The possibilities are endless. There is beauty in art; he could become a photographer or a sculptor. There is beauty in sound; he could write music, sing, design lovely bells, or build violins. Beauty can also be expressed in words, poems for instance; perhaps our friend should consider writing. There is beauty in form; he could become a furniture or industrial designer. There is also beauty in motion, expressed in classical ballet, the dance, or athletics. On a less literal plane, our friend could express beauty as a member of a hospice by helping those in the dying process. In fact, he could be a street cleaner and express the quality of beauty by bringing beauty to the city.

What ideas does this evoke in you? As I looked at these possibilities, I came to the conclusion that the form the job takes doesn't really matter. What matters is seeing, choosing, and experiencing the tie to the quality the job represents—in this instance, beauty. The power is in the connection.

Let's consider street sweeping as the job of choice. If any of us had such a job and approached it in the typical way, without seeing any connection to a quality such as beauty, we would probably feel lowly or unimportant. But what would happen if we looked at the task in the context of

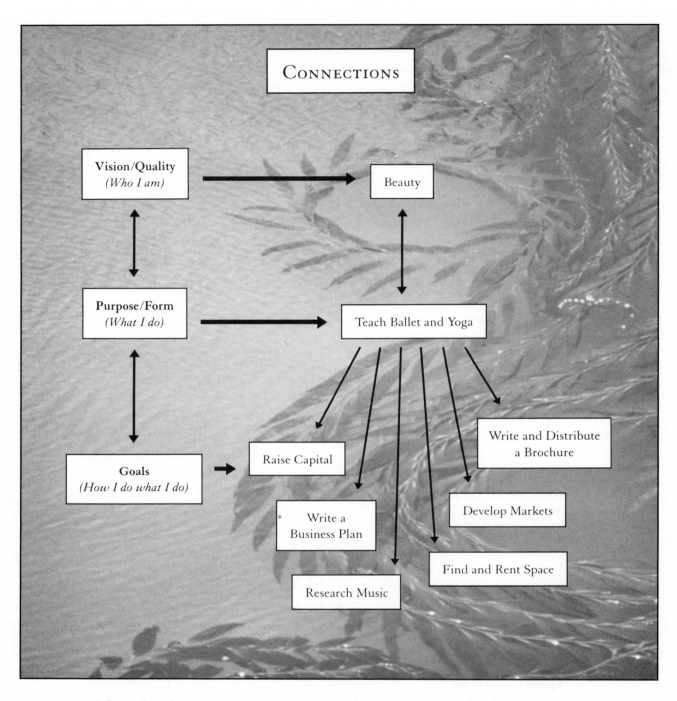

CONNECTIONS

Vision/Quality
(Who I am)

Beauty

Purpose/Form
(What I do)

Teach Ballet and Yoga

Goals
(How I do what I do)

Raise Capital

Write and Distribute
a Brochure

Write a
Business Plan

Develop Markets

Find and Rent Space

Research Music

expressing a life quality that was important to us? Suddenly, because of the connection with beauty, the job would take on importance. It would be elevated. We could hold our heads high as we performed it. Moreover, the work would be especially well done because we would consciously be associating the task of sweeping and the qual-

ity it represented—that is, making the city beautiful.

It is this conscious connection with a life quality that brings wealth. In fact, wealth seems to be something we experience more than possess. The Connections map expresses this idea graphically, elaborating on the vision-purpose-goal progression of the Investment Process map in chapter 1, but now within the context of connection. In the case illustrated here, a person chooses to express her vision, beauty, through a business of teaching ballet and yoga (purpose), and she develops specific goals to make it all happen.

Notice all the functions undertaken at the goal level. Typically, most of us live at this level of detail. We become very focused on marketing, locating space, and developing a curriculum for our classes. We collect financial resources and recognize risks, some of which we protect against with insurance. We hire advisors and study the market. We do a business plan. Maybe we raise venture funding for the business. We become outwardly very busy.

In other words, we tend to start our lives with goals and to bypass the guiding and inner-directed vision and purpose.

We often fail to experience the link between an activity like teaching ballet and yoga and the quality of beauty that it represents. We see our work as (in this case) teaching, when our true concern is expressing beauty in our life. Were we to experience this link, we would gain opportunities to manifest beauty in all the other aspects of our life as well, such as raising a family or nurturing the many contacts we have with others. We would receive a more rewarding by-product!

Jim Nicholson of the *Philadelphia Daily News* is an example of someone who has made the connection. In listening to him on a radio talk show, I was struck by a strong sense of rightness in what he was doing. He writes obituaries for the paper.

His profession seemed a bit grim to me at first. However, as I listened, I understood why he has become well known for the way in which he does his work. He brings both humanness and creativity to his subject. He digs well below the surface facts of a person's life to get at the elements of humanity in each individual. Moreover, he does all of his research by phone with relatives.

MAKING A CONSCIOUS CONNECTION WITH A QUALITY

Nicholas Roerich, the Russian painter who was nominated for the Nobel Peace Prize in 1929, is a perfect example of one whose work was deeply connected to who he was. From the start, he felt a link to beauty. He wrote, "In Beauty we are united, through Beauty we pray, with Beauty we conquer."* Throughout his life, he *was* beauty—and he knew it.

*In *Nicholas Roerich*, by Jacqueline Decter. Copyright © Nicholas Roerich Museum, published by Park Street Press, Rochester VT 05767.

His column is so filled with life stories that hold meaning that ministers forge whole sermons around them. Surviving family members have been known to clip the obit and paste it into their family Bibles. He is in demand to write obituaries from callers all over the country.

Why is he so successful? Because he has linked who he is (a creative humanitarian) with what he does (write obituaries).

Whenever any of us does the same, our day-to-day life seems to be more productive and to have less stress. We obtain a sense of well-being, or wealth. That is why there is such an emphasis in this book on becoming aware of who we are and what qualities represent our core strength. For people who make the connection, work takes on a joyousness that replaces drudgery. By contrast, those who are unconscious of the link can be financially successful and yet feel an emptiness in their lives.

We tend to segment our lives. As business people, for example, we are usually obsessed with the bottom line. We look at market share, competition, cost containment, quality-control issues, and all the other things that affect profit margins. In our intimate contacts with spouses, on the other hand, we express compassion and love. When we walk in the woods or along a beach, meditate, or listen quietly to great music, we become inner-directed. In this way we "divide and conquer" isolated segments of our lives but fail to address the whole. When we connect with the qualities that are important to us—which make us who we are—we are able to combine instead of separate all these aspects and thus are more nearly able "to be in the world without being of it." By joining our inner and outer selves, we bring our life qualities all the way through into our everyday lives.

Connecting the Financial and Nonfinancial Aspects of Life—An Example

A businessman I know was fired from his job. He was despondent; he felt that his record was irrevocably harmed. We talked for some time about what he sought in life. From that line of intuitive exploring, he began to get some sense of his worth and his values.

I asked him to make a financial and a nonfinancial balance sheet. The first came easily, but the second was a new idea to him. I explained that it comprised all of those assets—and liabilities—in his life that couldn't be labeled with a price tag.

His first item on the nonfinancial balance sheet was health. He felt well and had nearly always enjoyed good health. Nonetheless, he felt he could improve his health habits. He acknowledged that his lack of exercise was not a plus. In saying that, he was starting to value an asset

(health) that he had previously taken for granted. He connected with a nonfinancial asset, and making that connection resulted in a resolve to do something—exercise—that would lead to more well-being.

He next acknowledged that his family was an important asset and that he valued his relationships with extended family as well. Probably because he was between jobs and was at home all the time, he found himself especially aware of family as an asset. So this acknowledgment linked an unhappy event (being fired) with an ability to see special value in family. The connection heightened his sense of well-being.

At that point he drew a blank. When I suggested that his education might be valued as well, he agreed. I asked him about listing friends as a category of asset. Once more he looked puzzled. How could friends be of value in the present situation? Further, he said, he didn't really have any friends he felt he could call on. I asked if perhaps I could be counted as one; after all, he had come to me for help. Perhaps I was of value.

I began a list of all my business contacts who might help him get another job. The links I noted surprised even me, as potential leads came to mind that I had forgotten about. Looking at this list sparked new ideas from him. He began to regain confidence as he remembered others who could help. Eventually, by contacting friends (nonfinancial assets), he was led to work (a financial asset) that was better than his former situation. He became a very successful consultant in his specialization.

This result came about after he connected with the value of his intangible strengths, which had been there all along. He simply began to see, value, and link them in a new way, relating them to his task of new employment. He began to experience that his financial resources were nonfinancially driven. His contacts with friends had a real impact on his ability to find work.

Connections as an Important Source of Motivation

All of us make purchases. Some are small ones like daily food; others are much larger, like buying education, a home, or a car. Is there any relationship between these purchases and the values we hold? Definitely!

Some people buy food only because they're hungry; they may select certain items simply because they like the taste. Food is just food to them. Others, seeing a link between food and health, choose more carefully. For the first type of person, giving up a certain food or eating habit is difficult, while for the second, it has the specific purpose of promoting health and is therefore easier. The motivation is stronger because of the connection to a life quality—health.

Or consider a car purchase. What are we really buying when we purchase a car? The person who buys a modest car is probably buying transportation. Someone who buys a costly one is buying more than that, perhaps prestige or quality. Does it matter?

Judgment is not at issue here; it is neither good nor bad to buy an expensive item. The task in making a purchase is to recognize the connection between what is being bought and the value or life quality it may represent. Buying a car to keep up with the Joneses is simply not as powerful as buying one because it connects to a value held as important. For some—teenagers, for instance—the purchase of a car represents freedom. For others, the ability to drive to the wilderness could represent a reach for peace or beauty. When motivation is associated with a life quality, there is more meaning to the purchase and hence a sense of well-being.

Similarly, one can travel for education and learning, or one can go because others are "doing Europe" this year. Our son saved for two years in order to travel around the world. His travel represented his need to experience other peoples because he felt a connection with all human beings. Although it took all of his money, it was meaningful because it brought him closer to his value of wanting to be at peace with the world. He connected education, travel, and brotherhood. His experiences—and the memories he returned with—were thus different from those of the person whose travel is unmotivated by the pursuit of a life quality.

Another example from education: We have all seen students who are in college simply because it is the thing to do at their age in their socioeconomic group. We have also seen highly motivated students who hold a dream of entering a certain profession. They work during the day to earn money for night school. The long hours seem manageable because the education is clearly related to a dream. It is the connection that provides the motivation.

———

The potential for links between events and things abounds. We are presented with options all the time. Some allow us to connect with ourselves; others offer opportunities to relate to things and other people. The idea is simply to spot the possibilities that interact with one another and then to tie them back into our values or vision—and to let the other options go. Doing this takes a conscious effort.

This book includes a series of steps that will aid in bringing the process of connection to a fully conscious level—the level at which we can act and initiate change.

What comes to mind comes to pass.

3

VISION AND PURPOSE

All of us hold visions. Perhaps we call them dreams. Their essence is a sense or an image of what *could be*. These images are stored within us, and although we may not visit these inner places very often, they exist and we can reach them. They are at the core of who we are able to become. In them we can find information that is vital to our lives.

Visions are important because action follows thought. Very often our dreams, hopes, and fears do materialize. Someone who fears losing a valued object, a diamond ring for instance, often ends up misplacing it. Conversely, someone who holds a dream of doing something and really wants to do it is apt to fulfill that dream.

Mountains are climbed by people who see themselves on the summit long before they start the ascent. People with cancer have gone into remission through the process of visualization. Many discoveries and inventions have followed from visualization. I recall a software engineer saying that he "saw" electrons rushing through silicon chips when he was designing break-

through software packages. I also recall a computer salesman recounting how he envisioned his customer signing the purchase order long before the deal for a multimillion-dollar computer system was completed.

The best golfers see the ball land on the green long before they actually swing. Witness Jack Nicklaus, who said,

> I never hit the shot, not even in practice, without having a very sharp, in-focus picture of it in my head. It's like a color movie. First I "see" the ball where I want it to finish, nice and white and sitting up high on the bright green grass. Then the scene quickly changes and I "see" the ball going there—its path, trajectory, and shape, even its behavior on landing. Then there is a sort of fade-out and the next scene shows me making the kind of swing that will turn the previous images into reality.

There are many such stories. All of us visualize every day, although we may not be aware of it. The stories of how successful people use vision to succeed are well publicized. However, people who fail also visualize; they have visions of failure. Often we are unaware of our negative programming.

In short, visions hold power. That is why the True Wealth process starts with vision. When we make decisions and moves within the context of our conscious vision, we have a sense of achieving something that is right for us. All of us either express or do not express our visions or dreams in our everyday life. It is when we don't that the problems arise. The necessary complement of vision is *purpose*—what we do. Expressing who we are—our vision—through what we do—our purpose—is all-important in bestowing a sense of well-being.

This chapter will help you answer the question "Who am I?" based on an identification of your vision. Self-awareness is the foundation for everything else in this book. The final step in this chapter will be to determine whether what you do really connects with who you are. Are you following the right purpose in your life?

Responding to Life Challenges That Shake Us Up and Make Us Ask, "Who Am I?"

As we go through life, we all take care of the necessities first—clothing, housing, food, sex, our jobs, health/illness, family and other key relationships. These are the things that affect us most directly on a material and physical level at any given point in time.

For most of us, this emphasis *seems* to work for a while. Then, as we pass beyond the survival level, we start to feel safer and more successful. We continue to pursue material success because it appears to work, and we collect things that make us feel more successful. Our cars become bigger

and our homes are better located. We move up in our jobs. Everything appears to be going well.

We begin to feel supported by the things around us. The sight of others following the same course confirms us in our process. In fact, we see others who are more successful than ourselves as role models. The outer-directed side of our culture seems to be the primary force in our lives.

Eventually, though, a time comes when we start to wonder and to see things differently. As a result of business crises, illness, accident, a death in the family, the breakup of a key relationship, or even a hike on the beach, we begin to reflect on life values. Such moments are jarring and present us with opportunities to look deeply within ourselves. We ask questions: What is death/life? What is evil and how do I deal with it? More specifically we might ask, Why am I not being promoted? How do I deal with my own competitiveness? Are people out to get me? How do I make the most of who I am? Why did I have this accident or illness? All of these questions represent the beginning of a search for *meanings*—a search that will take us well beyond our personal selves.

We may find, though, that no one really has suitable answers. This is when we are obliged to look to ourselves for answers.

In this introspection there is both pain and joy. Without fully realizing that we are looking at values, we experience regrets:

- Why didn't I spend more time with my children?
- Why did I not help my friend after his car accident?
- What could I have done to prevent my divorce?
- Why didn't I give up smoking, alcohol, drugs?

At the same time we feel joy and thankfulness:

- I have raised fine children.
- I live my life with honesty.

- I am glad I spent time hiking in the mountains.
- I truly value my marriage.

In the course of our introspection we return to earlier dreams of what could be. We start to hold a vision about our lives and to look at it deeply. This is the beginning of the process of rediscovering who we are.

The following pages contain exercises designed to help you explore who you really are. Some deal with your present life; others will examine goals from a standpoint in the future. You will probably find one or two exercises more helpful than the others because they will trigger insights. Do them all, though, and collect your thoughts and feelings at the end. The process is really a simple one. It entails bringing your dreams, values, and vision of yourself to the surface so that you can relate them to your day-to-day activities and in this way give your life a more meaningful context. Put another way, you will simply be getting back in touch with what has been there all along—a realization of who you really are.

❧EXERCISE
FINDING OUT WHERE YOU ARE NOW

Start by sitting quietly in a comfortable chair at a time when you will not be interrupted for a half hour or so. Try to do this in what I call your prime time. For me it is early in the morning before anyone is up. For you it may be midnight. Take a look at your life. What is good about it? What is worrisome? What does it *feel like* right now? Take a look at all of it and realize that this is IT right now. There is nothing else.

Is this what you want?

What is happening at work? What is satisfying and what is not? How are your relation-

ships—with family, friends, business associates, enemies? How do you relate to the earth, the sea, sky, mountains, trees, flowers, the environment?

As you look into all this, what values seem to surface? Where have you put most of your time and energy? Where is your pride—in family, work, sports, a hobby?

How would you like to be remembered?

When you talk to others, how do you identify yourself—as a business person, a parent or spouse, a person with a hobby?

What seems to be most constant in your life? What is not?

Now write the responses to these and other questions that came to mind as you thought about your present situation. Take all the time you need. At first you may want to just note key words.

HOW ONE PERSON RESPONDED TO THIS EXERCISE

John is thirty-five, married, and has two children. He is a middle manager in a large company where he has worked for seven years. He drives a Toyota. He and his thirty-two-year-old wife, Cindy, own a modest home in an area with other young parents.

These are some of the thoughts and feelings that ran through his mind as he did the exercise.

"I have felt something was missing. I work fifty hours a week but I don't really see a clear career path. I owe a lot on my home loan and credit cards, and I can't go more than five months without a job. At times I get a bit nervous about this. I am often tense about my job, especially before a deadline. I guess I worry a lot about money. Maybe we buy too many things.

"I have a lot, I know, but I feel like I'm in a rat race. I get home late, am sometimes anxious about my work, and am short with the family. Cindy works also and she comes home just as tired.

"On weekends we are both tired. We go out to dinner and movies with friends but the high never seems to last. Sometimes we just plonk ourselves down in front of the TV and vegetate. It seems like I wake up tired too often.

"I have a lot to be thankful for: We are all healthy, both our parents are well. Our children seem to be getting along fine. Oh, there are the usual moments of frustration when the kids want attention and I don't have time, or I want to watch the ball game on TV when Cindy's parents stop by. I sometimes get angry with Cindy, when down deep, I love her. We fight unnecessarily. Our sex life is okay but I wish it were better.

"I don't think I use all of what I have to offer, but I'm not really sure what it is I have to offer. I don't feel comfortable talking about this at work or with Cindy—there just isn't time.

"I like my work and I get a high when it's recognized. I'm proud of how far I've come—I put myself through school in part. I feel I'm respected by my peers.

"I would like to make a real success, have more money, drive better cars, live in a better

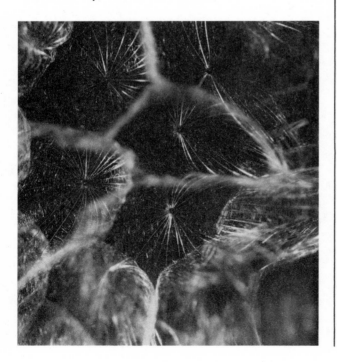

home in a different neighborhood—not that ours is bad or anything.

"I love to play the jazz piano, go to the beach, and go to restaurants. Cindy goes along with this. The problem is I just don't have time to do all these things and also be a spouse and parent.

"How would I like to be remembered? That is a hard one. I'll have to think about that. It's a deeper question than I want to handle just now."

Values Point to Life Qualities, Which Define Vision, Which Tells Us Who We Are

The preceding chapter, "Connections," introduced the concept of relating who we are with what we do as a means of bringing well-being to a life. It emphasized the important relationship between a life quality—a transcendent value that holds special meaning for us—and the form that quality takes in our lives. For example, a quality like beauty can be expressed in many ways, but regardless of the form, the beauty is always there. People who see their work in relation to some value-based quality always seem to have meaning in their lives.

Because qualities can seem rather abstract, I have found it is easiest to come at the life quality that is most meaningful to you by looking at what you *value*. Maybe you have started getting a feeling for what you value from looking at your current situation in the preceding exercise. But if the thoughts and feelings you just noted seem like a jumble, don't worry. You have begun something important, from which empowerment and a sense of direction will emerge.

As I already observed, values often come to us from a point of pain or crisis. Someone close to us dies or is hurt. We become ill, or a close relationship ends in divorce or some other rupture. We get fired from a job, or a plane we are on nearly crashes. Such events give rise to emotions—grief, fear, a sense of failure—that cause us to stop and look at values.

Then, beyond the dramatic personal events of life are the external changes that shake our worlds and make us ask questions. One of these is the rapid growth of technology. As rampant change is brought about by technology, we wonder where we fit in. The ordinary airplane now travels almost as fast as the speed of sound. Space vehicles go well beyond that. Communications technology and television coverage allow us to bridge space, so that everyone can witness, and thus be a part of, any war. We watch people in far-off places die right in front of us as we prepare the evening meal. We worry about nuclear war. Computers keep detailed track of nearly everything, putting our privacy in jeopardy. In medicine, technology has advanced to the point where the dying can be kept alive almost indefinitely. Such change is almost always upsetting, causing us to grasp for a sea anchor to steady us. That anchor is our tie to some system of timeless values that have a sense of rightness about them.

However, sometimes our spiritual values come into conflict with the events life presents. This happens particularly around issues that touch something deep within us and that affect many other people, too. An example is the current uproar over abortion. When does life really start? At the other end, when does life really end? The subject of euthanasia, like that of abortion, stirs deep feelings and fears. How can one be allowed to die in dignity, we ask? There are many other areas of conflict as well. Someone in a chemical plant making pesticides wrestles with the impact these materials have on the environment. A person who seeks peace wonders how to find resolution in a world at war. Poverty is evident everywhere, and someone like Mother Teresa, who

leads a very directed life, makes us wonder about our own.

Great paintings or sculpture can also urge us to STOP and assess. I am thinking of the *Pietà* of Michelangelo, *The Potato Eaters* of Van Gogh, and *Supper at Emmaus* by Rembrandt. Something deep within is affected by what we are seeing—there is a link. The very same thing can happen when we hear a piece of great music, be it a Bach requiem or a Beatles song. Writing, too, can call up thoughts about values. All of these art forms can touch something very deep. That *something* is a universally recognized value—what I have called a life quality.

When we get in touch with a deep value like love, peace, beauty, freedom, faith, brotherhood, harmony, friendship, compassion, serenity, or simplicity, to name only a few, we are relating to a life quality that shapes our lives and gives meaning.

The exercise that follows will help you identify the life quality, or qualities, of greatest value to you. This book includes other exercises designed to bring you to the same place. By doing all of them, you will see how certain qualities will recur, thus confirming their importance to you.

EXERCISE
A PAST EXPERIENCE THAT CAUSED YOU TO QUESTION VALUES

Sit quietly in a chair with a pencil and paper and become comfortable and peaceful. Let go of the distractions of work, dinner preparation, children, or the traffic ticket you just received. Gently return to an event in your life that raised a question about a life value. Maybe it happened yesterday. Maybe you extended help to someone and that made you feel good at a deep level. Perhaps you heard some music that touched off something. Whatever it was, the test is in whether or

QUALITIES*

Definition: A quality is the superior characteristic or property of something. As used in this book, a life quality represents a deep attribute that characterizes an important part of your life. It is a distinguishing property of life, corresponding to something intangible that is of great value to you. The qualities you identify with define your wholeness.

Appreciation—Admiration

Beauty—Brotherhood—Bliss—Balance

Compassion—Communion—Calm

Courage—Communication—Connection

Creativity

Detachment

Energy—Enthusiasm—Eternity—Excellence

Entrepreneurship

Freedom—Faith—Friendship

Generosity—Goodwill—Goodness—Gratitude

Harmony—Humor—Humanitarianism

Infinity—Inclusiveness

Joy

Love—Light—Liberation

Order

Patience—Positiveness—Power

Quiet

Reality—Renewal—Resonance

Service—Serenity—Silence—Simplicity

Synthesis

Trust—Tranquillity—Truth

Understanding

Vitality

Will—Wisdom—Wholeness

Wonder

*Adapted from an uncopyrighted list of qualities developed by the Psychosynthesis Institute of San Francisco in the 1970s.

not you resonate to the experience, whether it called up some life value that is important to you. The event does not have to be dramatic or a near-death encounter. Life offers all sorts of experiences that call up values. The task is to become aware of some of them.

Take a minute to write down the event and the value it recalled for you. When you are finished, put the papers aside. We will come back to them.

Before you begin, you may want to look over the accompanying list of qualities. It suggests qualities that have been valued by people over the years. Include others as you come upon them in the course of any of these exercises.

EXAMPLES OF VALUE-RELATED EVENTS IN OTHERS' LIVES

John and Cindy chose to do this exercise at different times. John preferred early morning before he went to work. Cindy decided to do it after the children were in bed.

John:

"The work at the office has been killing lately. As a middle manager I get a lot of heat and not much direction. We have had layoffs in management over the past six months, and though I don't think I'm a target, I am concerned. I feel tense, stressed, fearful—as if I'm on a treadmill. Even if my work is done I don't go home at 5:30 because I'm afraid someone will see that as not working hard enough. I would really like the freedom to work and take off when I have time. Instead I feel like I am being paced by someone else's drummer. I feel I cannot be self-determined. I like my work, but I feel trapped.

"I have a back that goes out now and again. It is fine right now, but I recall a year ago I was flat on the floor with a pillow under my knees and in a lot of pain. I slowly got better, but I was away from work, couldn't jog, and I guess I felt sorry for myself. I had a lot of time to think—I wondered why this was happening to me. I had always taken health for granted. Oh, I had been through the flu and the occasional cold, and a broken arm as a kid, but this was different. This time I could not move for a week. Now I could see the need for health in order to have freedom. Having money was not enough.

"During this time, I had to depend on Cindy. She had to be a nurse and take care of all my physical needs. I suddenly realized how important she was to me. I saw her and our relationship as something vital. We did a lot of talking about what we were going through. I made resolutions about doing exercises and yoga, and eating more sensibly. I felt helpless and at the same time powerful in the sense that I could DO something about my back."

What this experience meant to John:

"Out of all this, it became clear that I sought freedom and a sense of my own power. I saw that I wanted these things for both Cindy and myself in our relationship. I saw that I needed to honor her individuality and freedom if I was to enjoy the same values myself."

Cindy:

"When I was a teenager, an uncle died of cancer after having been sick a long time. Except for a couple of friends, no one wanted to talk about it, so I was mostly alone with my thoughts. When the subject came to mind, I felt afraid, and fragile. I wondered what death was like and when I would die. Because others didn't want to talk about it, I was hesitant to raise the questions that were in my mind.

"My children are important to me. I realize this especially when they get sick. I work to help pay for the house and to buy things for them. I wish John could spend more time with them. I really want them to grow up and be capable people with opportunity. Much of the time I have left over from my work I give to them.

"When I was learning to drive, I had a small accident. No one was seriously hurt, but we were all scared. I stopped taking my life for granted! All of us in the car were teenagers, and we talked a lot about our fear at the time. Then, as time passed, we forgot about it. As I recall this event now, I am reminded about the value of life.

"John has been so busy that we haven't been seeing a lot of each other. He's often on business trips and I become occupied with the children. I sometimes feel like a single parent. John is so involved in his work that he doesn't miss us as much as we miss him. The demands on him are sometimes crushing. I wonder if it is all worth it. He says it will not be this way forever, but I don't believe it.

"I love the symphony. Whenever we go, I am in a different world. The music touches something within me, something I value. I wouldn't say this out loud, but listening to some music is like a religious experience. It is so beautiful.

"With elections coming up, I think about the possibility of atomic war. We do not need to build so many warheads. I feel helpless. Also we are destroying the environment with pollution and endangering the lives of our children. The planet will heal if only we stop hurting it. I love to walk in the mountains, where the air and water are clear and the surroundings seem so wild."

What Cindy's experiences meant to her:

"Having had some brushes with death and the dying, I really value my life. I love music and feel as if it speaks to something spiritual within me that's bigger than me. I get a feeling of balance from it. My relationship with my family is the most important thing in my life, more than my job. I also value the environment and wild places. Love, wildness, harmony, and balance—I guess those are the qualities I value most."

Relating Money to Our Life Vision

In our search to uncover the qualities that are at the core of who we are, let's now look at vision in another way. But first, what is *vision*?

> [Vision is] the faculty of sight . . . unusual competence in discernment or perception . . . the manner in which one sees or conceives of something . . . a mental image produced by the imagination . . . the mystical experience of seeing as if with the eyes of the supernatural. (*American Heritage Dictionary*)

When we deal with vision, therefore, we are working with the eyes of the mind and the heart, using the language of physical sight. In the following exercises, we will rely on intuitive ways of knowing to bring us closer to the life qualities that speak to who we are. First we looked at values; now we will let *insight* work for us.

Refer for a moment to the Investment Process map on page 3. Most of us begin the investment process with a look at all the financial possibilities available to us. Some people may begin by examining their longer-term goals, but hardly anyone examines vision or qualities as a foundation on which to base final choices. Further, no matter where people begin, most never realize that there are nonfinancial investment choices to consider in addition to the usual financial ones.

In other words, most of us express who we are by what we have instead of through the life qualities we represent. Now, I don't mean to imply for a moment that in order to live your values or life qualities, you need give up having things.

THE EXAMPLE OF MARTIN LUTHER KING JR.

Martin Luther King Jr. was a humanitarian who saw his life as one of dedication to service. He seems to have made all his financial and nonfinancial decisions based on his vision of service. From his first civil rights march to the day he died, he had a clear value map to follow. He knew who he was—a humanitarian—and he did the things that expressed just that. In other words, he was fully conscious of the link between who he was and what he did.

In a speech in Atlanta in 1968, he spoke about his vision:

"Every now and then I think about my own death, and I think about my own funeral. I don't want a long funeral. And if you get somebody to deliver the eulogy, tell them not to talk too long. Tell them not to mention that I have a Nobel Peace Prize. Tell them not to mention that I have three or four hundred other awards. I'd like somebody to mention that day that Martin Luther King Jr. tried to give his life to serving others. I'd like for somebody to say that day that Martin Luther King Jr. tried to love somebody.

"Say that I was a drum major for justice. Say that I was a drum major for righteousness. And all the other shallow things will not matter. I won't have any money to leave behind. I won't have the fine and luxurious things of life to leave behind. But I just want to leave a committed life behind."

Clearly, his life was driven by the qualities of service and humanitarianism. His power came from within, for he connected who he was (service) with what he did (being a minister). All of his outer activities related to his inner vision. From what we know of him, although his life had tensions and anguish, it also had peace.

Quite the contrary. There is nothing intrinsically wrong with possessions. Money and the things money can buy are neutral when the goal is connecting who you are with what you do. It is the context in which they are used that is the test.

Take the case of the industrialist Armand Hammer, for example. He is enormously rich. Like Martin Luther King Jr., he has based his life on humanitarianism. But while the Reverend King took buses, Dr. Hammer flies all over the world in his private Boeing 727. As an M.D. early in life, he brought wheat to the newly formed and starving Soviet Union. Most recently, he paid for and flew medical supplies to those in need after the Chernobyl nuclear plant disaster.

In other words, if you are driven by a quality rather than a quest for acquisitions, the material goods you collect are simply assets with which to manifest your vision or values. Instead of becoming a burden, "things" become just another resource you can allocate to realizing your vision. So if riches are what you want, by all means collect them. Wanting an expensive car and a plush home is fine if you go after them within the context of a life quality with which you feel connected. The link with that quality is what makes the difference and brings True Wealth.

As money is a symbol for material things, it is worth giving some thought to how we relate to it. Over a lifetime we spend vast amounts of time on money and we also handle a lot of it. Take a minute to estimate how much of your life is spent on work done to earn and invest money. After eight hours for sleep and eight hours for work per day, we have a like amount for eating, nurturing a family, shopping, playing, and all the other things we do. So we spend about a third of our time collecting money.

At this point, compute how much passes through your hands. At an average annual inflow of, say, $50,000 per year for forty years, you would earn $2,000,000 over a working life, not counting money from investments over the same period. In short, in terms of both the time spent making it and the quantity made, money plays an important role in our lives. It has come to symbolize our measure of success.

Books, magazines, and speeches are devoted to money. World progress is measured in economic terms because money is used as a medium of exchange. We soon learn a lot about how to work for it, invest it, account for it, preserve it, and be responsible for it.

We also learn about its flip side—debt.

Clearly, money can shape the very fabric of our lives, both for the good and the not-so-good. We therefore learn very early what we will or won't do to obtain it. We form a lot of judgments and develop a lot of feelings about money.

Because of its central role in our lives, we will next do a reflective exercise about money. Again, the purpose is to assess how the material fits in with our vision in life. It will be another way of deriving an insight into who we are by looking at the qualities we most value.

EXERCISE
WHAT, REALLY, IS MONEY?

You will need a dollar bill, a pad of paper, and a pencil. Get comfortable. Become in touch with your breathing. Become free of tensions.

Now pick up the dollar bill. With your eyes closed, feel it in your hand. Concentrate on this piece of paper and become aware of its presence. How does it feel?

After a few moments, allow an image to appear. It may be a picture, or just color and form. Or you may hear sound rather than getting a visual image. Do not hold any expectations about what it should be. Just allow anything to emerge. Keep breathing slowly and deeply. Take a few minutes to be with this experience.

Open your eyes. Draw a picture of what you saw, or write about any sound you may have heard. Take whatever time you need to complete this.

Then ask yourself the following questions. Read each one, close your eyes and get a sense of the answer, then open your eyes and write the answer. Go to the next question. Take a minute or two with each one. As you will note, they are all associated with each other and will stir up a lot of feelings and thought.

- What qualities do you attribute to money?
- What purpose does it hold for you?
- What are you willing to do for money?
- What are you not willing to do for it?
- What are you willing to do with money?
- What are you not willing to do with it?

Finally, take a few minutes to look over your responses. Did one or two of them strike a special note, raise particular feelings, or create tensions? Think about the image that came to you as you

felt the dollar bill in your hand. Were you able to relate the symbol you received to a life quality? Take a look at some of the symbols that money has evoked for people doing this exercise. Note the qualities that the symbols may represent.

ONE PERSON'S RESPONSE TO THE MONEY EXERCISE

John decided to do this exercise on a flight to New York. He had a window seat and simply went quietly through the steps. In the first part of the exercise he visualized an eagle soaring freely and easily in the sky. He could feel the fun and joy of flight. He had a deep sense of freedom and creativity.

Regarding the questions, he saw money as having the quality of power. Its purpose was to be used as a tool to get things done. He saw it mostly within the context of business, where he saw the effect of its power every day.

John affirmed that he was willing to work hard for money. He was already doing so, although he knew that he was not willing to go on this way forever. The long hours took him away from his family, and that bothered him. He decided that if he had to choose, he would put family relationships above money. He was not sure, however, where the line was. He had the feeling that as he got closer to it, it would move farther away.

John wanted a lot of things—a new car, a bigger home, education for the children, time to travel. There were also some charitable projects he wanted to support more fully.

He was not willing to be dishonest with money. He was also not willing to use it as a power hammer over others the way it had sometimes been used on him. This question was especially important for him because of these experiences. The other question that provoked a lot of feeling was the one dealing with what he was not willing

---

MONEY SYMBOLS AND THEIR MEANINGS

The relationship of the symbol to a quality helps you get in touch with who you are— the goal of this chapter. The exercise about money, like all the others, is designed to lead you to your own intuitive knowing.

Symbol	Quality
Jaguar	Power
Steam	Energy
Car battery	Energy
Bird	Freedom
Light switch	Instant control
Pyramid	Strength
Rose	Beauty

to do for money. The long hours at work were starting to take their toll, and he had been wondering if it was worth it.

───────────

When I did this exercise myself, holding the dollar bill and opening my mind to whatever image might appear, I got a picture of a car battery. I saw money, therefore, as a source of passive energy being stored for later use. As I thought about it, that is really all money is anyway. By itself, it doesn't *do* anything. It just represents latent purchasing power waiting to be released. As a venture capitalist, I have found this perspective to be useful. The real power is never in the money invested in a new company, but in the people who align themselves with a given purpose and goal. In the same vein, when I solicit funds for a foundation I am really looking for donors who share the same values. Money passes *through* us. In this sense, no one ever really owns money. Our conscious link with a life quality has a lot to do with how we dispose of and relate to money.

After doing the exercise I also realized that money for me is "pure energy," which takes on the values, morality, and judgments of its owner at any given point in time. By itself, it is neutral. Thus money does not "contaminate"; only those who use—or misuse—money do that. For me, it is what we attribute to money that gives it the power and generates the fear we often associate with it.

Money means different things to different people—probably as a function of their experience of it. One woman I recall saw the image of a flower that symbolized the quality of beauty. This was very appropriate for her. Everything she did revolved around beauty—the way she set a table; her interest and work in art; her success in persuading her employer, a large technology company, to plant a rose garden. Her work place seemed very removed from beauty, yet this person brought beauty to everything she did, including how she worked with people. Eventually, having come in contact with her special relationship to beauty, she started her own company arranging flowers for corporate lobbies.

Some people use money to collect art. Unless they see these purchases as an expression of some quality—beauty being one possibility—their collection is just an investment. When they connect with a quality in a given piece of art (beauty, power, etc.), they have something related to who they are in addition to a possible investment. It is the connection with the quality that makes the difference—that creates a sense of well-being and thus supplies wealth.

As we have discovered, qualities can emerge through intangibles as well as through "things" such as a picture or a home (which can symbolize peace or a refuge). Helping someone through a crisis or performing some other act of service would also call up the qualities expressed in the act. Thus, if compassion is the quality being expressed in helping a friend, you *are* compassion at that moment. Put another way, whatever you do or feel is always an expression of who you are. Being able to recognize that link between what you do and who you are is the source of well-being.

As noted in the preface ("The Question That Began It All . . . "), **wealth has more to do with experiencing than with having.** Now you have an experiential means with which to "know" this truth. When you read the preface, that knowledge was perhaps only intellectual.

More Ways to Identify Life Qualities

In the four exercises that follow, two will deal with the present, and two will involve looking at the present from a point in the future. When you have completed them, you will be able to collate all the experiences to see which life qualities most closely define who you are. The exercises are:

- What do I most like to do? What upsets me the most?
- The guided daydream (a reflective exercise that will take you deeply within yourself)
- Writing your own obituary
- Listening to an older person as he or she looks back on life

EXERCISE
WHAT DO I MOST LIKE TO DO? WHAT UPSETS ME THE MOST?

Part 1—Things I Like to Do

Because what we enjoy doing is connected to who we are, you will next make a list of the ten or twelve things you most like to do and then relate each one to a quality that captures the meaning of that activity for you. Some activities may express more than a single quality.

Choose a time when you will not be interrupted. On a piece of paper, start by making a list, down the left-hand side of the page, of those things that are meaningful, joyful, or exciting to you. Do not try to put them in any kind of order. Just write them as they pop into your head.

If twenty items emerge, don't stop at ten. On the other hand, you will not need to use up several pages to fulfill the purpose of this exercise.

Now, opposite each activity, write the life quality that it reflects. Refer to the sample list of qualities on page 24 for ideas if needed. You will probably note that many of the same qualities reappear—a confirmation of their importance to you. Certainly, new ones will show up, too, adding to your emerging insight into who you are.

If you are doing this exercise with someone else, be mindful that two people may list the same activity and yet associate it with different qualities. For example, of two people who love golf, one may connect it with health while the other relates it to a drive for excellence.

THREE EXAMPLES—
RESPONSES FROM INDIVIDUALS
AT DIFFERENT STAGES
OF THEIR LIVES

The following cases will demonstrate what you already know to be true, that we choose new activities as we go through life. The interesting discovery, however, is that the qualities reflected in these new interests do not themselves change all that much—unless there is a change in awareness that uncovers what was always there anyway. Such a shift may totally change your life direction in terms of what you do to express the newly discovered quality.

YOUNG SINGLE PERSON

Activity or Source of Pleasure	Quality
Dancing	Vitality
Jogging	Vitality, reward
Sports car	Power, liberation
Music	Beauty
Travel	Freedom, friendship
Restaurants	Renewal, friendship
Success	Courage, creativity, renewal
Skiing	Freedom, energy
Wine	Appreciation
Dog	Goodwill, friendship

YOUNG COUPLE

Activity or Source of Pleasure	Quality
Home	Joy, renewal, nurture
Children	Nurture, creativity, cooperation
A night out	Harmony, communication, love
Exercise	Health, vitality
Time alone	Serenity
Professional success	Power, energy, creativity
Time with family	Joy, renewal
Friends	Harmony, renewal, humor
Reading	Renewal, understanding
Political action	Service, positiveness

RETIRED COUPLE

Walks	Energy, health
Mobility	Independence, liberation
Friends	Brotherhood, love
Travel	Freedom, wisdom, brotherhood
Grandchildren	Wonder, nurture, continuity, hope, vision
Natural environment	Nature, wholeness
Photography	Beauty, nature
Being useful	Generosity, purpose, appreciation
Gardening	Renewal, nature, nurture
Home	Generosity, nurture

Part 2—Things That Upset Me

In this part of the exercise, you will make a list of the situations or things you find most upsetting. Then you will relate each one to a missing quality or qualities. What you come up with this time will be a mirror image of your previous responses. As you will see, there is as much to learn from the upsetting situations as the pleasant ones. The polarities are natural—rather like being able to experience health most vividly in the context of illness.

If you need help with this exercise, look at the following responses from the same individuals who listed and assessed their likes.

THREE EXAMPLES

YOUNG SINGLE PERSON

Upsetting Situation	Missing Quality
Traffic jams	Freedom, harmony
Late for meetings	Order
Inefficiency	Order, power

YOUNG COUPLE

Arguments	Love, tranquillity
Car trouble	Order
Smog	Health
Corrupt politics	Harmony, trust, truth
Late-night telephone calls	Compassion, calm
Waste of resources	Order, gratitude

RETIRED COUPLE

Upsetting Situation	Missing Quality
Stiff joints	Movement, flexibility
Being ignored	Appreciation, connectedness
Gophers in garden	Harmony
Violence in streets	Love, tranquillity

EXERCISE
THE GUIDED DAYDREAM

The visualization process prompted by this exercise is simply another way of putting you in touch with your own vision and purpose in life. The intuitive response far exceeds the power of the conscious mind, drawing instead on the greater knowing of the unconscious. Through deep relaxation, you can tap natural creativity.

You will be getting in touch with images. The pictures you draw will be like blueprints. They are a way of giving form to your creative imagination.

Gather some colored crayons or pencils, drawing paper, and a writing pad. If at all possible, have another person slowly read the daydreamlike sequence that follows. If this is not possible, then record the guiding words on tape and play it back to yourself.

It is most important that you be relaxed, quiet, and in a receptive state of mind. Don't try this exercise if you are tense or under pressure at the moment. To help you relax, you may want to listen to music before you begin. In any event, choose a time when you have at least half an hour to devote to this effort.

1. Enter the daydream

Close your eyes. Let go of all distractions. Allow yourself to relax comfortably in a chair. Don't lie down, as that may encourage sleep. Notice your deep, unhurried breathing . . . in and out . . . expansion and contraction. Just be in touch with your whole body. Continue to be attentive to your breathing without changing it. Feel your body adjusting as you inhale and exhale.

Now, exhale fully, and then take a deep, relaxing breath. Do this two more times and let go of any tension you may be holding in your body. Watch any residual tension float away as tiny bubbles of vapor.

Ask yourself *who* is aware of your breathing. Who is it that pays attention to this process that continues automatically through your whole life? *Who is NOW aware?*

Focus your attention on your body sitting in the chair. Feel your back and seat as they make contact with the chair. Feel, also, your feet upon the floor. Be aware of your clothing as it touches your body. *Who feels? Who is aware of these sensations?*

Shift your attention now to any sounds that you may hear. Allow yourself to go deeper into the layers of sound. Some sounds are immediate, and as you go deeper into this awareness, you will notice that some sounds seem to be more distant and others closer. Perhaps you hear the sound of your heart beating or the sound of a pulse in your ears. *Who is aware of these sounds?*

Shifting your attention once again, imagine a blackboard with a large white circle in the center. Within this circle there is a white dot. *Who is aware of this dot? Who is aware?*

The sensations throughout your body come and go. The sounds pass. Images are fleeting. As all of these sensations and perceptions change, *who remains? Who is aware? Who is constant? Who remains unchanging while all else changes?*

You are a deep center of consciousness—a center of love and will. Realizing this unchanging deeper sense of *who you are*, you are looking for *your own* unique way to express the qualities of love and will that you represent, in harmony with the principles that govern the universe. As you become aware of your vision of yourself expressing these principles or qualities, you become aware of your purpose in living your life.

Ask yourself from this deep sense of knowing what your individual expression of this energy is in your lifetime. *Let an image of that come to your mind.* It may come in the form of a symbol, a picture of something, or a sense. Allow whatever comes to remain there.

2. Draw the Image

When you feel ready, gently open your eyes and draw the symbol or image. If nothing visual comes, just choose colors that most attract you and begin to draw. Allow yourself to draw without judgment.

3. Collect Your Reflections

When you complete the drawing, write down your feelings, sensations, and insights about your vision experience and the purpose of your life. Note which qualities came up for you—either in the course of making the drawing or within the drawing itself.

Take time to summarize your thoughts *and* feelings. Relate this exercise to the preceding ones. Did some of the same life qualities come up? Save your drawings and notes so that you can refer to them easily later.

Do not expect to wring out all of the feelings and images at this initial sitting. Self-awareness develops slowly. You may want to return to this guided imagery exercise and do it again. This sort of process is ongoing; once begun, it continues. Just be patient, relax a bit, and let things "marinate," incubate, and otherwise develop.

What is emerging is the expression of your

life vision as it looks today. This may seem pretty distant from your investment planning process, but it is actually the foundation for it. If you have any doubt, look again at the vision and purpose section of the Investment Process map on page 3, to see where it all is heading.

SOME RESPONSES TO THIS EXERCISE

Citing representative responses to this exercise is difficult because we are all so wonderfully varied. Some people draw pictures of a bright sun which symbolizes joy, love, or hope for them. Others see flowers representing beauty. I seem always to get images of high mountains, which symbolize a deep sense of freedom, strength, and eternity for me. One of my avocations is wilderness backpacking, and I have spent a lot of time trekking among the peaks of the Himalaya. Thus what I most like to do connects with the imagery I get in this reflective exercise. The experience is therefore a confirming one. You will want to look for similar confirmations in your own responses, both to this and all the other exercises in this chapter.

EXERCISE
WRITING YOUR OWN OBITUARY

Do you remember the story *A Christmas Carol* by Charles Dickens? Scrooge awakes from his deep "sleep" and discovers that Christmas has not come and gone after all. He sees that he still has his life ahead of him and that he has time to make changes.

In a sense, we will be doing the same thing in this exercise. We will be looking at our life qualities from another angle. To do this, we will need to move forward in time to the point of our death and look backwards at our whole life. *What do we see? Who were we?*

Until we get in touch with death and dying at some level, we are not fully connected with life or living. In a similar vein, we experience the meaning of health best during a bout of illness. Without shadow, there is no perception of light. An Ansel Adams image or a Rembrandt painting is vividly alive in part because the shadow offers a context for light.

Often enough, life "provides" us with experiences that force us to become more deeply in touch with our life and living. Those who have been near death reenter the world with a totally new view of life. I recall a less dramatic version of such an experience in my own life. I was startled one day when I urinated blood. Then I was terrified. I can still feel the chill of fear as I confronted the stark probability of my own death, announced by this potential symptom of advanced cancer.

Suddenly I remembered things I had put off doing and saying. I was reminded of relationships I wanted to heal. There were many unfinished tasks. I called the doctor, who told me that the incident was probably trivial and not to worry. He was right, and I had my life back.

But there was a vast difference. I now saw my life differently.

This altered perspective is what we want to try to approximate in the following exercise. We do not have to pretend to die, and not many of us have been through deathlike experiences. The goal is to learn what is truly important for us as another way of examining the life qualities that represent who we are.

Guidelines for Writing an Obituary

Choose a time when you will not be interrupted, and find a quiet spot. With paper and pencil at hand, sit quietly and become centered and reflective.

Your aim is *not* to write the usual newspaper

account in the obituary column. You will not list all the jobs you have had, the degrees you hold, where you live, and who survives you. Nor is your purpose to eulogize yourself.

Instead, the goal is to acknowledge to yourself what your life has been all about. Put another way, if your name is "Bill," the aim is to express "Bill-ness."

Who was he, really?
What were his dreams, thoughts, feelings?
What visions guided his life?

Ideally, if an outsider were to read the completed obituary, he or she would get a clear sense of who you were as a person. What were you afraid of? What made you laugh? What was behind your interest in business, hobbies, and the like? Your obituary should convey a feeling for the highs, lows, successes, and failures.

Be as thorough as you can. Recall both good and bad happenings; don't omit unpleasant events or the sad feelings they may evoke. Remember, this is private. No one else need ever see it—although sharing with a spouse or close friend can be wonderfully healing. Be honest with yourself. Go slowly. If one sitting is not enough, take several to complete the writing. Reread it, make changes. I rewrite my obituary about every two years and get deeper insights every time.

Start by being conscious that you choose to do

this, that you see its utility and want to learn from the experience. Undertake it during your prime time, when it is easiest to be reflective. Let go of tensions. Breathe easily and consciously.

Now pick a death date. Start by writing, "Bill died at 93 in his sleep" (or flying an airplane or whatever). This will immediately transport you to the end point we seek.

Now let your feelings and thoughts merge and start to describe what "Bill-ness" was. You need not follow any chronological order. Just record what comes up for you. The recent birth of a child may bring up feelings that lead you to remember a distant child experience of your own. Be attentive to emotional charges. I cried during the first draft of my obituary. There are almost always deep feelings around divorce, death, loss of a job (a kind of death), severe illness, and other major life events. Stay with these; they are at the core of "Bill-ness."

If you need help, look over the sample obituaries that follow. However, use your own style. One person I know did it all in a few words in the form of an epitaph on his tombstone!

SAMPLE OBITUARY NO. 1

"He was stopped mostly by fears of taking full responsibility for doing what he wanted . . . he blamed others for his lack of courage . . . never learned to relax . . . never found peace but enjoyed the trip. Had a hard time accepting his deficiencies and pushed to change them . . . but could reconcile all the paradoxes with laughter. Maverick, Grecophile, mystic, artist, firewalker, passionate traveler, crazy wisdom, cowboy, therapist, builder, covert asshole, lover.

"He was someone who created a clear means for people to become extraordinary."

Without knowing whether this person is married or has children or what he does for a living, we get a real feeling of someone who dares, who has life and laughter within him, and who is in touch with his own struggle to become. The qualities of joy, humor, service, trust, vitality, and courage are all there.

SAMPLE OBITUARY NO. 2

This is the obituary of a professional photographer. Cleary, he has identified with the quality of beauty. Just as clearly, the experience of that connection has brought peace and joy and a sense of rightness to his life.

"He saw it first at seventeen on a lake in Ontario—beauty, unity, power beyond imagining. Once having seen, he was not the same. Though trapped as we all are in the shoulds of life, that vision called to him again and again—to leave advertising, to follow Muir and Frost, to have a son, to love a daughter.

"Success came easily; it was fear that almost did him in. Fear to be honest, fear of hurting someone, fear of having people hate him. Half of him was letting go so easily, the other half holding on so tightly. It almost literally tore him apart.

"That fear, that tightness, didn't leave all at once. It was an evolution, not a revolution—helped by his children, his loved ones, and the exquisite beauty of nature.

"Finally, though, it did leave. He was still human to be sure, full of foibles, but he was at peace. And in that peace was great power.

"The ends were now unimportant, the process all. It was the delight of being human that captivated him. To struggle with its paradoxes, to boggle at its complexity and its simplicity. To learn, to grow—but always to laugh and to love.

"Like Matisse with his doves, he grew to see beauty in everything. He created, but was unattached to the result. Connected with the source, he just overflowed.

"Life was now light and laughter. And, in the end, he simply expired from joy."

SAMPLE OBITUARY NO. 3

"If I had my life to live over again, I'd dare to make more mistakes. Next time I'd relax, I would limber up. I would be sillier than I have ever been this trip. I would take fewer things seriously. I would climb more mountains and swim more rivers. I would eat more ice cream and less beans. I would perhaps have more actual troubles, but I'd have fewer imaginary ones.

"You see, I'm one of those people who live sensibly and sanely hour after hour, day after day. Oh, I've had my moments, and if I had to do it over again, I'd have more of them. In fact, I'd try to have nothing else. Just moments, one after another, instead of living so many years ahead of each day. I've been one of those persons who never goes anywhere without a thermometer, a hot water bottle, a raincoat, and a parachute. If I had it to do again, I would travel lighter than I have.

"If I had my life to live over, I would start barefoot earlier in the Spring and stay that way later in the Fall. I would go to more dances and I would ride more merry-go-rounds. I would pick more daisies."*

This piece was not, strictly speaking, written as an obituary, but the writer was looking back and so clearly speaking to the issue of who she was that I felt it was important to include. Its special value is in the fact that she got in touch with qualities she had by noting what she lacked. By lamenting being too careful, she identified with the qualities of creativity, trust, and courage. By speaking of wanting to relax more and flow with life, she identified harmony. By wanting to dance more, she spoke to joy. She also demonstrated the qualities of humor and the courage to look at herself.

---

*From *AHP Perspective* (July 1975), the newsletter of the Association for Humanistic Psychology, 1772 Vallejo St., San Francisco, CA 94123. Reprinted with permission.

✕ EXERCISE
LISTENING TO AN OLDER PERSON AS HE OR SHE LOOKS BACK ON LIFE

Instead of looking back with your own eyes as in the preceding exercise, in this one you will do so through the eyes of someone else. Select an older person, someone in their seventies or eighties, who knows you and cares for you—someone who has your interests in mind. It could be an aunt or uncle, a friend of the family, a grandparent, a former teacher. Make sure it's someone you respect.

Pick a time when both of you can be undisturbed. Choose a quiet place to meet, and take along paper and pencil.

Ask your helper to do what you have just completed—to look back over his or her life and to search for the truly important parts of it. You need not explain what life qualities are.

The purpose is to *listen*.

But be a *reflective listener*. Play back what you hear so that the speaker can know you have heard and that you "got it." From this experience, you will see how others intuitively identify with qualities in their lives. They may not feel the connective context, but they will give you insights into how others see themselves and value certain aspects of their lives.

From this experience you will see, through another person, that life qualities *are* important. You will have external confirmation that the nonfinancial assets gathered during a lifetime are the crucial ones. You will see the wisdom in **making money to live life rather than living life to earn money.**

———

The exercises you have just completed are by far the most important ones in this book, and possibly the most foreign to your usual way of looking at things. Paradoxically they are also the most theoretical and the most practical at the same time. Without them the rest would be much less productive or illuminating.

Before you go on, please take time to sift through the notes and drawings you have made for each exercise. Look for the qualities that kept coming up. These are probably the most important ones, in that they reflect who you are just now.

Write a short summary of the qualities you have identified. Then, if you feel comfortable doing so, share your discoveries with another person. You may be surprised at the insights he or she will have for you. If you are married, share with your spouse, who may be engaged in this same process. If you are not married, talk to a close friend. At the very least, you will deepen your relationship with that person, which in itself represents an important nonfinancial resource.

Finally, take all of your drawings and writings and save them in a file labeled "Vision & Purpose." You will use them in writing your life plan, the last step in the True Wealth process.

✕ A FINAL EXERCISE
CONNECTING VISION AND PURPOSE BY WRITING A PURPOSE STATEMENT

Life qualities reflect who you are—your vision. *Purpose* represents what you do to give expression to your vision. You are now going to link who you are with what you do during the course of a day. This linkage is the conduit through which True Wealth flows.

Writing a description of your daily work—what I call a *purpose statement*—is important because it will give you an opportunity to see whether your job is in accord with who you are. In the end, this statement *should* reflect who you are. Your true purpose may be no different from what you do now. However, given this new context, the way you go about your same job may change.

This happened to a secretary who, realizing how important beauty was in her life, went about her job doing the usual things to add touches of beauty, but with a consciousness that had been lacking before. Making that conscious link gave new meaning to her work even though the job content remained unchanged.

It is possible, though, that your current work will turn out to be totally inappropriate to who you are. An engineering acquaintance of mine worked on pesticides. When he got in touch with his life quality of harmony with the environment, he realized that his values were at odds with his work. So he quit. He had never been really happy in his job, and linking who he was with what he did explained why. His new awareness helped him turn the corner.

Such a major change may not be necessary even if you find that a particular quality hasn't been manifested in your current work. You may want to see how your job could be altered to allow you to express that quality. If that isn't possible, maybe a different job within the same company would enable you to find an outlet for the quality. Failing that, you may decide to change companies or your line of work, or both. Perhaps you will want to go after more education to prepare for work more in line with the quality you deem important.

Remember that a given quality can be expressed in any number of forms. Don't throw out the baby with the bath water. Your present job may work out well if you just change the way you think and feel about it.

You can also look for other ways, not necessarily connected to your job, in which you already relate, or could relate, to the life qualities you feel drawn to. For example, I laugh a lot during the course of a day. It is one way I have noticed that I connect with the quality of joy.

In your purpose statement, you will be expressing your life qualities, or vision, in terms of what you do. For example, you might express an affinity for beauty through being an artist. Your statement should be short, simple, and direct. When complete, it should make the connection between who you are and what you do for a living immediately clear even to someone who doesn't know you. Don't worry about including time frames or specific goals for realizing your vision or expressing your qualities more fully. These aspects will be addressed in the following chapter.

For now, the task is simply to write a broad statement in which you think through what you are now doing in such a way that you can tell that it relates, or does not relate, to the qualities you identified in the preceding exercises.

Use the worksheet that follows to write your purpose statement. At the top of the statement, list the qualities that you have identified as most meaningful to you. Doing so will help you focus your statement. You may also wish to refer to the examples following the worksheet for guidance.

SAMPLE PURPOSE STATEMENTS

A Secretary:

"I am a corporate secretary. I have always been attentive to having a clean desk and up-to-date files. I enjoy having flowers on my desk. In fact I'm compulsive about that. Now I see that being ordered is peaceful and an expression of beauty. Knowing that makes my tasks seem more important. I now can consciously bring beauty to my work and work place."

A Banker:

"As a loan officer, I will now see my work as an extension of the quality of humanitarianism.

Your Statement of Purpose

The task is to relate what you do each day to the qualities that represent who you really are.

Core Qualities

_____   _____

_____   _____

_____   _____

Purpose Statement

_____

_____

_____

_____

_____

_____

_____

_____

_____

_____

_____

_____

_____

_____

_____

_____

_____

_____

_____

_____

Consistent with sound lending practice, I will listen more carefully to people and try to be supportive of their goals. I will see employees and customers as part of the same community of human beings and be open to their needs."

An Engineer:

"As a production engineer in a high-tech company, I express both creativity and peace in what is normally a frantic and chaotic environment. I do this by creating ways for the creativity in my people to come out and by acting peacefully in my relations with people as a way of being an example."

An Executive:

"I seek freedom. I have always felt trapped in my work. Long hours keep me from my young family. I am now going to make sure that the time I do spend with family is of high quality. I am going to do a life financial plan and develop a path to be economically free by age fifty-five. I am going to see how I can create freedom on the job for my people by enlisting their creative thoughts."

A Single Mother:

"I am divorced with one young child. When I was married, I saw my role as that of housewife and mother. I nurtured. Since I've been on my own, I've often felt scared. I seek serenity and freedom from fear. In my work as a physical therapist, I see that I can bring these qualities to my clients, who really want the same things. In giving them these qualities through the manner in which I work, I connect with the same qualities within me. I find them to be who I really am. My former frantic pace is now relaxed and peaceful. I get more done and feel more secure."

A Young Professional:

"As an unmarried professional, I have been busy with work and never thought about who I was. I focused on success. Now that I am on my way, that is not enough. The attainment seems hollow. I know I am creative, and I seek enthusiasm, joy, and lightness. I am going to go after these qualities by no longer practicing architecture alone but instead joining with two partners who are joyful and creative. In this way I will draw out these qualities in me through my work."

You now have the link between who you are and what you do. That connection will be one of the criteria by which you will choose among all the financial and nonfinancial possibilities presented to you every day. For instance, does returning to school for graduate study better relate who you are with what you do? Does buying a particular stock fund fit with your purpose?

Unconsciously you express yourself daily in what you do and have and in how you present yourself to the world. Your home, dress, car speaks of you in a material way. Your behavior and attitudes do the same in a nonfinancial manner. The aim of this chapter has been to make the essential aspects of your life conscious so that, from a place of knowing who you really already are, you can act more in line with that knowledge.

Goals are nothing more
than specific intentions about how
what we do actually gets done.

4

GOALS

Vision is an expression of our governing inner world. Important as it is, nothing *happens* with vision until we start to "bend metal," as they say in the automotive field. To make a quality show up in the outer world, it is necessary to act. Goals are an expression of intended future action. When we set goals in response to vision and purpose, the resulting action gives form to that vision.

Through vision and purpose, we have bridged the usual gap between the inner world of who we are and the outer one of what we do. We must now extend the connection by making what we do very specific. The next step is to list tasks describing how what we do will get done. With this step, we are moving toward the familiar ground of actually doing things, where all of us spend a lot of our time anyway. Everybody knows how to make a list, make the items on the list specific and measurable, attach time frames, and then do them. Sounds familiar, doesn't it?

The difference is in remaining conscious of the fact that everything we do reflects who we are. Moreover, we are all whole even though many-faceted—like the piece of cloth made up of many interconnected threads. Each life-thread element connects to all the others. Hence the importance of staying aware of the quality that represents who we are as we go about the task of doing what we do.

Staying aware of the connections is the bridge between inner and outer parts of ourselves. These connections that are the "stuff" of True Wealth. **They continuously makes conscious, in the present, the quality of who we are.**

"Getting the Doing Done"

The word *goal* comes from the Middle English root word *gol*, meaning boundary or limit. It has come to mean a "purpose toward which an endeavor is directed"—an end objective. So the word speaks to specificity; goal statements are precise. The dictionary also offers a synonym, "intention." This word is rich in connotation, for it implies that in order to get anything done, or achieve a goal, one needs to be in a state of tension. Without tension, we are dead. With wholesome tension we prosper; with negative tension we suffer and atrophy.

Thus a goal is something specific, objective, on purpose, directive, and filled with clarity.

Goals are developed as we move from the relatively abstract level of qualities through the more concrete but general level of purpose and on to the very pragmatic, detailed level of taking actions to realize our purpose. For example, someone may begin by identifying freedom as an important quality. Say she chooses the forest service as a profession that will allow her to realize that quality. Now, how does the work of a forest ranger get done? It gets done by completing tasks, and anticipated or planned tasks are goals. As one of her goals, our forest ranger might plan a new ecology program for visitors and give herself a six-month deadline for presenting it to management. She might also work on a departmental budget, gathering cost estimates for the coming year to be included in the overall national park budget. As these goals become tasks that she is actually doing, she sees the work as her link to freedom via her profession of being a forest ranger.

Thus what began as an awareness of the importance of freedom as a value has moved to choosing the forest service as a profession and on to a set of tasks—the nitty-gritty stuff we do each day. Only now the everyday stuff has meaning because of the connections we experience. Seeing the linkage is what brings meaning (wealth) to the work. This is why the connections are the conduit through which True Wealth flows.

GOALS IN THE LIFE OF MARTIN LUTHER KING JR.

Martin Luther King Jr. sought to express humanitarianism in his life as his vision of who he was. His purpose—what he did—took the form of being a minister. His goals therefore centered on the tasks that ministers do, such as preaching sermons and being an inspired model for others. Other goals grew out of his vision as well—like leading marches and being central to the black movement through nonviolent protest.

I suspect that the Reverend King fully experienced the link between his vision of humanitarianism and his everyday work. No doubt his strength came from this awareness. Moreover, he was able to use his own power to empower others.

HOW A SECRETARY REFOCUSED HER LIFE AROUND A QUALITY

Earlier I referred to a corporate secretary who identified with beauty as the core quality that best expressed who she was. This insight allowed her to appreciate her previously "automatic" ways of showing beauty. She had always enjoyed arranging flowers and invariably had a fresh bouquet on her desk. Colleagues passing by would remark on the pleasure it gave them to see these artful, colorful displays in the otherwise stiff corporate setting.

As she became increasingly aware that her flower arrangements brought out an appreciation of beauty in others as well, she decided to look for more opportunities to pursue her talent. That is, she decided to set specific *goals*. She started within her company by asking to be put in charge

VISION	PURPOSE	GOALS
Who I am	What I do	How I do it
Beauty	Flower arrangements	• Do some on spec
		• Get an order and fill it
		• Attend flower arranging classes

of arranging flowers in the lobby of her building, a paid job. That done, she made it a goal to supply other lobbies as well, so that a trip to the flower market would pay off. She learned the ins and outs of the professional flower mart. She bought bowls and baskets for the flowers, and in the evening took classes on flower arranging to enhance her intuitive talent.

In short, she established specific, measurable goals tied to the expression of who she was, and began to overflow with creativity. Her business has now expanded beyond her corporate clients to private parties and weddings. She knows she could pursue this work full-time if she chose. Her life seems to hold many options—all because she became aware of the link between who she already was (beauty) and what she could do (arrange flowers).

Goals Are Not Limited to the Financial Sphere

Goals can be divided into two categories, financial and nonfinancial. The two are closely tied, as we shall see in chapter 5. Both need to be included in our plans so that we will be bringing our whole selves to bear on the development of True Wealth. In this way, we will maximize the results by benefiting from the multiplier effect of multilevel connections.

FINANCIAL GOALS

When we talk about financial goals, we are on familiar turf. Most of us focus on this realm because this is where the world keeps score. Further, we associate financial matters with everyday pressures. Relationships, hobbies, or even being attentive to a child can somehow be put off, but paying the mortgage cannot. Making money is a preoc-

cupation that can divert us from other aspects of life that deserve attention.

And yet there is absolutely nothing wrong with having healthy financial goals. If you want to collect money—I do—then press on. My only hope is that you start to see money as a part of your overall life, rather than separate from it. **Earn money to live life; don't live to earn money.** Consider money as one of many resources at your disposal to help you fully become who you already are.

This idea is hard to sell because you are being asked to trade something tangible (money) for something intangible (well-being) in a culture where the scorecard for measuring success is marked with tangibles. The truth is, though, that *you can have both*. Balance is the overall objective. Becoming who you are does not mean giving up money. As you will see, nonfinancial assets often drive the financial ones and can spawn financial options.

NONFINANCIAL GOALS

The concept of nonfinancial goals may be new to you, although possibly you already set such goals intuitively. Nonfinancial goals have as their object something intangible—something not directly translatable into money terms. Health, education, friendships, community projects, personal or spiritual growth, and leisure goals such as travel and hobbies are all examples.

Nonfinancial goals are important because of their relationship to financial goals. When they are included with financial goals as equal partners, they have the power to generate new options. But they are also important in their own right.

When you think about nonfinancial goals you can concentrate on what you really want. What are the objectives that relate to the life qualities that represent who you are? For example, if you seek joy, what goal can you set to bring more

FOR EVERY QUALITY THERE ARE MANY GOALS—AN EXAMPLE

An engineer I know seeks freedom as a quality. Now, there are many ways to experience freedom—as many ways as there are people. He could have worked harder in order to collect more money and invest it in higher-risk options so that he could retire sooner. Seeing mobility as a kind of freedom, he could have gotten more education to enable him to change jobs. He could have decided to take more hikes in the wilderness. But for him, the goal was to take thirty minutes at his lunch hour to run. In this way he let go of the stress that had built up during the morning. Then, right after he returned home, he made a point of sitting quietly for twenty minutes as a way to clear everything before joining his family.

laughter and fun into your life? Perhaps a goal to make time each week to see a friend, to go to a movie or take a hike, or to follow an interest in music or a hobby would be in order. In other words, when you are setting nonfinancial goals, it is a good time to dream a little.

If peace was a quality with which you identified, then goals aimed at bringing peace into your life would be appropriate and connective. What could you do to *live* the quality of peace? You might become involved in groups that work toward world peace, or you might take a course in conflict resolution to learn new ways of achieving resolution. Possibly you would use your new skills to resolve a dispute with an enemy. You might simply strive to demonstrate peace in your actions as you go about your life.

Perhaps health is an issue for you. What goals might you set to make your life more healthful? Maybe you would decide to give up smoking or

drinking. Because these activities can be addictive, you might have to set further specific goals involving seeking professional help in order to meet the first goal. Perhaps you are overweight or have a high cholesterol count. Maybe your knees are weak because you have run so many marathons. Whatever the health problem, you would want to set goals that would help you come to grips with it.

Many people choose educational goals to bring them closer to a particular quality. For instance, a middle-aged woman whose children are grown might return to school to study business—a first step toward loosing the entrepreneurial spirit that she has recognized as an important, previously untapped quality. Someone for whom tolerance and understanding are key qualities might start to learn a new language as a means of getting to know other people better. Another popular area of intangible goal setting is improving family relationships. In other words, the options are legion once you are aware of the qualities that are important to you.

In any case, setting nonfinancial goals is a process of discovery or uncovering. It has more to do with "being" than "having." It is a time of dreaming and then acting on the dream to cause it to happen.

Setting Goals That Connect with Your Vision

Goals are specific, prioritized ways in which we can ground the values or qualities that represent our vision. Goals that are based on your vision and purpose are the proof that the connective bridge between inner and outer has been built.

Review what you wrote about vision. Does it still feel right?

In setting goals, it is essential that you connect with your purpose and vision. For example, the

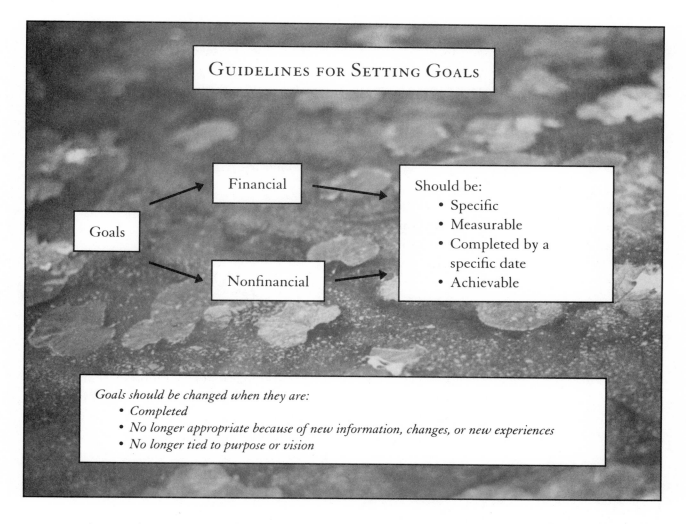

GUIDELINES FOR SETTING GOALS

Goals → Financial → Should be:
- Specific
- Measurable
- Completed by a specific date
- Achievable

Goals → Nonfinancial →

Goals should be changed when they are:
- *Completed*
- *No longer appropriate because of new information, changes, or new experiences*
- *No longer tied to purpose or vision*

child who elects to attend law school to please a parent is not true to his or her own vision and thus is planning an inappropriate action. Goals that are unconnected to who you are will take you off course and tend not to work. Thus, test each one for appropriateness.

Here are some general guidelines for setting goals:

1. Make them specific.
2. Make them measurable.
3. Set time frames for their completion.
4. Be sure they are achievable.

According to these guidelines, a goal to "become rich" or "get an education" is *not* satisfactory. What does "rich" or "education" mean? Neither one is specific enough to hold meaning and be measurable, nor is it really feasible to set a time frame for completing either one.

On the other hand, a goal to save $50,000 in two years is specific, measurable, and tied to a completion date. A goal to apply to an engineering college by next month is also specific and measurable.

Each goal should also be suitable and achievable. For example, someone seventy years old who decides to go to medical school would probably be unable to achieve this goal. If the quality of service was behind such a goal, undoubtedly other, more suitable forms for expressing it could be found. One possibility would be simply calling on bedridden people in convalescent homes once a week.

Finally, there must be intention and firm commitment behind each goal. To do anything worthwhile in life requires a measure of good old-fashioned passion for the task. Each of us has experienced excitement about doing something that truly interests us. Apply this feeling test. If the goal meets this review, it is probably fully appropriate.

I know of a woman who owns and runs a small business who would like instead to do charitable work full-time. Two qualities to which she relates are freedom and humanitarianism. She does not have enough net worth to quit, and the sale of the business would probably not yield enough capital to support her. She therefore set a goal to find a manager to run the business so that she could be free to do her charitable work. She also calculated the minimum amount of money she would need each month to keep herself and her business going. She set a date for accomplishing her goal. In the meantime, she decided to turn over some of her day-to-day responsibilities to

staff and to work primarily as a consultant, for which she would take a salary. Thus her goal of becoming financially free to do charitable work, which began with the search for a manager, has entailed setting other goals as well, all centered on bringing about the transfer. Her goals have been specific, measurable, time-based, achievable, *and* connected with who she is.

EXERCISE
BECOMING AWARE OF NONFINANCIAL GOALS BY EXAMINING WHAT YOU DO EVERY DAY

One way to approach nonfinancial goals and assure their connectedness to qualities you value is to watch what you do each day in order to discover the things that feel important. For example, I meditate each day. Nothing heroic. I just find it useful to sit quietly for twenty minutes or half an hour. Because I do this, I assume I must have a reason (connection) for doing it. Look for the connection. In my case, meditation furnishes a sense of inner peace, and peace is a quality with which I connect. I could just as easily work for peace in a number of other ways, but I choose this way. Thus, continuing to meditate is one of my nonfinancial goals.

Or look at freedom. A person who changes jobs may be reflecting this quality. Someone who dares to start a company may be doing the same thing. To escape from the stress of externally imposed work in a large company, many risk starting their own firm, perhaps finding self-imposed demands less stressful. Developing a long-range financial plan is another reach for freedom, in this case financial freedom.

Helping a friend points to the quality of service, while bringing laughter to people reflects joy. The form does not matter. Seeing the connection is the key.

Thus, take a few moments to look at the everyday activities that feel important to you and see if they reflect a quality with which you identify. I'll bet they do. Making this connection will indicate that you are onto a valuable nonfinancial goal.

Resolving Conflicting Goals in a Marriage or Other Close Relationship

When two people with intertwined lives set goals, they will inevitably come to conflicts of will. A husband wants a new car and a wife wants to complete her Ph.D. Unfortunately there is not enough money to do both at the same time. Another classic issue: He wants to get out of the corporate rat race, move to the country, and be a farmer. She wants to stay in the city where the children can get a better education and she has career ties. Even more common is the husband who has the opportunity to retire early at a time when his wife needs greater family income to support her goal of earning the master's degree that would lead to a whole new career for her.

What to do? Talk about it.

The by-product of communication may be more important than the initial issue that caused the contest. A wife may be offered a job in another city with a great promotion and salary increase. Who moves? Does the husband quit his job and find work in the new city? Talk about it. I know two young married musicians who were offered jobs in symphony orchestras in different cities. Both are tops in their chosen instrument. What do they do? Talk about it.

When situations of this sort arise, my "solution" is for each party in the conflict to return to the core qualities identified earlier and to search for alternative forms of expressing them. As you'll recall, any one quality can be expressed in a number of forms; examining alternatives can lead to a solution in which both partners' needs can be satisfied. Sometimes it is not a matter of finding alternative forms but of following nontraditional paths that allow the partners to continue pursuing the same forms. In the case of the musicians, they chose to live apart a lot of the time, having agreed that their musical careers took precedence. It seemed to work. After they had taken this decision, however, life dealt them another twist: miraculously, they both found jobs in the same orchestra!

My own experience is that conflict, in itself, is not the issue. It is how we handle the conflict and resolve it that matters. Examine the trade-offs and determine how they will affect both parties' ability to find a way to express an important life quality in their work. If nothing else happens in this process, both partners will have drawn closer together and learned more about each another.

✂ EXERCISE
WORKSHEETS TO HELP IN IDENTIFYING GOALS

This exercise provides two worksheets to fill out—a Goals Mind Map and a Life Goals Priority List. There are two because it is possible, and useful, to approach the selection of goals from different perspectives.

The Mind Map

Some of us think in pictures rather than lists. I know I do. If you are like me, it will probably be easier for you to start identifying goals by drawing a picture. The Mind Map supplied in this book shows sample subject areas. The categories are not exhaustive; you will use some and add others. A young couple with a new baby will select different areas than a recently retired couple in their sixties.

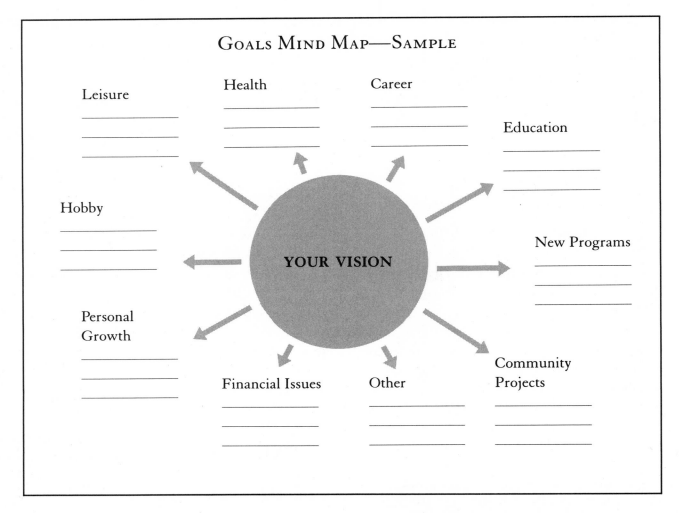

GOALS MIND MAP—SAMPLE

Leisure

Health
_____
_____
_____

Career
_____
_____
_____

Education
_____
_____
_____

Hobby
_____
_____

YOUR VISION

New Programs
_____
_____
_____

Personal
Growth
_____
_____

Financial Issues
_____
_____
_____

Other
_____
_____
_____

Community
Projects
_____
_____
_____

The Mind Map will help you sketch out broad goals. One of its key features is that it combines the financial and nonfinancial, thereby underscoring the connectedness of everything. You will start to see that money issues, important as they are, are only a portion of the total picture. The map will show the whole picture at a glance, and because it is a picture, you will remember it.

Life Goals Priority List

This list is the place for details, as well as for relating your goals to the life qualities that inspired them. Columns for measuring each goal and for setting completion dates are included. In this worksheet the goals are divided into financial and nonfinancial. You will measure financial

goals in dollars. Nonfinancial ones will have any number of measurement criteria; the choice is yours. Just be sure that whatever goal you select is specific and capable of being measured.

Don't select fifty goals. As you begin to work with this awareness process, keep it short and simple. You can add complexity after you're more familiar with the process. The Life Goals Priority List provides space for only five goals in each category, but if you have more, you can draw up your own sheet using this one as a model.

Beginning the Process

Work on this exercise during your prime time, that part of the day when you feel most alive. Don't be in a rush. Sit back and see what comes

LIFE GOALS PRIORITY LIST

GOALS	QUALITY EXPRESSED	HOW MEASURED?	COMPLETION DATE

FINANCIAL

NONFINANCIAL

to mind based on the qualities you identified in the chapter on vision and purpose. Let yourself dream a little.

Because I'm a visual person, I always start with the Mind Map. That may or may not be your preference. In any case, don't try to do it all in one sitting; keep coming back to it. Letting go of your thoughts for a while—letting them incubate—can give rise to new perspectives. In fact, letting go is a part of the creative process. Add new areas and goals within each area as they come to mind. Concentrate on seeing the financial goals as simply a part of the whole.

It also helps to relate each goal, as it comes up, to one or more of the qualities you chose earlier. Some people find it easier to begin with

qualities and select goals that seem to grow out of them. The point is to keep associating the qualities (your vision—who you are) with each goal.

After you finish the Mind Map (assuming you began with it), choose the top five or so goals, decide on their priority, and transfer them to the second worksheet. If you prefer to start with the Priority List, it might be convenient to note a number of goals on a separate sheet and then transfer them to the worksheet in order of importance. For each goal on the Priority List, write how the goal relates to a life quality. Then note how the goal is to be measured and when it should be completed.

If you are married, do a list separately from your spouse and then bring the two lists together.

Negotiate the final list. This step sounds a bit scary because "negotiating" can be hard business. The good news is that negotiation is dialogue, and a good debate is true communication. Many of us don't really talk to one another; we live together, alone. On a subject as important as money, talk can become close communication. It will probably encourage communication in other areas as well, and that is all to the good because it is contact.

When I introduced these ideas to a couple I know, they took a vacation to be alone together, so that they could talk about their separate visions and how they could work out any conflicts between the goals that each set. Previously they had spent relatively little time talking about things that really mattered to them.

In a sense, selecting financial goals with a spouse is an example of using a financial issue to develop a nonfinancial resource—communication. It is another illustration of multilevel linkage.

All Goals Have a Price Tag

Financial objectives usually involve investments. Some nonfinancial ones, such as going back to school, also involve the pocketbook, while others, such as bringing joy to people, do not. The price of the latter goal is taking time to develop awareness and then acting on it. Just as money is a resource, so is time. We are all constrained by our limited resources—of time, money, goodwill, personality, energy, etc. Although resources will be covered in depth in the next chapter, it is a good idea to open the subject by considering resource allocation in the context of goal selection.

Let's take as an example a young couple who have identified the qualities that define who they are, completed the worksheets in this chapter, and come up with the following four goals:

- On the financial side, they want to save for a house and start to invest for retirement thirty-five years away.
- Nonfinancially, they seek to improve their relationship and pursue further education.

Now let's help them figure the "resource cost"—both financial and nonfinancial—of implementing these goals over time.

A NEW HOME

Buying a home will require a down payment of $50,000. In addition, the couple wants to set aside $5,000 for fix-up costs in the two years after they move in. Landscaping, which will not cost a lot of money because they will do the work themselves, will nonetheless require time during weekends, using a nonfinancial resource that will thus be unavailable for other potential activities.

RETIREMENT GOALS

The couple wants to adopt an investment policy toward retirement over and above what their employers or social security may contribute. They would like to have a nest egg of $2,000,000 at the end of thirty-five years. They will begin by each paying into an IRA tax-deferred shelter each year. If they can reach this goal (that is, actually make the thirty-five annual contributions of $2,000 each) and if they can realize an average annual compounded return rate of 12 percent in mutual funds, they will have at retirement nearly $2,000,000 before taxes.

RELATIONSHIP ISSUES

Although they have chosen to make a commitment to their marriage, they are not really clear about what they can do to benefit their relationship. They have therefore decided to seek counseling as one means of achieving this goal. They estimate that the initial sessions will cost around $1,000. Workshops offer another possibility. Altogether, they feel they need to set aside $1,500 for the first year and see where that investment leads for subsequent periods.

EDUCATION

Both partners expect to want to pursue advanced degrees beginning in five years or so. This will involve night school as well as study time on weekends. They figure they will need $25,000 for tuition and supplies.

Expressed in chart form, the cost of their goals over time would look like this.

A Word about Nonrenewable Resources

Money can be regenerated. That is, a dollar lost can be re-earned. This is not true of *time*. Once a minute is past, it is lost forever. Consequently, time is a most important resource. Most of us tend not to attach much value to it. Only consultants who bill by the hour tend to value time in money terms. We need to attach both monetary and nonfinancial value to it. Time missed with children when they are young can never be regained. As parents, we should know that the early growing-up years with our children are critical. If we al-

| | RESOURCE ALLOCATION | | | TIME FRAME | | |
GOAL	Non-financial	Financial (Total)	NOW	2–5 Years	6–10 Years	11–35 Years
Home	Time	$ 55,000	$50,000	$ 5,000		
Retirement	Time	140,000	4,000	16,000	$20,000	$100,000
Relationships	Time	1,500	1,500	?	?	?
Education	Time	25,000			25,000	

Cost of Goals over 35 Years

The next step for this couple will be to examine their resources to confirm that they can entertain these goals. This will be the subject of the next chapter. For now, they have at least mapped out their gross financial need. Nonfinancially, their goals will consume a lot of time during certain periods. Additionally, they will need the asset of discipline.

Inevitably there will be conflicts with each other and between projects. The key connection will be their declared commitment to each other. That will probably drive all their other plans. Again, we can see how a nonfinancial goal like a commitment to a relationship provides the setting for all the rest, including the financial goals.

locate time away from them to any great extent, the lost experience can never be regained.

Emotional and physical energy are other reserves we all have. Overcommitment can drain either one of them. Thus it is wise to carefully weigh out any investment of these resources as well.

In the end, the important thing is to value each resource within the context of who you are and the qualities you choose to leave behind. (This might be a good time to reread the obituary you wrote in the preceding chapter, as a means of reaffirming values.) Goal setting lends a new and practical perspective to this task by connecting life's "everydayness" to your vision.

What we have is joined with who we are
to help us obtain what we want.

5

RESOURCES

According to the dictionary, a resource is "something that can be turned to for support or help." It is an "available supply that can be drawn upon when needed."

I offer that it is lots more. A resource is really not something separate from us into which we dip now and again. It is connected to us, a part of us that we have developed in the process of becoming who we are. Consequently, a resource represents an intangible value as well as a part of our net worth, which is both financial and nonfinancial.

What does this mean?

It means that our total resources are much more than the list of financial assets that bankers want to see when we apply for a loan. They are more than a list of the material things we have accumulated. They also embrace all of the intangibles we have and *are*. They are a part of us.

For example, if we went to college, that experience is a part of us. It is not something we can touch, but it has shaped us and in so doing become a part of us. If we are healthy, our health is a part of us. If we have an outgoing manner, that characteristic is a resource we can call on as we go about the process of living. Friendships we have developed form an integral part of who we are and what we can offer others. Travel, too, leaves its mark. Seeing other people and lands is a learning process, and all learning is influential. Our life experiences are as essential as our formal education.

We also have liabilities. Just as a financial liability is real, so are illness, a lack of experience or education, enemies, a sour disposition, fear or lack of trust, bad experiences, rigidness, and the like. We are shaped by everything we do and experience.

Why is this perspective useful?

To optimize the attainment of any goal, the odds are better if we use *all* of what we have. Unfortunately, few of us honor or even recognize ourselves as assets, thus neglecting a source of real power. We are our own key resource.

By becoming aware of all the assets we have, we optimize our chances for growth and progress, in a material sense as well as in the realm of intangibles. People often say that money isn't everything. Well then, what *is* "everything"? This chapter sets out to answer just that question, and then to propose doing something about attaining it in line with our goals.

As a way of including "everything," I have divided resources into two closely connected categories—financial and nonfinancial. Among our financial resources are all the material things we have gathered about us, things we can touch and for which we can financially account. Examples are our homes, cars, and investments such as stocks, bonds, and real estate. Usually we see such possessions as separate from us.

"Nonfinancial" is my word for all the non-material assets (or liabilities) we have gathered over the years. Examples are our dispositions, our education (both formal and informal), our health, friends, experiences, and the like—in other words, who we are. These intangible "belongings" are not only as relevant as financial assets,

---

Transforming a Nonfinancial Liability into a Valuable Financial Asset—A Story

SyberVision is a fast-growing and successful company creating and selling audio- and videotapes that promote personal achievement. These learning programs are based on a scientifically rooted learning technology that teaches patterning oneself after achievers as the best means of enhancing business, sports, or personal effectiveness. The approach is applicable in almost any field.

Steve DeVore is the founder and innovator of SyberVision. His story is a textbook example of connection.

As a child of two and a half, he contracted crippling polio. While his peers were running about in play and sport, Steve was confined to bed. His mother, refusing to accept the permanent disability prognosis offered by doctors, searched for solutions. She found one in the positive use of models. Each day she would take her son to a park and have him carefully watch people walk. Over and over, Steve would see natural walking patterns. Slowly, he was able to repattern his movements and regain the full use of both legs. The process was long but successful. In high school, he was an athlete.

Steve took a nonfinancial liability (polio) and transformed it into a nonfinancial asset (full mobility). But this story is just the beginning. Eventually he would take this nonfinancial experience and create a company that has now become a strong financial resource.

As a young adult, Steve looked back on his bout with polio. He had always wondered how he was able to regain the use of his legs. His inquiry into learning systems led to the formation of SyberVision. Using modeling tools not unlike the technique his mother had used, his company has developed over fifty learning products that span such topics as achievement, weight control, parenting, and foreign languages, as well as such sports as golf, tennis, self-defense, bowling, racketball, baseball, and skiing.

In effect, Steve moved from the nonfinancial liability of polio to create a fully financial asset in SyberVision. As is often the case, the financial asset was nonfinancially driven.

they are also, and more importantly, the creators of well-being and the drivers of our financial wealth.

I often refer to our combined financial and nonfinancial resources as the "means" by which we move and operate.

A Hidden Agenda— Connecting What We Have to Who We Are

Both categories of resources reflect who we have become to date and are therefore linked to the True Wealth process. Think about it. We dress as a statement of who we are. The cars we drive and the houses we live in are statements of who we are. So also are our dispositions, our formal and informal education, our health (a partial reflection of how we care for our bodies), the friends we keep, the enemies we create. The list is endless.

The point is that all of these aspects reflect *us*. They are mirrors of who we really are, and as such they can help us see ourselves. Therefore the effort to identify resources amounts to much more than cataloging our assets and liabilities for use in achieving goals—although this is the ostensible reason for doing it. This process will also enable us to see ourselves through what we have—another form of learning.

Most important, we will be addressing the question of whether our asset-gathering decisions are in line with our values and life vision. Having become clear about who we are (vision), what we do (purpose), and how we will carry out what we do (goals), we are now going to connect ourselves—our ultimate resource—and all of our other assets and bring everything to bear on achieving our goals. This task involves taking an inventory of all of our financial belongings and nonfinancial means. By clearly identifying each,

by seeing that they are all related to the task of achieving goals, we make them available to us.

Financial Assets Are Basically Nonfinancially Derived

The critical perception in linking financial and intangible resources is that financial assets are basically nonfinancially derived. In fact, this *is* the link. Seeing the connection allows us to move from an insight to something tangible.

We all know of people who have used their creative gifts to build businesses. Bob Hope, Jerry Lewis, Bill Cosby, and a host of other comedians have brought laughter to the world and built substantial businesses in the process. Walt Disney turned his form of creativity into a different kind of venture. In each case, a nonfinancial resource was used to create a financial one.

You have done the same thing, I am sure, but have not recognized the achievement. People routinely use their education as an asset to earn financially. In what ways have *you* used a nonfinancial asset to that end? This is not a theoretical question. Once you acknowledge having benefited financially from an intangible asset, you can proceed to pursue this result consciously. It is only necessary to become aware to make this connection work optimally.

You can also use a nonfinancial asset or even a liability to support another nonfinancial asset. I recall the young woman who used her bad back as a way of improving her health. When she accepted her back as a nonfinancial liability, she started to work on ways to transform it into a nonfinancial asset. As a result of doing yoga and other exercises and eating better, her overall health improved, her weight was under better control, and she experienced more energy and self-esteem.

Identifying and Working with Nonfinancial Assets— An Example

I am not a professional author. When I started to write the manuscript that has turned into this book, I knew very little about writing, publishing, or marketing books. However, as time passed, a table of contents emerged. I did some workshops around the ideas and concepts I had developed, and it became clear to me that I wanted to publish something that would empower people. Money and financial subjects seem to arouse a lot of fear and anxiety, and I felt I could help people resolve their fears through their own sense of themselves.

I began by putting into practice some of the ideas I was writing about.

One of the qualities I relate to is service, which seemed to me to be closely connected with what I was trying to do. I therefore set a goal to seek publication.

I then referred to my nonfinancial balance sheet. Among the assets, I found friends and contacts who had connections in publishing:

- An author friend had publisher and agent ties.
- Another friend knew an author who allowed me to use his name in approaching his publisher.
- A consultant friend who had done work for a major publisher wrote me a letter of introduction.
- A publisher I had met casually a year earlier came to mind; when I called, he offered leads.
- A friend who had started her own publishing company (in other subject areas) was helpful in explaining the industry.
- A fellow advisor on a foundation board introduced me to a newly formed West Coast publishing firm.

These were only the most direct links to publishing. I also got information from a professional contact of my wife's who had once been in publishing, and several business associates from my own financial consulting activities were able to offer leads which in turn led to other leads. Before I knew it, I had more connections with the publishing world than I would have imagined possible before I began.

My next step was to take what I had learned from my nonfinancial balance sheet and put it into action.

I began a lot of things in parallel. I wrote diligently, and when I wasn't writing I was calling friends who had themselves authored books to ask them for leads, thoughts, advice. These contacts led me to others who knew publishers, agents, or other authors. I began to collect information and war stories.

I circulated the manuscript to friends for comments, which I used to revise what I'd written. I gave small workshops using the material. I met with publishers. I listened.

There were dead ends. A publisher who had shown a keen interest didn't work out because our timing didn't mesh. After that, a published friend put me in touch with his agent in New York, who agreed to represent the work. He submitted the manuscript to some prominent publishers, all of whom turned it down. Finally the agent gave up.

What to do? I pulled on other pieces of string. I went back to my nonfinancial balance sheet and found additional ties to publishers. One was John Jeavons, with whom I had worked as a part of his network helping Third World people grow their own food. John had published through Ten Speed Press. That was the connection that proved meaningful.

It had taken a while, but I had successfully ended the search that had begun with a careful look at my nonfinancial balance sheet. And if the book does well, I will have derived a financial return with the help of a nonfinancial asset—my friends and business contacts.

What can you learn from this example?

First of all, value all of your resources, especially the nonfinancial ones. Be aware of the resource aspects of everyone you meet and everything you learn, and consider them in the light of your vision, purpose, and goals.

Then *use* your resources. They get better with use. Keep them current. Knowing what you have will help only if you link it to what you want (goals) and if you have access to it. **Being conscious of your resources provides the access.**

Also, be a resource for others. The connections work both ways. By being a resource, you will attract others to you and add to your nonfinancial balance sheet.

Gathering and Organizing Resource Information

As with so much of the True Wealth process, the prerequisite for identifying resources is an expansion of awareness. You must see things in a new light in order to gather and organize resource information in ways that make assets available for the completion of goals. In the end, you will have become more aware of your financial picture— the comings and goings of money in your life— as well as of your nonfinancial resource base. In the process you will learn more about who you are, this time from the perspective of your spending and investment patterns. You will have the opportunity to make changes in these patterns so that they better reflect who you really are.

STEP 1—GATHERING INFORMATION

An individual's or a firm's financial situation is usually expressed primarily in the form of balance sheets and income and expense statements.

We will take the same approach here. Gathering the data will require some inquiry into your monthly expenses and the value of your various assets. Initially you may have to guess at expense levels and asset values. But as time progresses, you will be able to refine these numbers.

On the nonfinancial side, you will develop a nonfinancial balance sheet. Because this is a novel tool, and because it requires a certain amount of self-awareness, it may take a bit more time than the financial statements.

Creating these statements is more a process than a task. As you do them, remember to connect resource identification to your goals. In this way you will see the ties that will suggest what to do with what you find.

The aim is to collect all of the resources available to you—financial as well as nonfinancial— so that you can invest them toward achieving your goals. Between the two kinds of statements, you will find you have an impressive resource base, and you will gain a sense of your own power. Self-empowerment, a quiet by-product of this effort, is something we all want.

STEP 2—INTERPRETING INFORMATION

Once collected, what does all this information mean? It is important to examine the statements from different perspectives to be sure that they yield all that they can show about you. Once a pattern of spending and investment emerges, the information can be used for financial and nonfinancial budget planning. That is, you will have a good enough understanding of your resource situation to know what is available for use and what should be held in reserve.

STEP 3—ACTING ON INFORMATION

Based on what you learn, you may decide to take corrective measures or to maintain the status quo. In either case you will want to take actions that reflect your goals. This means applying your resources in ways that are true to your vision and purpose.

EXERCISE
DEVELOPING A FINANCIAL BALANCE SHEET

The financial balance sheet is a statement of all of our material assets and liabilities at a given time. On the one hand it describes what we have; on the other, it lists how much of what we have is owned by others. The difference between the two—called net worth or equity—is what *we* own. As shown in the following figure, assets are typically listed on the left side of the statement and liabilities and net worth on the right. The two sides are meant to balance—hence the name.

Financial Balance Sheet
Date ———————

ASSETS	LIABILITIES & NET WORTH
What you have	Liabilities (What you have that is owned by others) Net worth (What you have that is owned by you)

The balance sheet is like a snapshot of the material things that traditionally have been considered of monetary value. The usual goal is to own as much of what we have as possible. With very expensive items, this can take many years. For instance, when we start out, most of us cannot afford to buy a home outright, so we borrow. Slowly, as the mortgage is paid off, the loan goes down and our net worth (the part we own) increases. At the end of our working life, the mortgage is paid off and the liability gone. Once we have no more debts, the only item on the right is our net worth, which equals our assets.

Assets are usually listed in order of how readily they can be converted to cash. The first group, called current assets, consists of items that can be converted into cash or its equivalent in a matter of days—bank deposits, listed stocks and bonds, listed mutual fund holdings, and the like. Because they are grouped together, it is easy to see how liquid the holder of these assets is, that is, how quickly he or she could respond to a need for ready cash.

The next group of assets consists of those with longer-term liquidity, such as real estate, unlisted stocks, and retirement investments. These are held with long-term intentions and are therefore usually unavailable for immediate cash transfer.

The sum of these two groups represents the total financial value of one's assets as of the date of the balance sheet.

The liability section is simply an inventory of the items listed as assets that are owned by others. Like assets, liabilities are divided into two groups: those due within one year (current liabilities) and those due beyond one year (long-term liabilities). For example, if one borrows to purchase a home, the amount owed the lender would be noted on the liability side. Because the loan would be a long-term one (say, fifteen or thirty years), the current year's portion of the debt would be shown as a current liability and the remainder under long-term debt.

The timing issue is important because it allows anyone reviewing the statement to see whether the owner of the assets has the funds available to meet short-term obligations.

The net worth section represents the portion of the assets listed that you actually own. Put another way, net worth (what you own) is the sum of assets (what you have) less the total of all your liabilities (the amounts owned by others until you pay off these debts).

How to Value Assets

In the traditional view, a balance sheet should be a conservative statement of one's financial status. Since we are not out to fool ourselves, and since our aim is to determine what we have that is available to support our goals, we will want to conform to the conservative rule.

This means that the value of a home is what the current market says it is worth—not what we might hope it is worth. For our purposes, we might consult a realtor for an informal estimate or extrapolate from recent sales of comparable properties in the neighborhood. The same goes for the value of a car. A new car, even if only a day or two old, is not worth nearly the purchase price, because it depreciated the minute it was driven off the dealer's lot. Art, antiques, and the like should also be valued conservatively. With art, the selling commissions are so high that they need to be figured into the valuation.

It is also important to date the statement as a warning to any reader (in this case ourselves) that the assets and liabilities had this particular value *as of this time*. Values change over time, and new statements will be needed to keep the financial picture current.

Worksheet for the Financial Balance Sheet

As you fill out the form on the following page, be sure to keep the conventions regarding current and long-term assets or liabilities in mind. This division will have real meaning when it comes to interpreting the entries.

To be sure you don't miss any of your assets, take a slow walk through your home and notice all the articles—large and small—that you have collected. Aside from such major belongings as the house itself, cars, and maybe a boat, you should list any other big-ticket items—art, sculpture, antiques, a family silver service, jewelry. Although you would not choose to sell such personal property, its value can be significant and thus can

be turned to in a crisis. Assets associated with hobbies can also be valuable. Examples are rare stamp collections, a lot of scuba gear or woodworking tools, looms for weaving, or camera equipment. On the other hand, ordinary home furniture, although expensive to acquire, depreciates straightaway and is often not worth noting.

The very act of looking for assets can cause you to reflect. For example, what does a hobby like photography, sewing, weaving, or writing tell you about who you are? Making an assets list is useful at several levels, as you will see during the interpretive stage of the process.

When you finish, lay the balance sheet aside while you go on to develop the other statements.

Financial Balance Sheet

Date _____

Assets (what I have)

CURRENT ASSETS		
CASH		
Checking	_____	
Savings	_____	
Total Cash		_____
LOANS Receivable	_____	
INVESTMENTS		
Bonds	_____	
Stocks	_____	
Mutual Funds	_____	
Cash Value:		
Insurance/Annuity	_____	
Other	_____	
Total Investments		_____
Total Current Assets		_____

LONG-TERM ASSETS		
INVESTMENTS		
Restricted Securities	_____	
Limited Partnerships	_____	
Real Estate	_____	
IRA/Keogh	_____	
Other	_____	
Total Investments		_____
OTHER ASSETS		
Home	_____	
Cars	_____	
Personal Property	_____	
Other	_____	
Other	_____	
Total Other Assets		_____
Total Long-Term Assets		_____

TOTAL ASSETS _____

Liabilities (what I have that is owned by others) **&**

Net Worth (what I have that I own myself)

CURRENT LIABILITIES		
UNPAID BILLS		
Rent	_____	
Utilities	_____	
Credit Cards	_____	
Charge Accounts	_____	
Insurance Premiums	_____	
Taxes	_____	
Other	_____	
Total Bills		_____
INSTALLMENT LOANS		
(Balance due within 1 year)		
Car	_____	
Bank	_____	
Home	_____	
Education	_____	
Other	_____	
Total Loans		_____
Total Current Liabilities		_____

LONG-TERM LIABILITIES		
(Balance due beyond 1 year)		
Home	_____	
Car	_____	
Taxes	_____	
Other	_____	
Total Long-Term Liabilities		_____

TOTAL LIABILITIES _____

NET WORTH _____
(Total assets less
total liabilities

TOTAL LIABILITIES & NET WORTH _____

EXERCISE
DEVELOPING AN INCOME AND EXPENSE STATEMENT

The income and expense statement is simply an accounting of our financial "comings and goings" over a given period of time. It describes what we buy and in what quantity. Usually the statement covers a month, year, or quarter. Ours will span a month because we usually think in terms of this period: we get paid monthly, and our expenses are billed monthly.

We all know to the penny how much money we earn, but we have only the foggiest notion of what we spend! Consequently, we tend to be vague about our net income or loss. With the availability of consumer credit through the credit card, many of us spend more than we make for some time before reality catches up with us.

The chart entitled "Financial Comings and Goings" describes how monies get divided and split off. Note that income from all the sources flows out to one of three areas:

· Expenses, those covering the bills that finance our everyday lives
· Major material possessions that appear on the financial balance sheet as assets
· Purchases of intangibles such as education, health, and travel that appear on the nonfinancial balance sheet

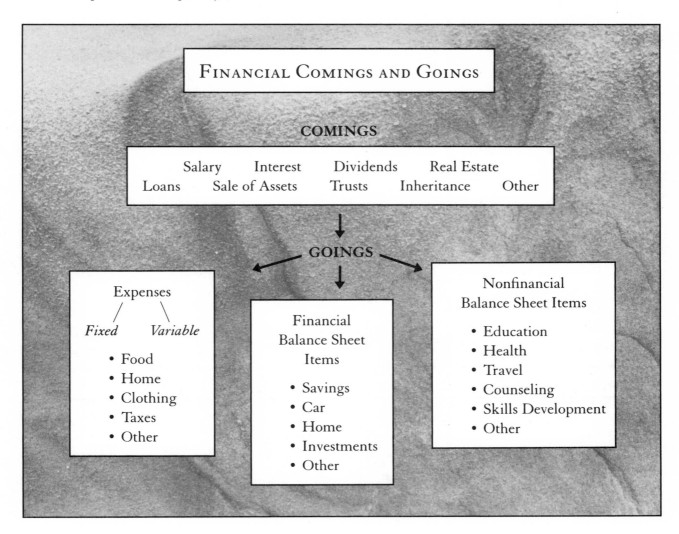

FINANCIAL COMINGS AND GOINGS

COMINGS

| Salary | Interest | Dividends | Real Estate |
| Loans | Sale of Assets | Trusts | Inheritance | Other |

GOINGS

Expenses
/ \
Fixed *Variable*
· Food
· Home
· Clothing
· Taxes
· Other

Financial Balance Sheet Items
· Savings
· Car
· Home
· Investments
· Other

Nonfinancial Balance Sheet Items
· Education
· Health
· Travel
· Counseling
· Skills Development
· Other

Income and Expense Statement

Period from _____ *to* _____

"Comings"

INCOME SOURCES

Salary
- Wife _____
- Husband _____

Interest _____

Dividends _____

Capital Gains _____

Rents, Pensions _____

Loans _____

Other _____

Total Income _____

"Goings"

LIVING EXPENSES	*Fixed* *(Not Controllable)*	*Variable* *(Controllable)*
Housing		
Rent or Mortgage	_____	
Utilities	_____	
Insurance	_____	
Taxes	_____	
Repairs		_____
Other	_____	_____
Food		_____
Transportation		_____
Medical		_____
Clothing		_____
Insurance (Life, Liability)	_____	
Personal Odds and Ends		_____
Federal and State Taxes	_____	
Entertainment		_____
Child Care	_____	_____
Other	_____	_____
Total Living Expenses		_____

"Leftovers"

Total Comings	_____
Less Total Goings	_____
Amount Left Over	_____

Leftovers to:
- Savings _____
- Investments _____
- Gifts _____
- Other _____

The income and expense statement reflects everyday expenses as well as monthly payments for such large items as a home or a car. Insofar as we might be paying off a loan for education or a special trip, these amounts too would appear in the expense portion of the statement.

Some of our expenses are fixed—that is, they are the same every month. Mortgage or rent payments are examples. By contrast, what we spend on items such as clothing or entertainment or even food can vary considerably from month to month. That is, we can control it. In the income and expense statement we will distinguish between these two kinds of expenses. In this way we start to see what is controllable and what is not, a helpful distinction from a management point of view. Once we are aware of what is controllable, we can adjust cash outflow more precisely in response to changes in income.

Worksheet for the Income and Expense Statement

In the form opposite, not all of the items will apply to everyone. Fill in the applicable spaces, and add other items as needed. The purpose is to get a close approximation of what it costs to live in comparison with what you earn.

If this is the first time you've prepared an income and expense statement, many of your expense entries will probably be guesses. Don't worry. As you continue with this process, you will see the need for keeping track, and the numbers will become more accurate. I suggest that you take at least two months during the year (make them fairly far apart and not months when you know you'll have extraordinary expenses) and note every penny you spend by category (food, housing, entertainment, etc.). In this way, you will be able to make more realistic estimates.

At the bottom of the form is a section called "Leftovers." This is not a part of the traditional income and expense statement. I added it so that you can note how much of what is left over after expenses—if anything—goes into investments or other forms of savings. Gifts to charities are included here because I consider them to be investments in society.

EXERCISE
DEVELOPING A NONFINANCIAL BALANCE SHEET

Now it is time to compile nonfinancial information to supplement the financial data we have already collected. We will develop a nonfinancial counterpart of the financial balance sheet. Although we will not do a nonfinancial income and expense statement, the concept *is* transferable, as the "Nonfinancial Resource Flow Chart" on the next page shows. Just as we spend money, we "spend" nonfinancial resources as well. Just as financial resources are often spent for nonfinancial assets, so nonfinancial resources are invested toward financial goals.

While the financial balance sheet records all of our material belongings, the nonfinancial one discloses the intangible "means" and capabilities that we have acquired over the years that are now available to us. Since the means create the ends, they are key elements in the search for well-being. And, as we have seen, financial assets are often nonfinancially driven, making our current endeavor all the more important.

As you start to consider your intangible resources, you will find that many insights will emerge. The name of a friend may trigger an idea. You may become aware of a liability and start to do something about it, thereby transforming it into an asset. Undoubtedly you will begin to value your enthusiasm, creativity, education, or family and to realize that not only do you have a lot going for you, you also have a lot to draw on in support of your goals—and that is the purpose of this exercise.

Worksheet for the Nonfinancial Balance Sheet

Earlier you walked through your home looking at everything you had bought and used this inspection to gain insights into your financial resources. Now "walk through your life" to see what intangibles you have collected. This review will be the basis for your nonfinancial balance sheet. As with every other step of the True Wealth process, awareness is crucial.

The balance sheet that follows contains items that are meant to be illustrative only. They are derived from statements done by many people and so may or may not be relevant to you. Their purpose is to trigger thought. You will want to come up with a statement that represents you as an individual.

Start work at a time when you will not be disturbed and can let your mind wander through your life to date. Go over your skills, your formal and informal education, your good and bad experiences, your attitudes, friends and enemies, health issues. Get in touch with liabilities as well as assets. After all, a liability can point you in the direction of an asset.

For example, if intimacy is missing from your life, and if you acknowledge its absence as a liability, the very fact that you were aware enough to identify it will encourage you to take steps to develop it. Put another way, if you don't realize

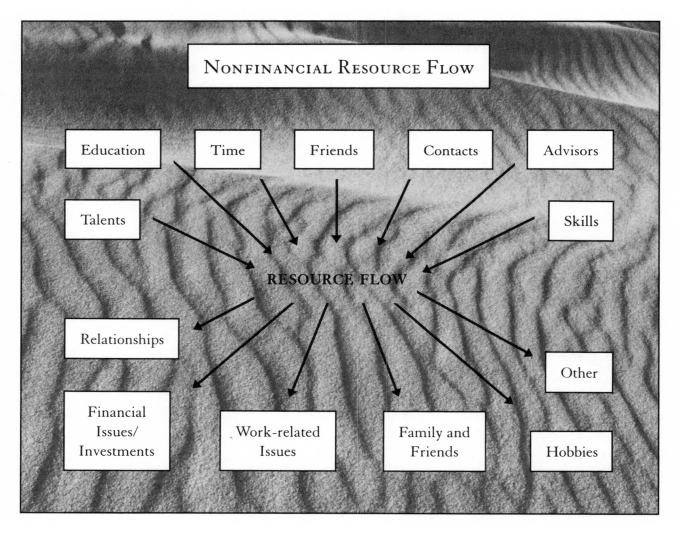

you are missing something, there is no way to obtain it.

Don't forget to consider the sports you participate in. They may offer some interesting insights.

The task is to sharpen awareness of all the intangibles we tend to take for granted. Remember, **your purpose is to become conscious of all of those resources that can be available for support of your goals.** It isn't important that you see an application for each resource right at this moment. Once they are on paper, though, they are available for use.

Do your nonfinancial balance sheet over several days, allowing time for statements because it requires more introspection. Probably you will be surprised at the number of nonfinancial resources you uncover. In fact, your nonfinancial balance sheet may end up being several pages long!

NONFINANCIAL BALANCE SHEET

Date _____

Resources   **Liabilities**

WHAT I HAVE

For instance:

Health/Illness

Education/Lack of education

Relationships/Lack of relationships or problem relationships

Friends/Enemies

Contacts/Lack of contacts

Talents/Undeveloped capabilities

Hobbies/No outside interests

HOW I AM

For instance:

Cheerful disposition/gloomy disposition

Age as a positive factor/Age as a negative factor

Flexibility/Rigidity

Broad interests/Narrow interests

Accepting attitude/Judgmental attitude

Note: These items are meant to be suggestive only. Use the blanks to fill in the items that hold meaning for you. Be sure to list all your important relationships, friends, and contacts, as well as any problem relationships or enemies.

Interpreting Resources and Connecting Them to Life Values

Because what you have is driven by who you are, your possessions provide a clue to your values. Interpreting your financial and nonfinancial statements will lead to insights about yourself and the relationships of different elements in the whole scheme of your life. It is important to start the interpretive process without judgment. There are no "shoulds"; whatever is, is. Just look at it within the context of your new self-awareness.

I know a young woman who is a ballet dancer. She lives to dance. Beauty expressed in motion is the quality she most cherishes. She will never be rich from dance. Her balance sheet is a disaster from a banker's point of view, but she uses her nonfinancial wealth—her body and her love of dance—to create great beauty.

The same utter commitment to a life vision must be true for a musician, a painter, or any other kind of artist. They fully express who they are by exploiting their intangible assets to an extreme. Some gain recognition in the marketplace but many do not. Irving Berlin and the Beatles did. Van Gogh did not, at least not during his lifetime. The only real issue is to live a life expressing the full potential of the qualities one sees in oneself. Keep an open mind, and to the extent that financial or nonfinancial resources can help you realize your potential, use them.

Before reviewing your statements, walk through your home again, either literally or in your mind's eye. Focus on what is there—a library of books, records, film; a stereo system and VCR; a piece of furniture handed down from grandparents (a link to the past); sports equipment; the car in the driveway; the home itself; the neighborhood.

What does all this say about you? Now that you are looking at it in a new light, what is your reaction? Take a minute to jot down some thoughts. I know that when I made this tour, I saw a lot of stuff I really didn't need. I wondered why I had ever bought it. Looking at my records and library I could see how my taste had changed over the years. On the walls I saw paintings given to me by family, and I was reminded of my boyhood. The memory brought with it an appreciation of my parents and their parenting. This in turn reminded me of my own role as a parent to my children. I found myself reaffirming the value that my wife and children hold for me.

In all these material goods I saw nonmaterial values! It was a powerful experience and took me back to my nonfinancial balance sheet to note, as an asset, my family ties.

INTERPRETING YOUR FINANCIAL BALANCE SHEET

The picture you obtain from a walk around your home should be broadly reflected in your financial balance sheet. Of course, small things like a bicycle are not on the balance sheet, but the big-ticket items are. On the other hand, you won't see stock certificates on a walk through the house, but they will appear on the balance sheet.

In any case, what is your reaction as you examine this statement? You may feel pride (if you have met a lot of your financial goals) or fear (if you have not saved much). Look at your level of debt relative to your assets. Do others own most of what you have collected, or do you?

Do the assets and liabilities reflect your vision and purpose? Do they fit with your new goals? If, for example, you identified with the quality of freedom, are the items you see in harmony with a life of freedom? A clutter of things made a friend of mine feel constrained. He "simplified" his life by calling the Goodwill folks and afterwards felt more free. See if you can find a tie between what you have and who you are. Making this link is one of the bonuses of this process. It takes us backwards from the material to the philosophical when, at the start, we were going the other way.

Here are some questions to stir thought.

1. How financially liquid are you? That is, what is your ability to meet short-term obligations? To find the answer, take the total of your short-term assets on the balance sheet and divide it by the total of your short-term liabilities. The result will be a ratio that expresses your liquidity. For example, if you have $10 in short-term assets and $5 in short-term liabilities, you have $2 for every $1 of debt, or a 2 to 1 quick ratio. This is pretty good coverage. If the opposite is true, you are pretty well leveraged, meaning that possibly you have overborrowed. You could have a problem if your source of income were cut off by a recession or the loss of your job due to disability, layoff, or some other reason.

At times, though, higher debt is reasonable—for instance when one is building a business or starting out in life generally. In any case, high debt with an offsetting asset is better than high debt without it. Borrow for a home, and you have the home to show for the money spent. Borrow to go on a vacation, and you have nothing to show for it, so to speak. On the other hand, a vacation or travel can be a form of education and thus represent a nonfinancial asset funded by a financial one. Interpretation is all a matter of context. Look at your situation and take your own readings. **The point is to determine whether what you have is in line with who you have discovered you already are.**

2. What is your debt in relation to your net worth? As debt can be a restraining force, this perspective is an important one. At issue is the role you want financial debt to play in your life plan. Debt is one of a number of financial tools. It is good or bad depending on how it is used or misused.

One measure of debt is its level relative to your net worth, or what you own. Put differently, how much of what you have is owned by others? This question is at the heart of the debt-to-net-worth ratio. By relating total debt to net worth, you can see to what extent you have used this tool and judge its appropriateness within the context of your vision and purpose.

For example, a couple who wants freedom in their life might find themselves very locked up if they owed $4 for every $1 of net worth. On the other hand, if that $4 represented borrowing on a home that was offsetting the debt, then this debt-to-net-worth ratio could be misleading—especially if the home investment reflected the couple's vision and purpose.

Or suppose a young family borrowed heavily to build a new business. The debt may represent a high risk but be completely in line with their purpose and therefore appropriate. On the other hand, using debt inappropriately can be dangerous. I heard about one young couple whose rental application was turned down when the landlord learned that their credit card debt was $46,000 and their joint income only $3,500 a month. If either one lost their job, they would not be able to cover their rent. This couple had gone on a spending spree that was completely out of line with their income. They had run up their twelve credit cards to the hilt. Their debt level was clearly too high. One wonders if their level of well-being was well served by the acquisition of so many material goods. Certainly they could not be experiencing financial freedom.

There are no hard-and-fast rules in evaluating debt. The important thing is to view your debt level within the context of who you are and what you are trying to achieve. If your debt looks out of hand, you will want to take note of the situation and consider it in contemplating any further big purchases. On the other hand, high debt may be reasonable given what you have obtained in return for the money spent. Or you may feel completely protected if your income can easily cover the periodic payments. Whatever the case, your new awareness is the first step toward making changes—if any changes seem called for.

3. How many of your assets are liquid or available for use in other forms? For example, if you have current assets worth $5 and your total assets are worth $25, most of your resources are tied up. This picture is typical for a young couple investing all of their money in a home. Things will be tight until they can boost their liquid assets through earnings. Still, their situation, tight as it may seem at times, may be right in line with their vision and goals even though a banker might be unwilling to lend them any money at the moment.

The relationship of liquid to long-term assets is worth looking at from time to time. I have a friend who has borrowed against his business, his home, and all of his investment property. His business is faltering, two tenants have canceled their leases on the two commercial properties he owns, and the bank is threatening foreclosure. His house of cards may be about to fall, and he has no reserves. In a chancy economic environment, his prospects don't look good. His situation might have been very different if he had looked at the relationship between his liquid and long-

term assets and realized that, although he had many material assets, he had woefully few liquid ones to turn to if trouble arose. On the other hand, he is a very creative person who is comfortable with risk. If everything collapses, he has such nonfinancial resources as youth (that is, time), experience, and an innovative spirit with which to earn it all back. In effect, he relies on his nonfinancial resources to compensate for his extreme lack of liquidity.

In general, then, you are examining your balance sheet for information that may be useful to you relative to your goals. What assets are available—or "arrangeable"—to meet goals? What can the balance sheet tell you about the financial goals you had in the past? What does it indicate about your willingness to take risks? In the next chapter we will use this same statement to assess your attitude toward risk.

INTERPRETING YOUR INCOME AND EXPENSE STATEMENT

In interpreting this statement, you will probably find few surprises. We all know how much income we bring in each month. Ask yourself, though, how secure the income streams are. Do you have more than one source of income? How well are your employers doing? (If you are self-employed, you know how well you are doing.) If you are in a couple, do both of you work? How dependent are you on that second income if there is one? What is it like with both of you working? If you were to lose your job, how secure would you be in your own self-worth?

If a family business is involved, what qualities of living emerge? How much of your time is taken up with working? What do you do with the time left over? Can life qualities you identified

A Personal Story about Saving

I have always sought the quality of freedom—freedom to work at what I do best and freedom to be of service (another quality that is important to me). I wanted my family to be free also. Most of all, I wanted never to be owned by any employer. I wanted to be able to change jobs if that seemed right, or to move if that seemed appropriate.

Freedom was more important to me than having things. But how to attain it? I decided to lay down a family policy of not having debt except for the purchase of a home, and to limit even that obligation as much as possible.

I was fully aware that this approach meant that we would have to defer having things. It also meant that investments were slow to grow, because we wouldn't borrow and we didn't have a lot of our own cash to invest. However, as time passed, our savings accumulated. Before we had children, our two incomes permitted a fairly rapid savings rate, and the interest compounded. We drove our cars over a hundred thousand miles before even considering buying new ones. We paid cash for everything, including our hiking vacations, which were inexpensive and wonderful.

As our jobs paid more, we invested our savings, and our net worth grew. There was nothing very heroic in any of this except that we knowingly lived the qualities that were important to us. We were never big spenders (and are not now) because *having* didn't seem as important as *being*. After our children left, we were back to the two of us again, pursuing the same policy. However, we are now able to travel and have been to many memorable places in the world. We are both self-employed and do work that is meaningful to us. I am writing more, and my wife has become a licensed counselor after returning to school and getting two master's degrees.

There have been lots of bumps along the way, and there will be more in the future. But no matter. The point is that we have held onto what is important to us and have used our resources—both financial and nonfinancial—to attain our goals.

as important be realized in the present financial context? In short, does the income statement say anything about the rest of your life?

On the expense side, where do the big expenses cluster? Do the fixed ones (rent or mortgage, taxes, insurance payments) dominate? Are the variable ones (entertainment, clothing, vacations, hobbies) under control? Is there room for savings? Interestingly, the Swiss—the world's greatest savers—consider a deposit to savings to be an expense. That is, they contribute to savings before paying the bills. Then if they have anything left over after paying the bills, they consider saving that, too. In contrast, we not only save little but borrow to spend. It is a whole different way of being.

Finally, ask yourself also whether there are expenses that perhaps ought to be there to support a nonfinancial goal such as a hobby, further education, or improving a relationship. The point is not so much to become Swiss-like, but to **tailor spending to match goals that emerge from an awareness of who you are**. The task is again one of connection—of relating who you are to what you have and using what you have to support who you are. Everything goes both ways.

INTERPRETING YOUR NONFINANCIAL BALANCE SHEET

The insights you obtain from your nonfinancial balance sheet will influence decisions you take about financial investments as well as nonfinancial measures. How complete do you think your statement is? If you have doubts, perhaps it would be best to let it rest for a while and return to it later with fresh ideas.

At first, just take note of the items that came up for you, since they represent the intangibles you value most. What qualities do they represent? Are the qualities you identified earlier reflected in these items? In other words, does this statement reflect who you are?

Do you see ways to draw on any of these resources to accomplish goals? Are there any conflicts between a financial goal and a nonfinancial one? For example, is there competition for the money to buy you the education you nonfinancially seek? Are there other demands on the same funds?

What does this balance sheet say about the value you place on relationships? What does it say about your interests?

Do you feel that you are appropriately using the education that you have? Is lack of education standing in the way of your doing something you really want to do? On the liability side, do you see anything that could be changed immediately?

Does the nonfinancial balance sheet reflect the skills you possess? After all, a skill is a resource. Consider skills you have developed in different parts of your life, not just your job—sports, hobbies, charitable activities, politics. Don't overlook behavioral skills, such as helping people resolve conflicts. Then look behind the skills and note their link to the person you have discovered yourself to be.

Acting on the Information Revealed in the Statements

Having gathered and interpreted your resources, you are now ready to bring all of your insights to bear upon achieving your goals by using these resources.

Start by relating financial and nonfinancial resources. For example, suppose you need a job. Is there a person (a nonfinancial resource) who can help you attain this financial goal? Or, if you are pursuing an intangible goal, is there a financial asset that can help you reach it? Cash, for example, can be used to buy education, pursue counseling to improve a relationship, or learn yoga to ease a back problem and thus promote health.

Look also for ties within the financial and nonfinancial categories. For example, a friend may be able to advise you on diet and health, or exercising may allow you to pursue an activity that you previously had to forego for health reasons. The options abound.

Now act on your insights. Return to your goals and start to relate a particular resource to a goal—as I did in finding a publisher to take on my manuscript or as Steve DeVore's mother did in beating the doctors' pessimistic prognosis for her son. Base your action on the theory that you have the inner and outer resources to achieve your objectives.

By the way, because financial assets *are* often nonfinancially driven, this approach works even if your goals do not relate to who you are. The effect is simply much more powerful if the goals connect to the qualities that represent who you are. You also avoid the destructive aspects of any disharmony that can occur if you do not follow your vision.

Before You Start Allocating Your Resources, Set Aside Reserves

Everyone needs reserves—be they energy, insights, love, friends, or money—to "run the operating system," to borrow a computer term. It does not make sense to run out of any resource. Therefore it is important to hold some resources in reserve for emergencies.

In chapter 10, "Investment Possibilities," we will come to the point of making investment decisions in line with your goals. We will also be returning to the issue of making full use of your total resources. Before choosing specific investments, though, we will want to provide for life's unforeseen needs by creating both financial and nonfinancial reserves. Many of us already do this in the financial realm, for instance by holding contingency funds in savings. In this way we insure against illness, being fired or laid off, or just deciding to leave a job without having an immediate offer in hand. Few of us, however, build nonfinancial reserves.

The maps on the following pages illustrate the place of reserves in the overall context of investment resources. Financial reserves can come from either resources in hand, borrowing, or a combination of the two. In looking for sources of funds, only the balance sheet is pertinent because that statement alone represents assets that are currently available. Income from a job or an investment is not considered because it is a *future* resource that may or may not materialize. Still, we can borrow against income, as on a personal loan, just as we can borrow against an asset in order to obtain funds.

Nonfinancial resources like time, friends, health, or energy cannot be so readily "borrowed." However, they can be developed in order to build reserves. Seeing a dearth, we can set about making friends, developing contacts, honing skills, improving our health, or getting more education, to mention only a few of the possibilities. Time is a particularly precious resource. If, for instance, we devote all of our time to financial or business objectives and have none left over for family relationships, we may find the quality of our life deteriorating as a child or a spouse becomes distant.

Holding resources in reserve is a means of ensuring balance. We need balance in order to remain whole.

But how large should a reserve be? That depends on you and your willingness to risk, both

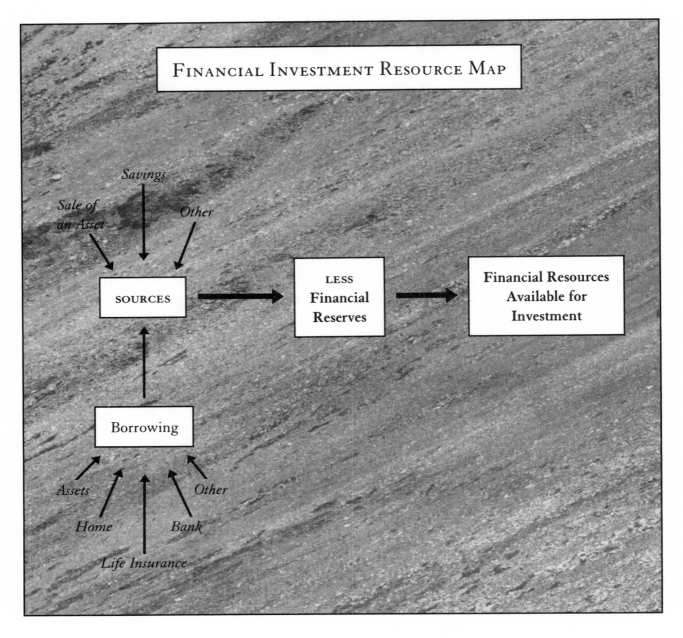

FINANCIAL INVESTMENT RESOURCE MAP

financially and nonfinancially. Some people insist on having three months' worth of living expenses in the bank at any time. I know one couple who is not comfortable with any less than two years' worth of expenses in a savings account or money market fund, where it is readily accessible. Others prefer to have their financial assets earning the maximum amount all the time and never hold liquid financial reserves; perhaps their income flow is large enough to cover sudden needs. Also,

people who have high confidence in themselves often feel comfortable betting all their financial resources on a new venture because they believe in their ability to get other work if the venture does not turn out as expected. In other words, their belief in themselves (a nonfinancial resource) serves as a financial reserve.

Nonfinancial reserves are as valuable as financial ones, and sometimes more so because they are irreplaceable. Time, for example, is a nonrenew-

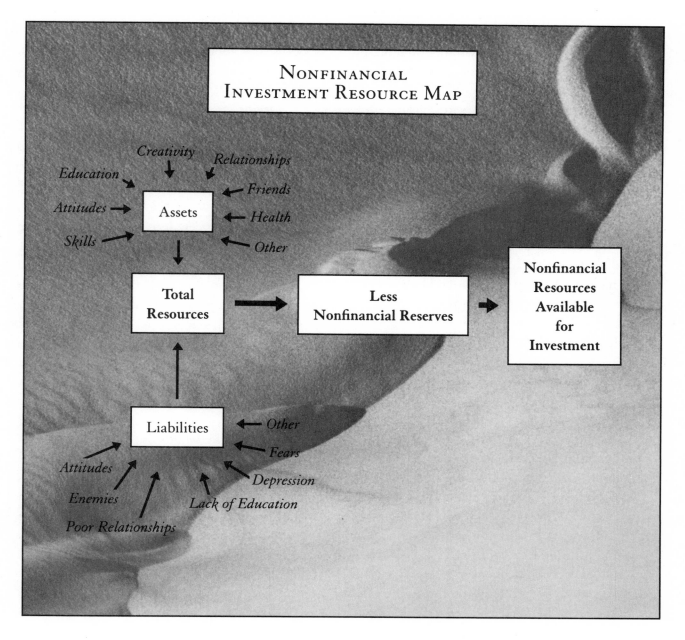

NONFINANCIAL INVESTMENT RESOURCE MAP

Creativity

Education

Relationships

Attitudes

Friends

Skills

Assets

Health

Other

Total Resources

Less Nonfinancial Reserves

Nonfinancial Resources Available for Investment

Liabilities

Other

Fears

Attitudes

Depression

Enemies

Lack of Education

Poor Relationships

able resource. It is impossible to relive the hour just passed. Health is a resource we need for pursuing most of life's activities, so we had best hold some of it in reserve. Health can suffer if we work all the time without relief. So can relationships.

You must simply feel your way through the question of how much of your total resources to hold back. The discussion of risk in the next chapter will help you decide. In the meantime you can make some general choices that you can

refine later. Your *written* responses to the following tasks will serve both as a commitment to yourself and as a reference later when you prepare your integrated plan at the end of this book.

1. Pick a preliminary number for your financial reserves. If you are married, consult with your spouse. What are the pros and cons of particular amounts? There may be more at issue than covering living expenses. You may have a debt to repay in four months, or a large tax or insurance payment coming up soon. In other words, what does your cash flow look like?

What feelings arise as you consider this question? Clearly, there are nonfinancial aspects to this seemingly financial matter. For example, someone with a lot of business self-confidence may not need a reserve. I know of a man who sold his car to start a company, leaving himself with no car and no reserves. He had a vision of what he sought, however, and he went after it. Being single and young, he had only himself to consider. His ability to get another job with ease was his only safety net. His own inner power was enough.

In this sense, True Wealth is really only a belief form. That is why empowerment is the real subject of this book. Once we are in touch with our own power, we see it as the ultimate resource available to us.

2. Examine your financial balance sheet to determine your liquidity level. Do you feel comfortable with the reserve provided by your current assets? If not, you may want to consider ways to increase your liquidity. Or you might find that your liquid assets exceed what you feel you really need as a reserve; you might want to put some of the funds into longer-term, higher-yield investments, apply them toward achieving a goal, or use them to develop another, nonfinancial, reserve. You might decide, for example, that investing in building your self-confidence through counseling is the best way to create a safety net.

I am pushing and pulling in all directions in order to encourage you to stretch your thinking and to include your feelings as input. Ultimately, you will probably reach your decisions through a combination of thinking, feeling, and intuition—which is great, because it is another way of bringing all of your personal resources into play.

3. Decide what intangible resources you need to be whole. The question of nonfinancial reserves is probably more important than the financial one because it will influence your financial outcome. It is a very inner-looking question. The answer is equally "inner."

The way to decide is by returning to the qualities that you associated with your life vision. Let us say that beauty is one of them. Suppose that you seek time to experience beauty through an avocation like painting. You feel rejuvenated when you can relax through this activity. Thus a reserve of time to paint is an important nonfinancial resource to add to your safety net. A person who relates to the quality of peace might also want to reserve time, in this case for the purpose of walking in the woods once a week or meditating for an hour before or after work. Someone else may reserve time with family as his or her nonfinancial requirement. Or, if health is an important intangible, then a certain amount of energy would be held in reserve. The list is as long as there are qualities that people cherish.

For each intangible resource you want to hold in reserve, specify an amount to be held back. Then look at your nonfinancial balance sheet to see whether withholding a resource like time will conflict with the pursuit of other goals. In other words, what is the trade-off, if any, of holding back the resource in question?

Sometimes decisions about nonfinancial reserves can lead to dramatic changes. A Silicon Valley engineer quit his well-paying but very time-consuming job to take another, less demanding one so that he could have more time with his family. A Boston executive who sought peace and freedom from the stress of city life decided to quit and form a new company in the Iowa countryside.

Remember, "deficit spending" of any resource, financial or intangible, can be harmful. Lost money can re-earned, but the loss of someone's love or the absence of a sense of peace can be devastating. Therefore, an inquiry of this sort can lead to upheavals. Beware—and be encouraged!

We all need to experience something to really know it. As Einstein said, "All knowing begins with experience and ends with it." In our context, the important thing is to act on what we experience. Action is often the connection between all the parts—between the inner and outer. With a clear idea of the resources available to us, and with the heightened inner sense of empowerment that comes from constantly associating the financial and the nonfinancial as one, we can now proceed to develop a plan to employ our resources toward the accomplishment of our goals.

The way we feel *about something often*
governs what we do *about it.*

6

RISKS AND RISK TAKING

The subject of risk can send shock waves through our brains. Then when something bad really does happen—as in the stock market crash of October 1987—a lot of fear is generated. Risk is almost always considered a negative factor and associated with impending doom and loss. Yet risking has two sides, just like the polarities health/illness, life/death, and light/shadow. It is impossible to experience one except in the context of the other. To laugh is to risk being the fool. To reach out is to risk involvement. To hope is to risk despair. For every "up," there is the possibility of a "down."

Usually, though, we tend to see only the downside of risking. Even the dictionary deals with risk as "undefined danger." Why not also look at it as "undefined opportunity"? The Chinese nicely combine the two perceptions in their definition of a crisis as a "dangerous opportunity!" In so doing, they acknowledge both the up- and the downside simultaneously—a wise perspective, since that is the way life works.

Money inspires a lot of fear. We worry about how we will get it, and then after acquiring some we worry about losing it. We constantly feel insecure, as if what we have might be taken from us at any moment. But what is security anyway? The dictionary definition simply reinforces fear by characterizing security as "freedom from fear [or] anxiety . . . anything that gives or assumes safety." Yet where does security really come from? The great samurai swordsmen were never afraid to die because they were secure in death. Their security came from within.

For us, too, security must come from within. We must not let a desire for external security keep us from experiencing life. I recall Alan Watts's remark about the "wisdom of insecurity." To risk is to come alive. Risks create change, and change promotes growth and acts as a safeguard against boredom.

What, then, is the nature of risk?

Where there is life, there is movement and change. With change, some of which is unforeseeable, there is the potential for danger. This potential is also, however, opportunity. Whether we see danger or opportunity depends on our perception of risk, and we all tend to perceive and respond to risk differently. It is this variety of perceptions that "makes for horse races." Remember, whenever one person sells a stock, there is a buyer who is betting on the other side. Each of them sees the same world differently.

What makes us respond as we do?

Our attitude toward risking is probably determined by how we experienced life as we were growing up. In fact, researchers theorize that risk takers come from certain environments. For example, those growing up in families where there is great difficulty or uncertainty—economic or otherwise—learn that they must risk to achieve. Similarly, children whose parents have high expectations quickly learn to risk in order to reach that higher level of achievement. An environment of rivalry also promotes risk taking. Further, those who learn a strong sense of self-worth are often willing to risk beyond the norm.

Because risk taking is driven from within, it is very much connected to who we are. As a result, we will learn more about ourselves as we move through this area of learning toward being fully in charge of what happens to us—the point of empowerment.

We Are Our Own Best Risk Managers

All of life involves choices, and choosing inherently involves risking, which in turn involves feeling. The more aware we are of our resources and of the interconnectedness of all things, the broader our range of options becomes. Since risk is unavoidable, it is essential to learn how to work with it to achieve goals. We cannot abdicate the ultimate responsibility for the management of our lives. We can delegate, but we are responsible for the results. As Harry Truman used to say,

"The buck stops here."

Which leads us back to the issue of empowerment. Taking an inventory of resources has made us aware of how much we have going for us. However, power does not come from resources; it stems from knowing who we are and being able to act from that place in ourselves. Acting involves taking risks using our total resources. If we know we are a particular quality and we act accordingly, we can take all sorts of risks that would not have felt possible to us earlier. We can do this because **our ability to risk is inner driven**.

However, even after we've gotten in touch with our resources and connected them to who we are, we may choose not to take a given risk. The important thing is to have explored the options.

To help sharpen our risk-taking awareness, we will do a number of exercises to discover where the "driver" is for us. We will look at factors that cause risk levels to rise, and we will see how to lower them. We will relate risking to who we are and to our purpose and goals. In effect, we will connect how we feel about a course of action with the action.

Throughout, awareness will be a key ingredient. It is our awareness that will most help us when we come to choosing between investment possibilities.

Financial and Nonfinancial Aspects of Risking

As we have already seen, the nonfinancial aspects of our lives are often the key to the financial side. The childhood experiences that shape us are nonfinancial factors that often govern our approach to financial risks such as making investments.

We react to risk with either fear or exhilaration; sometimes we feel a combination of the two.

Sky divers are clearly enthusiastic about throwing themselves out of an airplane at several thousand feet. Others get chills just thinking about it. Actually, the sky diver probably feels both emotions simultaneously.

One thing is sure, however. Whenever we take risks we feel *very alive*. Feeling alive is a part of wealth. Risking is a part of life and living. We must not hide from the risk that growth necessarily involves—financially or nonfinancially.

This book is about the investment process. Probably the greatest risk any of us ever take is when we "invest" ourselves in an effort such as a marriage, relationships generally, a job, or healing. We bet everything on the outcome because it is so important to us. The process gets our attention and energy, and we become intensely alive.

When I decided to marry, for instance, I really had no idea what I was going to experience. Looking back, it was the single most important decision I ever made, and one on which many other things have depended. Marriages so often end in divorce nowadays, which takes a terrible inner toll on the partners and severely affects any children. Yet when I married, I knew about divorce intellectually but never gave it a thought. I saw only what I now refer to as the "upside of risk." I saw the life-giving aspects of a close relationship.

Soon enough I discovered that to realize that potential would take maturity, inner work, and faith. In retrospect I see that getting married was the biggest risk I have taken to date, it was entirely a nonfinancial risk, and it has been important to my wealth.

As we work through this chapter, keep a weather eye open for the nonfinancial risks you have taken. Look especially for risks that have caused you to feel excitement. In this way you will reexperience the upside of taking risks, and you will be more willing to entertain new risks in the future.

A Sampling of Nonfinancial Risks

Life presents seemingly endless occasions for taking risks. Here are some typical nonfinancial examples.

- Marriage, or the risk of making a commitment to a key relationship. This risk is so great for some that they never take it.

- Initiating a divorce. This is a big risk, for it generally means going into the unknown again, which always generates fear.

- Changing careers—again the feeling of traveling new roads. How will it be? What are the dangers?

- Telling an employer that his or her policies are poor—another major risk.

- Smoking, drinking, overeating, or otherwise misusing our bodies.

- Facing (or not facing) one's own death. People dying of a terminal disease frequently will not risk acknowledging what is happening to them. Yet those who work with the dying say that there is healing in dying, provided the process is conscious. Unfortunately, the risk is too frightening for many of us.

- Physically rescuing another person. Perhaps you heard about the man who jumped into freezing water to save someone whose plane had crashed into a river upon takeoff. Such incidents happen over and over.

- Following one's intuition or heart instead of logic. The life of Mother Teresa is a case in point. She so connected with the quality of love—who she is—that she probably never saw the risks involved in what she has done to express that quality.

Connections Are
Implicit in Risking

Risking can have far-reaching effects. At the very least, an exploration of risking connects us with who we are and choose to become. I have observed the following general attributes of risking:

Link 1. Risking is a connective activity. In a marriage it illuminates who we are, making both us and our spouse a bit more conscious of our true selfhood.

Link 2. When we risk, we touch the lives of others. Marriage or performing a rescue are obvious examples of this effect. On the financial side, when we make a risky investment, we are financially backing other people and thus connecting with them. When we give to a charity, we are doing the same thing, which is why I always consider such gifts as investments.

Link 3. Sometimes when we take a risk, we place others at risk. Smoking and drinking are clear examples. So is driving a car or flying an airplane. These activities hold the potential for an adverse link with someone else.

Link 4. Our willingness to take risks affects our ability to make financial investments and thus our financial resources as well. As the old lady in New York said, "If you don't 'speculate,' you can't 'accumulate.'" **Our financial and nonfinancial risks are deeply connected.**

Link 5. Some risks are nonelective; they are forced on us. Consider what would happen if your spouse divorced you. Suddenly you would be on your own. If you had children and were granted custody, you would become a single parent, a scary prospect for some. With one connection broken, you would reach out for new ones. At such a time, you would rely on your inner power to see you through—the power that was there all the time anyway. When you make *that* connection, you realize your real wealth. Divorced people rarely see themselves as risk takers,

but they are and they often manage very well. They are simply not aware that risking is inherent in such a situation. When the awareness comes through, they can better appreciate their risk-taking abilities.

Refer to the Investment Process map on page 3. You will see that both resources and risk tolerance play a supportive role in the achievement of goals. They can also affect each other. As we have already seen, our attitude toward risk can limit our resource base or it can help it grow. Similarly, a resource can influence the way we tend to take risks. If, for example, a friend discourages us from making an investment, this is a case of a nonfinancial resource (the friend) offering advice about the *risk* of making an investment. The same would be true if the friend had encouraged us instead. We make connections of this kind all the time without being conscious of it. Doing it consciously allows for a more efficient process.

❦EXERCISE
WHAT IS YOUR HISTORY OF RISK TAKING?

Pick a quiet time and reflect on the major financial and nonfinancial risks you have taken over the years. Write them down so that you can see them all together. Start with the financial ones because they will trigger the others. You will see the links to the nonfinancial risks as you go along.

Here are some examples of areas in which you might have taken risks.

Financial	Nonfinancial
Investment in stocks, bonds, real estate, etc.	Health
The purchase of a home	Relationships, including work relationships
Self-employment	Education
A request for a raise	Sports, hobbies
Loans of money to a friend or relative	Public speaking

Now look to see how you treated each risk. Probably you responded in one of the following ways:

- You avoided the risk. That is what I do when offered the opportunity to go sky diving.
- You transferred the risk, for instance by purchasing insurance.
- You assumed the risk and took your chances, or you assumed it and did things to lower your exposure. An example would be eating properly to sidestep cholesterol and heart problems. This is prevention.

How have you chosen to handle each risk in the past?

How do you handle risk taking now? Do you get nervous or sweaty? Do you worry a lot and think about it all the time? Or are you able to pass it off?

Do you treat all risks in the same way? What is the difference if you treat some of them differently?

Now that you are becoming more aware that you risk all the time anyway, how does this knowledge affect you?

One Way to Insure Is to Self-Insure

Generally speaking, women appear to be more able to risk in relationships than men, while men are willing to risk more with investments. No doubt there are sociological reasons for this, but the point is that we all feel most comfortable in familiar areas. What are the areas in which you feel comfortable, and why do you suppose you treat them in this way?

Those who are unsure of themselves will probably have difficulty with risking. If you are aware of a lack of confidence, be sure to note it as a liability on your nonfinancial balance sheet. This link with your resources is important because in being aware of it, you can start to think about changing things if you choose to. In a sense, being "self-sure" is one of the best ways to insure.

Although we often think of risk taking as something we do in the outside world, it is actually something that happens inside us, involving feelings that rest squarely on our own perceptions. What is out there doesn't determine the risk; it is how we see it that defines the risk. This fact is encouraging, for whatever is inner is "in our court" and thus is something that we can influence.

Another perspective that can be helpful in coping with risk is this: Risks taken in pursuit of our vision and goals have a totally different quality than risks unrelated to our aims. The difference is in the sense of rightness that comes from taking actions in line with who we really are. We are more confident because what we are doing feels right.

Police officers often take great risks in their work. If they perform their duties from a quality of service, and if they are fully in touch with this connection, then the risks become tolerable because their work is congruent with who they are. A teacher in a ghetto area or a pilot flying medical supplies into a war zone may have similar reasons for assuming the risks.

Look back at the exercise you just completed to see if you are making a distinction between your willingness to risk financially and nonfinancially. Risking is risking. While the trigger is always different, the experience is the same. The important thing is to sharpen your awareness, just as you did when recording your resources.

EXERCISE
WHAT RISKS ARE YOU TAKING NOW?

Make a list of risks you are currently taking and think about which ones are easy and which cause concern. Use this as a starting point for becoming more aware of all the risks you take in your life. Later in this chapter, you will learn ways to lower risk and otherwise manage this area of your life.

Then list the risks you would be willing to take in the future. List also the risks you would *not* be willing to take. What can you learn about your feelings by looking at the gap between the two? Where do you draw the line? Don't make any judgments. Just discover where the line is for you.

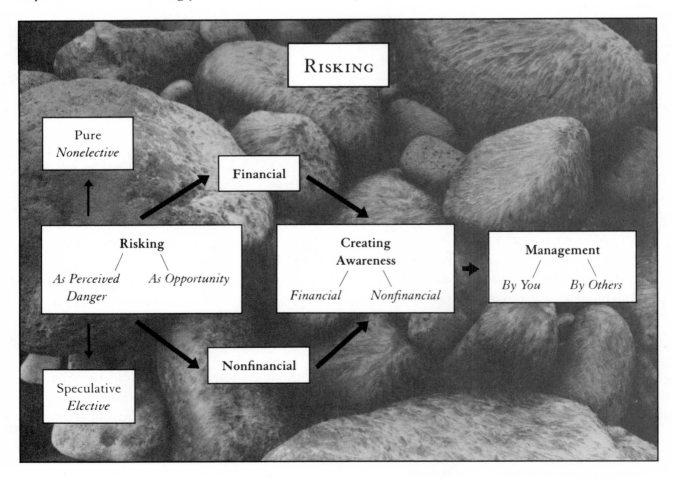

84

The Risk Environment, Inside and Out

Risks are everywhere. Instead of thinking of them as "lurking about waiting to get us," we should see them as the shadow side of opportunities, without which we would not be able to recognize the opportunities. As we saw earlier, light does not exist except in the context of shadow.

The Risking diagram maps out the big picture by very broadly categorizing risk in terms of how it is perceived, whether it is forced on us (pure) or chosen (speculative), and whether it is financial or nonfinancial. Awareness is the prerequisite for managing any risk, regardless of category.

A pure (nonelective) risk has the additional characteristic of being without perceived gain. Examples are fire, theft, and earthquakes. On the other hand, a speculative (elective) risk is taken on with the hope of gain. Speculative risks can be either financial or nonfinancial. A nonfinancial example would be a risk taken within a relationship, in which the gain sought might be better communication or intimacy.

The individual risks within the categories are not really qualitatively different, but it helps to categorize them in order to clarify the whole subject of risking. Admittedly the divisions are artificial and occasionally overlapping.

Risks are to be sought. Taking on a new job that stretches our capabilities is both a risk and a tremendous opening. I once took a job for which I had little direct experience. I was a bit unsure, but I took the risk and learned a lot, did well, and made valuable life contacts that came importantly into play later on.

Heart surgery is certainly a risk, but it also represents a route to life. Driving and flying are both risky activities, but without them we could not get about the world nearly as handily.

Risk can almost be seen as a friend instead of as a portent of loss and disaster. Because it is associated with change, it will always have a substantial impact on our lives, irrespective of its origin. But we can change our thinking about it and thus be better able to address the issues it presents and to use them as opportunities.

THE INNER WORLD OF RISKING

Risks are something we feel or experience. Although we do think about them, the thinking is shaped by what we feel. It is therefore very important to monitor how and what we feel. Have you ever woken up with a lot of worries? Looked out the window at a gray day and just felt "poopy"? Then the very next day, although you still have the same concerns and the sky is still overcast, you see life as good and get up with energy? Nothing has changed, but there is a great difference—the way you feel and think.

Our inner response to risk consists of feelings we have about the world around us, including fears we may not even be aware of. These feelings are rooted in life experiences, some of them very old indeed. They have become embedded in our unconscious minds, and pop out reactively to influence the way we respond to situations and choices.

Since risk taking creates fears in most of us, we often have a gloom-and-doom attitude toward it. A rare few of us see risks as energizing. Some people are enthusiastic about some forms of risk taking and afraid of others. For an entrepreneur, starting a new company is a source of great creativity and excitement, but the same person can be paralyzed when it comes to risking in a relationship. Ever experience that duality? I have.

What to do to deal with risk in such a situation?

First of all, realize that there is no requirement to change yourself. Being who you are is the goal of this book, and how you feel about risk is a part of who you are. There are no judgments or shoulds. The goal is simply to know your risk tolerance so that you can consciously bring this knowing to bear on making financial and nonfinancial choices.

For now, let's look at the opportunity side of the risk/reward polarity, not as a way to persuade you to go beyond your comfort level, but as a way to reexplore how you may feel about risking. If you see a scary risk as an opportunity, you can transform the energy from a risk-taking side of yourself (say, your entrepreneurial side) to make it available to the part of you that wants intimacy or whatever else previously seemed too risky. Just implant this new thought and see what happens. No blinding light will come on. It's not like hitting "undo" on your computer after a key stroke error and having things magically right again. However, you *will* start to experience a new outlook and a daring where fear reigned before. You will begin to see that risking opens the way for hope and possibilities. The effects can be extraordinary. Try working with this idea. After all, ideas are thoughts, and thoughts control actions.

THE OUTER WORLD OF RISKING

Our inner responses are directed toward various life possibilities or situations in the external world. Externally derived risks can be divided into three subgroups which I like to express as the polarities they represent:

- Those we recognize/those we do not
- Those within our control/those beyond our control
- Pure risks (those that are nonelective and don't involve gain)/speculative risks (those that are elective and involve gain)

Many risks fit into more than one group at a time. For example, an investment in a venture stock or bond whose success depends on market developments (that is, the economy) is both a recognizable financial risk *and* one whose outcome is beyond our control. The nonfinancial hazard of illness involves recognizable, pure risks that are partially within our control. Marriage is an example of another nonfinancial risk that we may not recognize as such but that is both controllable and fully elective.

As our own risk managers, we deal with the obvious risks—health, fire, theft, disability—by deferring them to others. We hire insurance companies. These risks are recognizable, pure, and within our control; they are the easier ones.

Some people approach risks in a different way. They find peace of mind by handling them from within. An example would be a person who addresses the health risk by eating and exercising properly, engaging in less stressful work, and being sure his or her relationships are in order. This approach may not cover the hazards of car accidents, natural disasters, genetic illnesses, or health damage caused by leaky atomic reactors or air pollution. However, such people handle what they can handle, and do so largely by way of inner interventions.

(Sometimes we have no choice about whether to insure or not. In much of the Third World, for instance, insurance is not an option: there is none to be had and no money to pay for it if there were. In our own country, we are sometimes forced to insure. For example, if we have financed our home, we have to insure it for the protection of the lender whose collateral it is.)

When we invest in a stock or in real estate, we recognize the risk and we take it in order to make money. Such a financial risk therefore involves the gain/no gain polarity as well as the seen/unseen one. We tend to limit such a risk by knowing as much as possible about the situation.

ONE PERSON'S RISK IS ANOTHER PERSON'S OPPORTUNITY

Let's look at pure risk—the kind we can insure against—from an insurance company's point of view. They see the same hazard, so why do they take it on? In the case of fire, we care only about our home. The insurance company does not. Their only concern is the predictability of how many homes in our area will burn. Using statistical data about past experience, they set premiums to cover their losses plus earn a profit. If your home burns, they will be pleased to build you another because the chances are that the cost to them will be within the amount they've anticipated through their actuarial studies for your area. Thus everyone wins. You transfer the risk and the company enjoys a profit.

The same goes for car insurance. Who wants to take on the liability risk alone? We transfer that one, too. No one can foresee a specific accident, but a company can predict occurrences by age group, general location, make of car, etc. Based on that information, a company will quote rates that cover their

losses and still allow them to earn a profit.

What is the lesson in this? That risk is seen and felt differently by different people.

Because we are typically fearful of risks like fire and theft, we take a direct way out and get rid of the fear by passing the risk to others whose very business derives from our fear or our inability to fully self-insure. In this way we transfer our fear from within to the outer world and address it there instead of from within. This is very smart risk management.

This means being aware of *all* of the elements that can affect our success.

I recall the secretary of a large electronics firm who borrowed money to make an investment in real estate. She figured that her job paid enough that she could easily handle the loan payments and still earn well on the investment. What she didn't foresee was the loss of her job when her employer had to lay off a number of people due to a shaky market. This story demonstrates again that everything is connected. In losing the job, she lost the investment. Her mistake was in failing to see the multiple risks involved in making the investment. The connection between the real estate

purchase and her job was the link she missed. Her risk experience involved all three polarity groups at once.

Choosing a spouse is often not seen as a risk, but as anyone who gets divorced knows, it can be a big one. Marriage can have both financial and nonfinancial (emotional) consequences that can lead to divorce. Can these consequences be foreseen? Sometimes. The probability of a marriage ending in divorce can be predicted statistically but not specifically.

Choosing a job is another move that presents risks that are often not recognized. If you were an auto worker and did not look into the competitive status of a potential employer before signing on, you could get a rude shock if the company failed to make its volume goals and you were laid off. Sometimes, though, you can take all precautions and still find that your employer has failed, not because of mismanagement but because the economy has collapsed. An engineer I know transferred to a division that had just been acquired, only to find after one year that the parent company had decided to sell to a foreign buyer. Many were laid off in the transaction.

All job selections are examples of risks taken for gain, but some of the conditions are foreseeable and others are not. Usually we can control or at least influence the risks we can foresee.

We lay ourselves open to another risk in choosing a job if the field we enter is not congruent with who we are. By ignoring our skills and what we like, we increase the potential for failure. Take the example of the doctor's son who was really an artist but who went into medicine because his father wanted him to. His nonfinancial decision (choosing work out of a sense of duty) created financial distress (the eventual loss of all the money that had been put into his education) as well as nonfinancial problems (poor health caused by stress and depression). Clearly, the nonfinancial aspects of our choices are as important as the financial ones.

Now, what have we learned from this survey of the risk environment?

Risk taking is a part of life. It involves a lose/win polarity, meaning that just as there is always a chance of loss, there is the possibility of gain, too. The one factor most likely to tip the scales toward gain is *you*. The "inner you" often sets up a context for winning or losing. The key is to discover how you experience risk and to recognize in what areas you are able and not able to risk.

Risks accompany both financial and nonfinancial ventures. However, nonfinancial risk tak-

ing probably has more to do with True Wealth than financial risking.

Becoming aware of the presence of a risk is the first step in addressing that risk. If you are not aware, you simply face the risk without the opportunity to do something about it. For example, you might ignore diet because you were unaware of heart disease in your family. With awareness, you could focus on dietary interventions that might significantly lower your own risk of heart trouble.

Finally, watch for multiple risks associated with any one apparently risky activity.

Risk-taking Traps

Overconfidence can obscure risk factors that, if addressed, would actually lower—not raise— risk. The stock market crash of October 1987 is a case in point. Many people confused the ability to invest in the securities markets with a long-term bull market that they thought would rise indefinitely. I vividly recall investors boasting about their gains just two months before the crash. Like overconfidence, greed is a quality that can raise risk-taking levels. Because it is "blinding," it shuts us off from our better judgments. It breaks the connection between who we are and what we do at a time when it needs to be strongest.

Then, some people try to lower risk by being outright dishonest. Ivan Boesky is a recent prime example. By breaking trading rules and working with inside information, he lowered risk and profited handsomely. However, in lowering risk through dishonesty, he *raised* the risk of being caught. His willingness to be dishonest blinded him to the other risk he was taking.

We all fall into the overconfidence trap from time to time. I recall a start-up retail chain that was wildly successful with its first two stores. Flushed with success, the owners implemented a third, but without the careful site selection that had accompanied the first two stores. The third one failed dismally, leaving the management stunned—and aware that they had been overconfident.

These three cases all highlight the link between financial and nonfinancial risk taking. In each instance, overconfidence decisively affected a risky financial venture.

Managing Risk—Alternative Responses, Ways to Lower Risk, Ways to Make Risk Worse

We have it in our power to lower risk in a number of ways. At the same time, we should become aware of the things we do that typically raise risk. Because our inner responses to risk are closely connected to how we face risks presented by the outer world, it is important to work with both the inner and outer aspects of risk taking. Dealing with the inner aspects of risk is a deeply personal matter. For everyone, though, becoming more aware is the place to begin. Concerning the outer management of risk, let us look again at the options I mentioned in the first exercise in this chapter.

1. *You can avoid the risk by choosing not to take it.*

    Obviously, this approach works only when you have a choice. If a stock trade or a real estate deal looks too chancy, just don't do it. If someone suggests a hang-gliding date for next Saturday afternoon and you feel apprehensive about it, decline. If you have been invited to dinner and learn that there may be a risk of getting chicken pox because one of the household "just got over it," you might want to side-step that one, too.

2. *You can transfer the risk.*

    If someone will take on a risk that you face and is capable of following through on it, and if that intervention otherwise makes sense, do it. The most common examples of this approach are home, health, and auto insurance. Transferring the risk is a way of allaying fear and stress in the face of an unpredictable outcome.

3. *You can assume the risk.*

    Often you have no alternative but to take on a risk. For instance, you cannot avoid or transfer the risks involved in marriage or a new job. Once the decision is made, you are on your own. In such a situation, you can only seek ways to raise the odds in your favor and to transform the risk into the opportunity it can become. Lots of marriages work and jobs turn out well.

4. *Lower the risk and then take it on.*

    This is an extension of number 3. Take whatever steps are available to you to reduce the chance of loss and to sidestep hazard. For example, if the risk of fire is great, install sprinklers, use sheetrock with fiberglass in it, or install fireproof landscaping; if theft is an issue, put in burglar alarms or get a guard dog. The same approach works with relationships. If you want to lower the risk of divorce, improve your ability to communicate and to create intimacy by seeking counseling or by just plain talking to one another at a meaningful level.

    In other words, look for ways to control or contain the risk. Often it is up to you to make a move. In the case of a marriage, there is no one to offer insurance; you are very much on your own. But you are also the best one to address this issue—provided you are aware.

RISK IS LOWERED WHEN YOU . . .

· *Follow your vision, purpose, and goals.*

When you connect who you are with what you do, you have a sense of rightness about your life and tend to be much more centered. This connection creates the sort of balance that deflects the dangers of arrogance, overconfidence, and greed. It is probably not a guarantee, but it seems to help. Witness the lives of those who appear to follow their purpose with a deep sense of knowing; Martin Luther King Jr. and Mother Teresa are cases in point.

· *Improve your awareness of inner and outer reality.*

No one can avoid something they do not sense. Here are three ways to increase awareness:

1. *Practice living in the present.* Doing so will promote paying attention to what is going on now. For example, if you are gardening, stay with the gardening; don't be off somewhere else in your mind. If you are talking to someone, be completely present to that person. When it is your turn to listen, listen. Don't plan what you will say next. Be conscious of what is going on in the present.

2. *Be open to advice from others.* Sharing experiences that are pertinent to current issues can often be vital to risk taking.

3. *Accept that you may not know everything.* No one needs to have all the answers all of the time. The important thing is to network. Collect people. They are among the most valuable nonfinancial assets you can gather around you for support.

· *Become fully informed about the area of risk you contemplate entering.*

Recall that the dictionary defines risk as "undefined danger." The logical protection, then, is to bring definition to the danger and thereby make the situation more predictable. There is no excuse for entering any field without data if the information exists. Use your nonfinancial resource base for support in finding the people who have the knowledge necessary to lower risk. We will be looking at the role of advisors in the next chapter.

· *Hold onto the concept that risking involves opportunity.*

Instead of seeing risk exclusively as "undefined danger," include the "upside of risk" in your view of things—that is, the notion that the risks that present themselves offer opportunities to pursue your purpose and goals.

· *Write a life plan.*

As we will see later, a comprehensive plan and a network of people are key nonfinancial tools that can be used with great leverage in overcoming risk and combatting fear.

RISK IS RAISED WHEN YOU . . .

· Are out of touch with or are not following your vision, purpose, and goals.
· Are so consumed by fear that you are unable to take advantage of opportunities that could be prudently risked.
· Are unaware of either the risks you are taking now or those that may present themselves in the future.
· Are impulsive and do not wait to become as informed as is reasonably possible before taking risks.
· Are unattentive to the inner aspects of risking.

The Paradox of Risking More by NOT Risking

We tend to think that risk and security are at opposite poles. Although in one sense they are, in another they are not. That is the nature of any polarity. Its power comes from its inherent connectiveness.

Have you ever had the experience of realizing that in not taking a given risk, you would be taking a still greater one?

That is the paradox.

Staying in an unrewarding job because it is safe may be a larger risk to health and well-being than moving to a riskier situation that holds the possibility of growth and challenge. Not taking the risk of showing your true feelings can lead to the loss of the whole relationship. The same thing can happen if you avoid communicating on tough interpersonal issues at work or at home.

Our nation is stronger and more secure because people are willing to take risks. The most conspicuous example of this willingness is in new business start-ups. Some people choose to deal with job security by starting their own businesses and betting everything on their own creativity, endurance, and skills. In this way they manage their own risk rather than putting it in someone else's hands.

So consider the possible consequences of *not* taking risks as well as the consequences of taking them. Be on the lookout for all the connections. Remember that for every patch of sunlight there is adjacent shadow, without which the light would not be visible.

*We are all both teachers and students
and are responsible for what we teach
as well as what we are taught.*

7

ADVISORS

Up to this point, the True Wealth process has wholly involved you—your vision, the purpose that flows from your vision, your inventory of total resources, and your willingness to absorb risk in order to achieve goals. While others could be helpful as "connections," the process was yours and the insights came about largely because you recognized what was within.

We now turn to the world "without." Using advisors, you will be making investment decisions in the outer world based on the insights of the inner one. You will set about the task of choosing from the myriad of financial and nonfinancial possibilities within the structure of your own vision and purpose.

First, however, you need to be clear about the role you yourself want to play in the selection and execution of financial and nonfinancial investments. With this knowledge you can clearly define the roles you may invite anyone else to assume on your behalf.

Your own role will depend on your skills, time availability, ability to pay for advice, the complexity of your resources and goals, and your predisposition toward risk.

Who Needs Advisors?

Using advisors should not be at all a frightening experience. All of us rely on the services of various "advisors" every day. Examples are the experts who repair our cars, computers, and washing machines; the specialists who advise us about our health, from doctors and acupuncturists to holistic healers; and the therapists and counselors who help us work through relationship or conflict issues. We hire people who have expertise in areas where we have needs and lack the knowledge to do the job ourselves. We also use experts in areas where we may have competency (gardening, let's say) but not enough time to do the entire job ourselves.

Although all of us are used to seeking nonfinancial advice in one form or another, turning to someone for support on financial matters may be new. Here are some very good reasons for seeking financial advice.

1. Change is rampant on all fronts—political, social, environmental, technical, and international. If we are to prosper, we must recognize that all our actions are subject to the impact of change. Access to information about changes that could affect us is therefore vital.

2. Timely information is as valuable as money itself. If we buy oil stocks without knowledge of an impending drop in crude oil prices, we could be badly hurt financially. In our businesses, if we hire a new employee without waiting for the results of a background check, we might be stuck with someone who is completely inappropriate. To make sound decisions in the moment, we need to know about both past experiences and prognoses for the future.

3. With financial deregulation, new financial products abound and new players appear daily, each wanting to make their mark on the industry. Competition further fuels this trend.

   Discount brokers, department-store chains selling such financial products such as insurance, the increase in mutual funds in recent years, all make the offerings so varied that it is now possible to get a diversified portfolio at nearly every level of risk and purpose. Advisors can play a valuable role in keeping us current in the fields that affect us.

4. Financial markets will soon be open worldwide twenty-four hours a day; some already are. Communication and computer technologies are joining to make full-time trading possible and practical. This change will greatly expand the choices, the range of risk, and the opportunities—for profit or loss!

5. Because of the proliferation of products and services, the investment scene has necessarily become more complex. Add to this the detailed reporting and record-keeping requirements, and it becomes obvious that help is probably appropriate.

However, none of this is reason for you to delegate responsibility. You know more about your goals than anyone else, and you are in charge of accomplishing them. **Do not give up your own power.** Don't disengage any more than necessary. We all tend to give too much credit to experts. Use advisors purposefully for specific tasks about which you are clear before you engage them. Also, remember that you are the employer. They work for you on your programs. The good ones know this. Like good counselors, they serve as catalysts in *your* process.

Problems You May Encounter in Working with Advisors and How to Avoid Them

To get the most benefit from using an advisor, it helps to be aware of some hazards that can confuse the situation. These have to do in part with what you bring—or don't bring—to the relationship, and in part with the interests and disposition of the advisor.

AS ALWAYS, SELF-AWARENESS IS CRITICAL

The biggest hazard in working with an advisor is not to know your life dreams and the purpose on which your goals are based. Lack of clarity about your capacity for risk taking and about your resources is also hazardous. Be forewarned: if you are unclear or wishy-washy, an advisor is going to have to intuit or guess at your preferences and the degree of risk you are willing to take. If you leave your financial wealth in the hands of someone who cannot be sure what you really want or what you have in the way of financial resources, you put yourself at additional risk.

Another problem that can arise is miscommunication between spouses concerning goals. If you are trying to achieve multiple goals, they must all be compatible! If they're not, a good advisor will pick up on the split in purpose and won't be able to move. A poor advisor will not notice the differences and will plow ahead—an especially dangerous eventuality.

ACKNOWLEDGE YOUR OWN POWER

A financial advisor is a hired consultant being asked to advise about, or actually manage, your financial assets. He or she works for you, not the other way around. Remember that the assets an advisor is dealing with are a part of your wellbeing. Thus they are of great consequence. Approach the hiring process with confidence. Advisors may know more about financial assets than you do (that is the reason you engage them), but you know most about you and what it is you want.

So, although you need not be frightened of using financial or other advisors, you must guard against giving them inappropriate power. **Ultimately, you are responsible for the rightness of their advice.**

CONFLICTS OF INTEREST CAN MAKE IT HARD FOR AN ADVISOR TO SERVE YOU WELL

Be wary of the odd advisor who puts himself or herself in a conflict-of-interest position. Such a situation can sometimes work, but it can also be a problem. It depends on the advisor.

For example, some financial planners do not charge directly for their planning services. Instead they charge commissions on the financial products they sell to you. In this case, there is an obvious temptation to trade more than necessary, to sell you products you do not really need, or to sell only the products they carry, ignoring others that may be more appropriate.

Such problems can be avoided if you stay centered and approve only those financial moves that are in line with your purpose and goals. In this context, you can see how important it is to be clear about your goals and overall guiding life qualities.

PROTECT YOURSELF AGAINST INCOMPETENT ADVISORS

How does one test for incompetency? Financial planning is not yet an accredited or state-licensed profession. Persons of every description are entering the field; some estimates peg the number of planners in this country at more than 200,000. Some of these individuals are excellent and others next to worthless. As increasingly demanding jobs claim more and more of our attention, and as more and more families earn two incomes that put them in higher tax brackets, the need for sound planning grows. The number of practitioners increases to keep up with the growth in the market. In all fields, whether unlicensed or licensed, incompetence exists. As managers of our own wealth, we will want to ferret out the advisors who are both competent and appropriate to our needs.

Later in this chapter, we will discuss how to think through the selection process. For now, remember that one of the best defenses is to be clear about the direction in which you are going. This awareness is critical in assessing advice from a would-be advisor.

SOMETIMES YOU AND THE ADVISOR ARE JUST MISMATCHED

If you are looking for aggressive investment advice, it is counterproductive to engage a conservative planner. Similarly, if you are the conservative one, you and an aggressive planner will be pulling in different directions. It is nearly impossible, for example, for an otherwise venturesome investment advisor to become suddenly conservative with 30 percent of your financial assets. Best take the 30 percent and give it to a planner who has a conservative bent. Be sure to become aware of a particular advisor's predilection during the interview or referral-check process.

Also, advisors have different strong points. For example, one advisor may be better in down markets than up markets. Others specialize in particular risk niches.

Listen to or ask for information on how a given advisor operates. After learning about the advisor's inclinations, ask yourself if they fit with your goals and your way of being. The danger is in your being unclear about the degree of risk you want to take, ignorant about the extent of your resources, or vague about your goals. If you know these things, then the hazard of teaming up with an inappropriate advisor will not be a dangerous one. You will have lowered risk!

YOUR OWN ATTITUDE CAN BE THE BIGGEST HAZARD OF ALL

If you think you can simply hand over responsibility for all your financial problems, then you will be in the soup straightaway. There is nothing magical about the process of financial advising, and you cannot abdicate responsibility for the management of your financial and nonfinancial resources. Even if you do nothing, you are doing something. Having resources automatically carries burdens and responsibilities. Planning is often hard work; it requires alertness, a willingness to look at risk, and a sense of direction. You are a part of that process, and you cannot abdicate your responsibility without great risk.

Where Can You Go for Financial Advice?

For a fee, you can obtain financial advice from a variety of business people, some of whom provide related services that you may already be using. Or you can seek advice through various informal channels that will cost you little but time.

ACCOUNTANTS

If your tax situation is complex, you probably already have an accountant. A tax accountant's job is to guide you through tax issues, including advising on legally accelerating a deduction, shifting income from one year to another, and deferring taxes (for instance by opening an IRA). Accountants can also advise on changes in tax law and on tax considerations at times of marriage, divorce, or death. They can be critical in helping you understand how to create pension plans. The list of services is long. The point is that accountants can be very important in the preparation of a good financial plan.

ATTORNEYS

Like accounting, the legal specialty is complex. If you are active in real estate deals as a general or limited partner, an attorney is very important for looking over or casting agreements, reviewing tenant leases, and the like. Attorneys are also useful for drawing up wills, creating trusts, and preserving tax-exempt wealth. Since their work often overlaps that of accountants, especially in tax issues, you will frequently need to use both simultaneously.

The lawyer who drafts a limited partnership agreement may be different from the one who writes a will. Consequently, you may need to deal with a number of attorneys, depending on the tasks you are pursuing in line with your goals—even your nonfinancial ones. For example, to help an aging parent manage assets, you might have your attorney draw up a living trust so that you can better act as manager for your parent's account. Again, the list of services is long. Which ones you choose to take advantage of will be a function of your goals and available resources. The important thing is to become aware of how attorneys can help, and then judge whether their help would be appropriate in a particular instance.

INSURANCE AGENTS

Insurance plays a valuable part in risk management. As you learned in chapter 6, you can elect to manage risks such as fire, theft, and health by hiring someone to assume them for you. Such insurance is not an investment; people buy it to cover a situation, or exposure, that they perceive as risky. In general, insurance offers an important means of protecting financial wealth (homes, cars, valuables) as well as nonfinancial wealth (such as health and life itself).

The kinds and amounts of insurance you buy

FINANCIAL ADVISORS

Professional	*Informal*
Accountants	Investment clubs & other networking
Attorneys	
Insurance agents	Books, newsletters, referrals from friends
Financial planners	
Stockbrokers	Public libraries

---

depend on how you feel about using insurance as a means of dealing with coverable risks. Some people buy major medical insurance with a large (say, $15,000) deductible because they self-insure against lesser medical expenses by watching diet, exercising, and practicing holistic health methods. The majority of us, however, would probably not feel comfortable with this solution.

As you try to settle on appropriate types and levels of coverage, you will probably find that insurance agents can ably advise you on options that match your needs. Just be clear about their role, and your goals, before you engage them.

Most of us deal with one or more insurance advisors already, usually different ones for different specialties. Home owners use agents to provide coverage for fire, theft, earthquakes, or whatever. Some people use a different agent for personal liability, although the general agent can handle this, too. Business insurance may involve still another agent. Health insurance, which is often covered by employers, is a separate insurance cost for many self-employed people. Some people have an agent for disability insurance as well.

Finally, there is the life insurance agent, whose product is the one most likely to provoke questions. Life insurance tends to be pushed by the seller more than sought by the buyer, and a lot of life insurance is sold on fear. Since you have

IF YOU ARE THINKING ABOUT LIFE INSURANCE . . .

The overall task is to see your life insurance needs within the context of your goals and resources. This will require some homework that will help objectify your decision.

First, be aware that life insurance primarily involves survivor needs. Children and single people without financial responsibilities tend not to need it at all, at any price. Second, because of recent changes in the tax law (the kind of information a tax accountant could provide), it is no longer necessary to have life insurance to protect retired or non-working spouses except in special circumstances. Previously, the taxes due upon the death of a spouse were the reason for a lot of insurance. Since there is now no tax liability upon the death of a spouse, no insurance is needed. (But the law can change again, so stay current.) However, when the remaining spouse dies, insurance can be useful for paying taxes then due, especially in cases where estate liquidity is low.

If you do require coverage, what is your approach to it? Having thought through your resources and knowing your goals, you are in a good position to make use of a reputable agent. Over time, one's income usually increases. Over the same time, needs decline as children grow up and leave the roost. At a certain point you will want to rethink whether you need continued coverage. Certainly in some cases you might. Because each of our situations is unique, advisors can be very helpful.

The "investment" side of life insurance raises other questions. With term insurance you are buying coverage only (or sometimes an employer buys it for you). With whole life insurance, you are buying both coverage and an investment. As with any investment, it is best to compare a particular policy with competitive investments at similar risk. Be aware of the differences between the two kinds of insurance, and be clear on which is appropriate for your plan—if insurance is a part of the plan at all.

New life insurance products emerge with changes in financial markets. We are only covering basic principles here. The point is to be clear about your insurance needs and buy only the product that meets those needs and is in line with your goals.

to die to "win," the stakes are death, and few of us want to think about that. Nonetheless, it is important. The issue is made more complicated because life insurance can also have an investment component (see sidebar).

All of us see risk in some areas and not in others. The certainty of death—and thus the possible need for life insurance—is something we all recognize, but what about something like disability? We tend to think that "it won't happen to me" and therefore to disregard it as a risk not worth covering. Whether it is worth it or not is entirely up to you. No one else knows how you feel, and your feeling—a nonfinancial input—is what governs in the end.

The important thing is to become aware of your exposures (where you are at risk) and know your needs. You are your own risk manager and must make the decisions about how to deal with the various risks you face. There are many areas to consider. You must simply start looking into the whole issue of risk in order to find the exposures that seem most real to you. Then you can do something about them.

EXERCISE
FINDING YOUR EXPOSURE LEVELS

Use the following form to get an overall picture of your risk exposure. If you decide you need more insurance, remember that insurance advisors can be important resources. Just be sure to use them selectively and to choose those who are competent and well-versed in your area of need.

EXPOSURE COVERAGE	COVERED BY ME	COVERED BY OTHERS
Life (term or whole life)	☐	☐
Home	☐	☐
Liability	☐	☐
Disability	☐	☐
Health	☐	☐
Earthquake	☐	☐
Business	☐	☐
Other	☐	☐

FINANCIAL PLANNERS

We usually think of financial planners as the key players in the investment process. However, they are only one part of a group. In seeking advice to further our goals, it is often a *team* that we need to enlist.

What can a financial planner do for you?

If you were the average client, engaging a financial planner would force you to survey your financial assets and take an inventory by preparing financial statements. Since you have already done this, and since you understand the financial and nonfinancial meaning of these statements, your need for a planner on this account is perhaps limited.

Since you have already identified your vision and purpose and set prioritized goals in line with your purpose, you are also not in need of another service planners often provide—getting their clients to set goals. What the best planners can

offer is a good sense of financial markets and the full spectrum of financial products—stocks, bonds, real estate deals, venture stocks, commodities, collectibles, legal tax-avoidance investments, cash equivalents, U.S. Treasury bonds, overseas markets for financial products, etc.

Many planners have an understanding of the economic environment and are thus aware of interest rate movements, inflation, and political fallout that could have a financial impact. The competent ones know how debt levels can help or hurt corporate America and how earnings are doing. They are familiar with the technical aspects of the various markets and the international events that shape our domestic financial products as well as those offered abroad. With their wide range of experience, they represent an important resource to you in those areas where their knowledge is appropriate to the implementation of goals. To employ them properly, of course, you must be clear about your objectives.

If you are a beginner in all this, I would suggest reading and discussing such a book as *The Only Investment Guide You'll Ever Need*, by Andrew Tobias. This will give you some basis for starting a dialogue with a planner.

STOCKBROKERS

Generally speaking, stockbrokers fall into two broad categories: the first advise and execute orders, and the second, called discount brokers, only execute orders without giving any advice.

Again, in selecting one, be clear about your needs based on your resources, goals, knowledge of the field, and any financial planning advice you may have sought. Brokers are knowledgeable resources, too. They are in touch with certain financial markets (listed stocks and bonds, U.S. Treasury bills, cash equivalent possibilities, and real estate investment trusts, or REITs, to name only a few). They often know, or can find out, about possible interest rate changes and other factors that can affect current investments. Brokers are an especially good resource to tap if you are doing your own planning or at least executing your own buy/sell orders.

The Importance of Getting Second Opinions

Suppose you hire a financial planner who proposes a strategy that is a departure from what you are used to or feel comfortable with. What should you do?

First, take the time to reflect and see if you can get a sense of rightness or wrongness about the proposal. Check it out with your purpose statement and goals. Then, if you are still unsure, get a second opinion.

For example, one man was advised by a planner to borrow to the hilt on his home and to put the proceeds into a moderately risky investment. It just didn't feel right. Mortgaging his home simply struck him as too risky, and he decided not to do it. Trust such feelings. Nothing is worse than taking risks beyond your comfort level and suffering stress just to make (or lose) money that may not be in line with your purpose.

Another example: A client was advised to borrow in order to buy tax-free bonds on the theory that the interest was deductible and the income exempt from taxes. On the surface it sounded wonderful. To be safe, however, the client decided to get a second opinion. The next planner explained that the interest on the loan to buy tax-deferred bonds was *not* deductible. Obviously, this difference made the investment prospect much less attractive. Although current tax law has changed, this story illustrates both the importance of second opinions and the valuable role advisors can play in planning one's wealth.

INVESTMENT CLUBS AND OTHER NETWORKING

Most of us do not realize that we are capable of putting together the resources to develop a financial plan and to execute that plan ourselves. In fact, people do this all the time in investment clubs. They pool resources, research investments, discuss the pros and cons, and then make investments together. Some groups do all the preparatory work together but the actual investing separately. This approach is clearly not the answer for all of us, but it is an option that should be examined.

Actually we do much the same thing when we ask friends for advice on buying a home, a car, or a new set of golf clubs. We seek other people's experience, and we combine what we get with all the other information we have gathered on the subject. Networks play a large part in our lives already. Simply use them more consciously and in line with your goals.

BOOKS, NEWSLETTERS, REFERRALS FROM FRIENDS

Books and other literature contain a lot of information. The only problem is that reading and studying take time as well as a keen interest in order to pay off. This simply underscores the cold fact that any major program takes focus, time, and effort. Talk to those who are now making that effort. What steps have they taken? What books have they found valuable? How do they go about reading the *Wall Street Journal* in order to get the most out of it quickly, relative to their sense of purpose?

In any case, the list of possibilities is endless. Just start with questions, for they naturally precede answers. Keep in mind that the quality of the question determines the quality of the answer. Often just the careful framing and thought that go into a question will yield an answer.

PUBLIC LIBRARIES

Too few of us even think of our free libraries as a resource. Because we rarely visit them, we are unaware of their value. Yet today's public libraries are often up-to-date institutions. Because they share their collections with each other, you have access to an enormous pool of information.

To start with, libraries have all of the major local and regional newspapers, from the *Wall Street Journal* to such financial weeklies as *Barrons*. They also carry key business weekly magazines like *Business Week*. One evening a week could easily be devoted to reading these alone. In fact, if you assemble your own network of people, each person can read small sections of the entire literature and report to the group on the content, thus saving a great deal of time.

Libraries specializing in business and finance will also have prospectuses, annual reports, and the more detailed 10K forms issued by listed corporations. They often subscribe to a wide range of newsletters and guides, including such expensive ones as the *Value Line Investment Survey* and *Standard & Poor's Stock Reports* and *Stock Guide. Value Line* covers upwards of 1,700 stocks, reciting their histories, stock movements, rankings,

and the like. It also gives overviews of the economy and the possible effects of economic conditions on the securities markets. *Standard & Poor's* contains information on over 3,700 firms. All in all, these publications offer a wealth of financial data.

Finally, some libraries offer access to even more data through their on-line computers. Unfortunately the access is limited and the service not yet widely available.

Libraries are only one of the many resources available to all of us. Because it requires time and energy to use them, they will probably be most appealing to those who are more entrepreneurial and intend to invest themselves in the investment process.

Many of us may not want to devote ourselves to networking, books, or libraries; it may not be in line with our purpose to do so. If you choose to invest your time in other ways, relying on advisors for information is indicated. For those who see the investment challenge as a game they want to participate in, however, there is joy and purpose to be found in this route to both financial and nonfinancial wealth.

Where Can You Go for Nonfinancial Advice?

An advisor is simply anyone who can be supportive of your process of achieving goals based on purpose. There is nothing necessarily formal about the act of advising. We advise others when we aid in their process. Just as we identified many sources of information on preserving and expanding our financial wealth, we can also find many individuals and means to help us with the assets and liabilities on our nonfinancial balance sheet. The possibilities include friends, family, therapists, and ministers as well as college courses, seminars, and literature on the subjects of interest.

For example, if your goals include health issues, then doctors, chiropractors, therapists, holistic health practitioners, etc., become suitable

---

NONFINANCIAL ADVISORS

People	*"Things"*
Friends and family	College courses
Therapists	Seminars
Ministers, priests, rabbis, etc.	Workshops
Colleagues	Books and periodicals

---

advisors. A person with cancer might want to work toward a solution at many levels simultaneously, using doctors, therapists specializing in nontraditional approaches, literature on the subject, and so on.

A goal of going back to school for an advanced degree or a license might lead to contacts with a host of advisors, ranging from friends and teachers to people working in the chosen field.

The types of advisors are limited only by the area of interest. Review your nonfinancial balance sheet and look over your list of intangible goals. Start to think about which advisors may be useful. Then select each one with the same care and tests for appropriateness that you apply in the case of financial advisors.

A Selection Process for Finding Good Advisors

Once you have decided to use advisors, how do you go about it? How do you avoid just "anyone" and get someone who is both competent and appropriate?

The first requirement is to be clear about what you want. You do not usually just walk onto a car lot and buy a car. You look at brochures. You talk to people who have bought the kind of car you want. You read *Road & Track* magazine and *Consumer Reports*. Possibly you even check particular dealers' reputations with the Better Business Bureau. You test-drive the car. When you stop to think about it, you do a whole lot before spending ten to twenty thousand dollars for a car.

Selecting an advisor involves the same sort of research, yet few people do it. In fact, most of us do a lot less in committing all of our financial resources than we do when we buy a car!

This is really quite foolish. It happens, though, because we think we don't know enough about the subject to evaluate our choices and because we have a lot of fears about money.

In seeking advisors, you will want to check out credentials, type of practice, background, license (if any), and how they operate. Financial planning, for example, has attracted a diverse lot of people. Some have been around financial markets for years. Others come from different but helpful backgrounds. Therapists, for example, sometimes enter the field with a lot less experience in investments than other planners but a great deal of knowledge of human behavior. If you need help with goal selection, the person with a therapy background might well be a better "planner" to see than the financial whiz.

Consider how you choose a car mechanic. If the problem is elusive and you have only symptoms to go on, the dealer may be the best place to go. If you know you need new brakes, however, then you will possibly turn to specialists who do just brakes and who are less expensive. Who knows best where to go? You do!

Honor what you know. And before you do any selecting, know your goals and why you chose them.

GETTING STARTED

Begin the selection process by reviewing the money issues we discussed earlier and getting in touch with your own power again. Revisit your resources—especially the nonfinancial ones like friends—and begin to gather information.

You probably already have an accountant who helps you with tax preparation. Start to look at that person in a new light. Is he or she competent? Still suitable to your needs? Does he or she seem to have your best interests in mind? Make a thorough review.

Talk to friends about the advisors they use and ask what they think about them. Have they really performed? What does "performance" mean to your friends? Does it have the same meaning for you?

Talk to business associates in the same way. Keep "pulling on the piece of string." One question leads to the next. Pretty soon you will have become something of an expert. It is like buying your first TV. You had no idea what this hunk of electronics was all about, so you talked to people who had already bought one. Some had had good experiences, some bad ones. You began to see the importance of different features and the value of quality and repairs. You sought service. Perhaps you discovered that buying by mail for less, for example, was not such a good idea after all. When you look for advisors, you go through the same investigative process.

If you are dealing with a firm, who within it will actually do the work for you? Remember, accounting companies do not do anything—only a specific person does something. In selecting advisors, therefore, you are going after a person or persons rather than a whole company.

I recall the sad story of a man who chose a big law firm with "impeccable" credentials to do the legal work on the start-up of a new company. The person assigned to do his job was new and inexperienced and overlooked all the tax considerations. As a result he lost all chance to deduct the start-up costs—a matter of $150,000! His mistake was to choose a firm without checking out the person who would handle his business.

Determine what experience prospective advisors have in the area where your needs lie. Look at their track record, because we tend to be what we have *done* rather than what we say we will do. In the case of financial planners, beware of those who have not done the work for any length of time or do not have competent backup among their associates. Since your financial net worth is important to you and is part of your well-being, take the trouble to put your financial assets with those who have the experience.

This is a management function. You choose the advisor and are responsible for their advice.

INTERVIEWING

Start the interviews by asking advisor candidates (let's say financial planners) to tell you about their track record. You want to find out whether they have done well, especially during poor financial times. Then test them on hypothetical situations. Ask what they would do if interest rates fell; if interest rates were to jump radically in the next two years; if inflation were to return; and whatever other "if" scenarios you can think of. Where do they see the economy going and why? How do they intend to manage their accounts within the environment they see? Ask where they get their information. Listen for the responses and the way the answers are given. Do these would-be advisors take the time to explain things simply? Do they treat you respectfully?

My mother used to advise studying how a prospective spouse treats siblings in order to see how he or she will probably treat you after the

marriage. The same notion holds for prospective advisors. If they are impatient with you or act as if they consider you "small potatoes," these are clues about how they will treat you after they have your account.

A very prestigious investment firm I know agreed to take on a small account—several million dollars—as a favor. They were arrogant about the ease with which they could handle such a modest sum. The clients, awed by the firm's reputation, abdicated all management responsibility. In the end the firm lost money for them and had to be fired, but only after losses had been taken over a long period of time.

With your various testing methods you will learn a lot about the advisors. You will learn that each financial planner, for example, has a particular bent. Some are very conservative and others tend to play the odds a bit more than you might feel comfortable with. Some are really interested in you. Some make decisions themselves, while others go through lengthy committee processes. Some groups, fearing lawsuits, study things to death—behavior that can lead to being "a day late and a dollar short."

In the course of your interviews you will begin to see that there is nothing magical about financial planning. Planners make a profession out of the practical study of economics, a complex subject. They have to work within constraints just like everyone else; there are no easy answers. You begin to have respect for the task and the field and thus to become realistic in your search for the right person.

Conflicts of interest are a possibility you will want to look out for. Ask yourself whether you will be getting a crack at all the options if you are tied exclusively to what this particular planner can buy or knows about. The situation would be analogous to going to an insurance agent who works for a single company and represents only that company's offerings rather than to a general agent who deals with all the companies.

With a planner who gets paid by commission, you start to see the inherent temptation to trade you in and out of assets too much. You become straightforward with your questions, and you probe. How much will the commission-based advisor make on a proposed transaction? Is there a way to achieve the same objective without buying the product being suggested? If so, why not hold tight? In so doing you are owning your own power—and prospective advisors will start to see that they are dealing with someone who is willing to be *causal*, that is, to take charge and to actively manage his or her own life.

After a number of interviews you can tell the difference between a canned pitch and a genuinely individual response. You recognize advisors who try to surround themselves with mystique instead of being forthright. You get a feeling for how you will be treated as a client. Using the intuitive sixth sense we all have, you know whether the relationship will work out.

In the end the process turns interesting and also exciting. What began as a confusing task—something to be avoided—now seems manageable. You find that you have new confidence in an unfamiliar area and that you are getting closer to managing your resources to realize goals. However, don't get overconfident. Remember, this is a serious task. Stay with your reason for doing it—finding the advisor best suited to your needs because you do not know the field.

During all these interviews you will also be getting a feel for the fees advisors charge. No one gets something for nothing; ultimately we get what we pay for. The important thing is that you start to see that you can buy planning services at many levels. Some advisors consult for an hourly fee. Others take on clients for a yearly retainer. You start to see which extreme—or which point in between—best matches your needs in achieving your goals, and you choose.

A Reminder—Be Clear about Your Goals and Purpose

It bears repeating that you will get further if you are clear about your goals and purpose. I recall a person who went to see a planner and was told to mortgage her house to buy bonds. She was an apprehensive person to start with and did not feel comfortable with debt. That feeling of discomfort is what saved her. Because she listened to it, she got a second opinion (from a friend), started to get in touch with her true purpose, and realized that the planner saw her only as a balance sheet and not as a whole person. Once she looked at her nonfinancial wealth as well as her material assets and developed prioritized goals in line with her life purpose, she was clear that the advice to mortgage the home was just crazy—for her.

In another case, a young executive on the fast track in the electronics field went to a planner for "a plan." He and his wife wanted to take charge of the financial aspects of their lives. The planner told them that they should both work (even though they had small children) and demonstrated with a computerized projection that if their incomes grew according to his plan they would have $2.5 million by the time they were sixty-five. Then, the planner said, they could really live!

They were dissatisfied with the plan because both wanted to attend to the rearing of their children. Both wanted the qualities of freedom and peace in their lives, and both wanted to be able to pursue special interests, including outdoor photography and hiking. They talked things over and decided to ignore the planner's advice. After reviewing their financial and nonfinancial assets, they chose to take charge of their well-being in another way.

They sold their home in Silicon Valley for $285,000 and bought an old house in the country not far from a large city for $70,000. The zoning in their new location would allow them to convert the property to an apartment house if need be. Thus it had investment potential. The balance from the sale of their home was put into cash equivalents pending the development of their new life.

They moved—lock, stock, and barrel. They now have clean air to breathe and good water to drink, and they are close to hiking. Their living costs are lower. They are going about restructuring their lives and starting new careers in line with the qualities they want to have in their lives. They are excited about life. They paid their financial planner the agreed $1,500 for the plan and then threw it away. They were free.

All of this resulted from their being able to filter the advice of the planner through the insight of who they really were and wanted to become. Although they declined the advice, they learned a great deal in the process. They made major changes that left them feeling less stress and more connection to themselves. Perhaps this is the only real outcome to be desired of any planning effort—with or without advisors.

In the broad context of how we defined an advisor, **we are all both students and teachers**.

There is one overall awareness worth holding onto: whether you use advisors or not, you are always your own financial and nonfinancial manager. If you have advisors, you are their client, but as the buyer, you are also always the "employer." The final responsibility and the decisions are yours. Thus, do not totally disengage from the process. Even if you elect to turn over a portfolio to an investor or trustee, you are responsible for monitoring progress. Every move taken, whether financial or nonfinancial, has its impact on how successfully you bring your vision and purpose into being.

The last page of this chapter is a worksheet to help you identify the various people you might want to call on for advice.

Your Personal List of Advisors

Financial

	NAME	ADDRESS	PHONE

Planner

_____

_____

Accountant

_____

_____

Lawyer

_____

_____

Banker

_____

_____

Other

_____

_____

Nonfinancial

Health (doctor, etc.)

_____

_____

Learning (teacher, etc.)

_____

_____

Spouse, partner

_____

_____

Friend

_____

_____

Colleague

_____

_____

Minister, priest, rabbi, etc.

_____

_____

Other

_____

_____

People working with appropriate tools
get the job done.

8

INVESTMENT TOOLS

To construct anything you need tools. Making plans for creating wealth is no different. It is important to first recognize, and then integrate, both financial and nonfinancial tools so that you can address varying needs. To paraphrase Abraham Maslow, "If all you have is a hammer, everything looks like a nail." In this chapter we will be identifying a whole range of tools that you can consider using as you take steps to achieve True Wealth.

You will probably be familiar with most of these tools, though you may not recognize them as such. They are your means of making your dreams visible in the world. While your prior work has made you aware of your vision and purpose in life, you now need tools to help you achieve your goals and thus realize your purpose. The ultimate implements are your mind and your feelings for life, for they determine the context in which all the other tools can work.

Compounding—A Primary Financial Building Tool

Compounding, the process of earning upon earnings, is a powerful tool for creating riches in a very quiet, automatic way. We use compounding nonfinancially as well, in that each life experience builds on previous ones. Although we have all heard of financial compounding and probably understand it in a general sense, we tend not to give it the attention it deserves. Compounding should be the cornerstone of both financial and nonfinancial growth.

At first glance, the table on the next page may look like just a boring compilation of numbers, yet there is seeming magic in this list. It shows how $1 will grow over time at different rates of interest. The only requirements are that you refrain from withdrawing the interest and that you give it time to grow. **Time and discipline are the two essential ingredients**—both of them nonfinancial elements. They drive the financial outcome. Of the two, discipline is the more difficult. However, if you are clear about your purpose, and if gathering riches is a part of it, then discipline comes more easily, because you will have no strong purpose pulling you in other directions. Expressed differently, if you are clear about the need to get to New York as quickly as possible, you will not be tempted to stop off in Texas to see a friend on the way.

Compounding Table

Year	5%	7%	10%	12%	15%
1	$1.05	1.07	1.10	1.12	1.15
5	1.28	1.40	1.61	1.76	2.01
10	1.63	1.97	2.59	3.11	4.05
20	2.65	3.87	6.73	9.65	16.37
30	4.32	7.61	17.45	29.96	66.21
40	7.04	14.97	45.26	93.05	267.86

Source: David Thorndike, *Thorndike Encyclopedia of Banking and Financial Tables* (1987). Copyright © Warren, Gorham & Lamont, Boston, MA. Reprinted by permission of the publisher.

Note: Compounded annually for selected points of time and rates. These calculations are before tax and inflation considerations.

COMPOUNDING AT WORK IN A SAVINGS ACCOUNT

As an example, let's see how a dollar compounds in a savings account. In a certificate of deposit, or CD, it would multiply in basically the same way. To make the calculation easy, let's assume a 10 percent rate of interest. In one year, $1 grows to $1.10. In five years, it becomes $1.61, not all that spectacular. Now look at the end of ten years. The dollar has become $2.59, or a bit over two and a half times as much. We are beginning to make headway. After twenty years, the dollar is worth $6.73, or nearly seven times its original

value. At the end of thirty years, it becomes $17.45, or nearly seventeen and a half times its original value! (Note that these results are before taxes and that they do not account for inflation either; more on both subjects later.)

One major point emerges, the importance of *time* as a component of financial wealth. People who are young—those with thirty years or more ahead of them—are inherently rich because they have the time for compounding to work. That is why young people should have some form of savings or other investment program.

It takes time for the earnings base to get big enough so that "earnings on earnings" become a real factor, working automatically day after day. We tend to discount this process because it gets off to a slow start. Yet as the table shows, it is the earnings upon prior earnings that create the eventual snowball effect. At the end of only ten years, the earnings have dwarfed the original capital pool. People who save, like the Swiss (who do it for retirement purposes since they have no social security), do not seem very dramatic. But after thirty years of saving, they "suddenly" possess riches. It is like the tortoise and the hare: with all the hare's dashing about, the tortoise eventually catches up and passes him.

Another major point emerges: in order to earn in this way, we must have the *discipline* to keep at it and not cave in to the temptation to pull out money to buy something. If money is drawn out in dribs and drabs, then the compounding is set back because we are withdrawing the earnings (the real investment base) on which earnings are earned. There must be intention around a financial investment goal, and money should be left in, or added to, in order to achieve that goal.

In compounding, everything depends on having the discipline to hang in there over time. That said, it is also true that money is energy to be used toward a goal, as the diagram indicates. It has little value by itself. If your goal was to save until

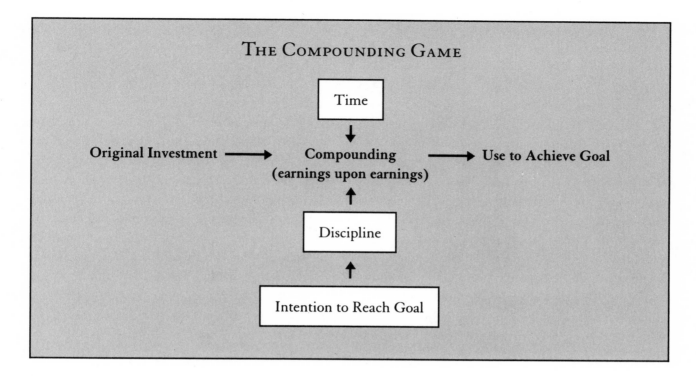

you had the down payment to buy a house, then withdrawing funds for that purpose would be totally appropriate.

COMPOUNDING IN MUTUAL FUNDS AND REAL ESTATE

Compounding applies to any type of investment. Most mutual funds, for example, strive to create capital gains and often earn dividends, too. If earnings are left in the fund to buy additional shares, then the capital base (that is, the number of shares) rises as shares are accumulated.

In the table on the next page, you can see what would happen to a $10,000 investment in a mutual fund. The left-hand column shows the various return rates expressed as a percentage. Along the top are years, or time. Because stocks tend to protect against inflation and (if capital gains are counted as well) to outstrip savings interest, let's take a 15 percent rate over a thirty-year period. During this time, $10,000 becomes $662,117.

One day you wake up to the fact that you have

riches. In effect, you bought additional shares with the gains on the original base, and these shares earned on themselves to create yet more gains for further share purchases. You earned upon earnings by having the discipline and focus to let the earnings accumulate.

However, unlike a savings account where interest earned is added to savings, the new shares purchased from gains left in the fund are bought at varying prices as the fund's share price fluctuates with the market. In a low market, shares are bought at low prices, in a high market at high. This is called dollar averaging and is a dynamic that works with, and in addition to, compounding. With a savings account there is no dollar averaging because we are not dealing with a fluctuating dollar; each addition of interest to savings is made at the same dollar value.

Before you get too excited, remember that returns are typically a function of risk. Stocks represent more risk than an insured money market account in a bank or a long-term government bond. Still, a mutual fund offers professional diversified management, and funds can be selected from an enormous list ranging from very aggressive, high-risk, high-yield options to more benign, lower-risk funds that are slower growing and yield a lower return.

The fact that a mutual fund stock is subject to market fluctuations while a dollar in a bank account is not imposes an important management responsibility on the investor. The compounding principle aside, one would not tend to leave a given stock fund at market risk unattended for years on end. We do not live in a vacuum. We must always be responsive to the changing world around us. For that matter, one would not want to leave funds in a savings account unattended either, even though they are less subject to the wider fluctuations attributed to stocks. Inflation

alone might be a reason not to house funds in a bank account. As we shall see, inflation can silently rob an investment of value in a short time.

The concept of compounding applies to real estate investments as well. In the case of income property, instead of taking out rents as cash, we can reinvest the income in the project in order to enhance value. At the time of sale, reinvestment in a new venture compounds previous earnings. Buying a home is another illustration. By making monthly payments of interest *and* principal, we are saving by paying down the amount owed. By the time the loan is fully repaid, we own the home and, if neighborhood values have increased as a result of inflation or other factors, such as a change in supply and demand relationships, we have also enjoyed capital appreciation.

What a $10,000 Investment Will Grow To

Years Gain	5	10	15	20	25	30	40
5%	12,762	16,288	20,789	26,532	33,863	43,219	70,399
6%	13,382	17,908	23,965	32,071	42,918	57,434	102,857
7%	14,025	19,671	27,590	38,696	54,274	76,122	149,744
8%	14,693	21,589	31,721	46,609	68,484	100,626	217,245
9%	15,386	23,673	36,424	56,044	86,230	132,676	314,094
10%	16,105	25,937	41,772	67,274	108,347	174,494	492,592
11%	16,850	28,394	47,845	80,623	135,854	228,922	650,008
12%	17,623	31,058	54,735	96,462	170,000	299,599	930,509
13%	18,424	33,945	62,542	115,230	212,305	391,158	1,327,815
14%	19,254	37,072	71,379	137,434	264,619	509,501	1,888,835
15%	20,113	40,455	81,370	163,665	329,189	662,117	2,678,635
16%	21,003	44,114	92,655	194,607	408,742	858,498	3,787,211
17%	21,924	48,068	105,387	231,055	506,578	1,110,646	5,338,687
18%	22,877	52,338	119,737	273,930	626,686	1,433,706	7,503,783
19%	23,863	56,946	135,895	324,294	773,880	1,846,753	10,516,675
20%	24,883	61,917	154,070	383,375	953,962	2,373,763	14,697,715
21%	25,937	67,274	174,494	452,592	1,173,908	3,044,816	20,484,002
22%	27,027	73,046	197,422	533,576	1,442,101	3,897,578	28,470,377
23%	28,153	79,259	223,139	628,206	1,768,592	4,979,128	39,464,304
24%	29,316	85,944	251,956	738,641	2,165,419	6,348,199	54,559,126
25%	30,517	93,132	284,217	867,361	2,646,698	8,077,935	75,231,638

Source: Reprinted from *Growth Fund Guide*, Box 666, Rapid City, SD 57709.

COMPOUNDING WITH MIXED INVESTMENTS

Even if investments are mixed, compounding can still work. Let's take an example. We all probably began with a savings account. We let earnings earn upon themselves until we had enough money to buy a home. We perhaps added a room or a deck to the house, thus compounding its value further.

We then borrowed on the home to buy another piece of real estate or a mutual fund or securities. The discovery in all this is that compounding tools figure in many of our choices. Moreover, when we take money and buy an intangible like education, we add to experience—a kind of nonfinancial compounding—and we may also derive financial benefit (a better-paying job, for instance). When we use tools with the intention of furthering our purpose, we remain focused and can head straight for our goal.

ENVIRONMENTAL FACTORS AFFECTING COMPOUNDING

To explain how compounding works, I assumed a steady interest rate. In reality, interest rates fluctuate. This is simply a given of the business environment with which we must contend. One solution is to lock in an interest rate by buying a very long-term government or corporate bond that has an attractive rate. Some years ago it was possible to find 11 percent bonds for thirty years. However, tying up money for the really long term can work against us at times. In a recent example, interest rates went as high as 20 percent on a short-term basis—and then fell to 6¼ percent not long afterwards. The point is that any investment requires attention.

Another way to work with interest rate fluc-tuations is by investing in vehicles for which there are offsetting factors. Stocks and real estate, for example, have historically been considered infla-tion hedges because, unlike cash, their value tends to rise as prices do. They need to be watched, though, since they don't always follow this rule.

Regardless of the investment tool or goal, the key to addressing "uncontrollable" external forces is alert management. We are responsible for monitoring change. Interest rates are only one of the factors that need to be monitored. Compounding is subject to numerous other environmental influences, about which you will learn in the next chapter. Two of the most pernicious are taxes and inflation.

Taxes and Inflation— The Enemies of Compounding

Taxes and inflation seem to work against our best efforts to accumulate financial wealth. Even as compounding builds, inflation silently robs and taxes deplete. Inflation can be especially insidious, because it reflects complex economic—and non-economic—forces that tend to be unpredictable.

TAXES

Taxes are here to stay. They annually lower the capital base on which earnings and gains are made. To make things even more difficult, tax laws change constantly, sometimes to increase taxes and at other times to lower them. Given these realities, it would seem that there is little one can do about taxes. In fact, there is a lot.

First off, you can learn about the legitimate tax avoidance measures allowed by the tax law, for instance such tax-deferred retirement plans as IRAs (Individual Retirement Accounts), Keoghs, and SEPs (Simplified Employee Pensions) for individuals and 401(K) plans for employees of corporations. Because they allow you to put money into any number of investments and to defer tax payments until retirement, you not only get to compound earning, but you also get to earn money that would otherwise go to taxes.

Age at Start	Total at Age 65 ($2,000/Yr.)	Fund Value (at 10% Interest Rate)
25	$80,000	$973,704
30	70,000	596,254
35	60,000	361,887
40	50,000	216,364
45	40,000	126,005
50	30,000	69,899
55	20,000	35,062

Source: Fidelity Investments, Boston, MA.
Note: Double amount for fund value if husband and wife both work and both contribute $2,000 annually. Increase by $1/8$ for married couple with nonworking spouse, contributing the maximum $2,250 allowed annually.

Note the table above, which assumes a compounding rate of 10 percent over different time periods. It clearly shows how tax-deferred earnings can accumulate over time. For someone thirty years old who is able to contribute $2,000 per year and willing to leave the money to compound in such a shelter for thirty-five years, the accumulated earnings (before taxes and inflation) come to $596,254.

Such an increase is impressive. It is also very real. In fact, it is so real that just about everyone who is eligible should participate. You should even consider borrowing to do so. The only exceptions might be young couples saving for a home and people paying for education, who would need funds earlier. Retirement saving is long term.

One caution: These plans allow tax deferment, not tax elimination. Ultimately, when funds are withdrawn, you will have to pay taxes. If, however, your retirement needs are less, you will pay taxes at a lower rate, assuming the amount you withdraw puts you in a lower tax bracket.

What role do advisors (a nonfinancial tool) have in all this?

Because tax laws change so often, it is worthwhile consulting people who make a profession of keeping up with the changes. Advisors can tell you which tax-deferment plans you are eligible for. They can help you estimate your tax burdens given potential investment opportunities. They can also point you toward perfectly legal investments that can limit taxes. For example, the law often provides loopholes as incentives for investment.

However, beware of "iffy" tax avoidance propositions that may be offered from time to time. Such schemes can be hazardous because they often fall into a gray area—a place of unclear and untested tax law. In the end, the call is yours, for *you*—and not an expert advisor or an ardent salesperson—are the one who must face the IRS.

INFLATION

Although inflation is beyond our control, it—like taxes—needs to be taken into account and "managed." Inflation fluctuates over time. Recently we have been in a period of disinflation, one conducive to saving. By contrast, during the period when oil prices were being rapidly driven up by OPEC, we saw the "thievery" of inflation as living costs went up dramatically. At such times, savers are hurt. That is, the bathtub drain lets more water out than the spigot lets in. The result? The water level in the tub—our purchasing power—gets progressively lower.

Forecasting major economic change is a difficult task for the professionals, let alone nonprofessionals. I only wish to underscore the significance of the inflation factor and to encourage you to consider it in your planning. It can have an especially large impact on retirement income.

For example, my own father, a retired senior executive in a New York bank, lived nearly thirty years after retiring at age sixty-eight. Beginning in the early 1950s he received a monthly pension check of $998, which seemed fine at the time. However, when he died at ninety-four in 1985, this amount was clearly not enough. Inflation had robbed him of his lifestyle. What will it do to you and me?

Debt/Leverage—A Useful Financial Tool If Not Misused

Debt is neither good nor bad in itself. It is simply another investment tool with which to make both tangible and intangible investments in line with our purpose.

As defined by the dictionary, debt sounds just awful: "something owed, an obligation or liability, an offense requiring forgiveness" (*American Heritage*). The definition of *mortgage* is even worse, for the root meaning in Middle English or old French is "dead hand"—or just plain "death" if you prefer the Latin root! No one likes obligations, nor do we take joy in death. Nonetheless, there can be purpose in using debt as a tool with which to achieve goals.

THE POSITIVE SIDE OF DEBT

Few of us could ever afford a home without incurring debt. We need to purchase time (one sense of borrowing) in order to buy such a big-ticket item. In taking on a promise to pay, we buy the time necessary to acquire the resources to eventually own the home outright.

Debt makes sense for other financial reasons as well. A real estate investment, like a home purchase, is capital intensive and involves not only the purchase of time but also the use of *leverage*. Leverage quite simply means using money belonging to others to fund an investment.

ONE ADDITIONAL WORD OF CAUTION ABOUT TAX AVOIDANCE MEASURES

If a tax avoidance scheme conflicts with one of your financial or nonfinancial goals, be especially careful because the life quality behind that goal is on the line. Always select in favor of the goal. Stay connected.

This rule took on new meaning for me when I attended a financial planning conference at which several planning advisors spoke. One was a woman whose subject was tax avoidance issues. During her talk, she made the comment that wives perhaps ought not to work for pay because the extra income could put the couple filing jointly into a higher tax bracket that could wipe out or diminish the wife's income. She gave examples.

She made *her* point and completely missed THE point! She ignored the fact that work is an actualizing activity and that a wife may need work to feel complete and to meet a nonfinancial goal like broadening her life, using her mind in new ways, or experiencing her own power in a new context.

Therefore, **be goal oriented, not tax driven**. Stay linked to who you are and the qualities you represent. Limiting tax exposure by legal means makes sense as long as it is viewed within the greater context of your purpose and goals. You are the only one who can make these decisions.

An example: An office building is bought for $100,000 with $30,000 in cash and a $70,000 note at interest. In due course, the building might be sold for $150,000. Two things are evident: (1) the whole asset was controlled for less than its purchase cost, and (2) upon sale, the seller (after paying off the debt) could receive a return of $50,000 on the $30,000 of cash invested—versus the same return on $100,000 had the owners elected not to use debt. Clearly, the return is greatly enhanced by the use of debt.

The disadvantage would become evident if the market value of the building fell instead of going up. The debt would be just as payable, and the cash down payment, and the property itself, could be lost.

Leverage through debt is hardly limited to real estate. Investors buy stocks, bonds, and dress shirts with debt. For this last purchase, credit cards are often used as a debt vehicle. In buying stocks, the goal is the same as for a real estate purchase. In the case of the dress shirt, people defer payment because they do not have the money just then (but will have it later, they hope), because they have a more profitable use for the funds elsewhere, or because they thereby get a thirty-day interest-free loan if the credit card balance is paid off each month. In any case, the leverage obtained through debt is clear: one gains a sort of mechanical advantage, as in using a lever to pry an object up (hence the name).

There are also nonfinancial reasons for debt. For example, a student borrows from a university to go to graduate school, promising to pay the money back over time after graduating. The asset (the borrower) is more valuable (in an appropriate field) after the graduate work than before, and this added value can be translated into income as the source of repayment. In this case, debt is being used to create an offsetting intangible asset (a more educated individual) that will create a financial return from a nonfinancial purchase (education).

As in the real estate example, money is being used to buy time—the time needed to get a degree and then to translate that intangible learning into a financial income stream from which the debt can be repaid. Again we see the recycling between financial and nonfinancial resources to achieve a goal and purpose. The important thing is to see these connections and act on them.

Homes can be seen as both financial and non-financial assets. If a home is viewed as an intangible—something to provide shelter or a place to raise a family—then buying a home is another illustration of using financial leverage for a non-financial goal.

We spend money to become or to stay healthy. Sometimes we borrow to finance this nonfinancial goal.

Barter is another example of leverage. Someone skilled in counseling may trade—or leverage—that skill for the planning skills offered by another person. All on-the-side trades are leverage situations. In a sense, any time any of us materially helps another, there often is an implied obligation (debt) to return the favor.

THE NEGATIVE SIDE OF DEBT

Leveraging cuts in both directions. If you buy a stock at $30 per share using debt to finance $15 of the price, and if that stock tumbles to $20 per share and is sold, you get back only $5 for the $30 paid, a considerable loss. If the share were to drop to $5 per share, you would not only lose all your money but be required to pay off the loan of another $10 per share of liability as well.

As we saw, credit card use can also be a form of debt if the balance is not paid off each month. Although credit cards have important advantages—such as allowing you to travel without carrying cash and providing receipts for tax purposes—they can also be traps. Too frequently people use them to buy more than they can readily repay, and in so doing, they also make themselves liable for hefty financing charges. Still, credit cards are neither good nor bad in themselves; they become negative only if misused. The important thing is to use them in line with your purpose.

In short, borrowing involves responsibility and proper risk management. Look at debt as only one of many available tools, and use it to further goals within the context of your resources, earning power, and propensity for taking risks.

Nonfinancial Building Tools

The idea that financial resources are essentially nonfinancially driven carries over into the area of tools as well. Most of our intangible power is vested in tangible connections—those that we forge with education, our outlook on life, our health, and the people with whom we associate as we go about building our financial and nonfinancial net worth. Another intangible tool is time itself. How we choose to use it within the context of our goals will have an impact on both riches and wealth.

The following are examples of nonfinancial building tools that are widely recognized and used. I hope they will prompt you to identify others that you will find helpful as you build value in your life.

VISUALIZATION

As we saw in the chapter on vision and purpose, what comes to mind comes to pass. Action follows thought. The brain holds a picture of what we envision and can often prepare for the ultimate manifestation of what was seen. The striking story of Steve DeVore is a case in point.

TIME—THE FORGOTTEN RESOURCE

Time is both a component and a tool of wealth that we often overlook. We have already seen how money multiplies, or compounds, with time. In that narrow context, time *is* money. Thus youth is inherently rich because young people have the time to accumulate riches. Time is also a form of wealth and can be used to create other nonfinancial aspects of wealth as well, for example joy, friendships, and education.

Money (another component of wealth) can be used to purchase time. For example, we can either do our own gardening or hire a gardener. By choosing the latter route, we are buying time to do some other thing that is hopefully more in line with our purpose. In other words, we are using a financial resource (money) to free time (a nonfinancial asset) so that it can be reinvested in some other activity, which may be financial or nonfinancial. We have all witnessed people buying time in this way in order to go back to school in midlife, with the goal of creating second careers or making other new options available.

Whether it is viewed as an intangible asset or a tool, time is an essential resource that we should invest wisely and take care not to waste.

NETWORKS—THE BUILDING OF ALLIANCES

It is difficult to go it alone. We need one another. Besides, doing things without others is lonely and not much fun. Almost any activity, business included, is a way of making contact.

There is real power in community. Doing things together allows our individual strengths to shine while our weaker spots can be covered by those who are effective in ways we are not. Marriage can be thought of as a mini-network, and so can a partnership in commerce—which is a sort of business marriage.

If you haven't already done so, begin networking now. Set about joining with people who share your financial and nonfinancial planning goals. Select people of different backgrounds and abilities so that a strengthening diversity results.

In building networks, keep your purpose in mind. That is, be clear about what you want from any network. Without such clarity, you will not find harmony in your collective activities, and conflicts of purpose may arise at a time when you really want to go forward.

How do you start networking?

I suggest that you begin by writing down your specific reason for wanting to network. Others can read your statement and either agree that it fits their purpose or decide that they need to look somewhere else. If the group's goal is not made clear at the outset, people with differing needs will oppose each other, and "deformation" will soon follow formation.

Look at your situation and decide what your particular needs are. If you already have a lot of knowledge, your needs will differ from those of a beginner, and you will be frustrated in a group that mainly discusses fundamentals. Some networks are small, closed investment communities where each member puts up investment capital and the group makes the investment decisions. In other networks, the members gather solely to discuss investment information, and each person then goes his or her own investment way. In the former situation, it is crucial that the investment goal of each person be the same. In the latter, it doesn't matter. There is no norm in choosing a

network group. The only guiding principle is need. Be certain that the group's goal meets your need.

I know of one group that meets to share information. Because it is difficult to read and assimilate every relevant periodical, members are assigned specific pieces to read and report on at each monthly meeting. In this way the whole group is able to cover, in some depth, over fifty periodicals plus the odd investment book. This saves a lot of time.

Another group formed around a computer whiz who uses statistical analysis to make investment and market calls. They invest together, with the expert advising the rest of the group. For those who want to follow and learn (with their own money at risk), such an arrangement can work out.

Look over your list of friends and contacts. These may be neighbors or people you meet casually in business or through social activities. Prioritize the list according to who you think your best prospects are, and start interviewing. Share your purpose with each candidate and get a sense of his or her requirements and interests. Remember, you do not need to do it all. Those you approach will suggest others, and the number of potential members will expand dramatically. That is the power of networking. You discover you are not alone at all. There are others with similar needs, and you end up meeting wonderful people as a by-product! Everyone wins, and the win-win approach magnifies the investment return.

Nonfinancial networking is also effective. For example, women's or men's groups often form for the purpose of offering a supportive environment. Great books groups come together for educational reasons. Those working for a charity—from giants like the Red Cross to tiny local groups in a hospice—are still other examples. Then there are the political groups who work to save the redwoods, clean up water, or elect someone to office. All of these groups meet to focus on something that holds meaning and represents a life quality. The important thing is to be sure that the quality associated with any activity is one you share. If it is, then your own purpose will be furthered along with that of the group.

Finally, build your network in such a way that you can integrate whatever comes out of it into your own plan. After all, that was the purpose of going about this process in the first place.

AWARENESS

Awareness is a prerequisite for bringing about change. Before we can intervene, we must be aware of the need for change and have ideas about new directions.

The need for awareness extends to all aspects of our lives. In both the financial and nonfinancial realms, we are touched by forces beyond our control but with which we must deal if we are to achieve goals. The overall economy, corporate profits, interest rates, the international balance of payments, the national debt level, and annual deficits are examples of the financial elements we must be conscious of. Our health, outlook on life, and the quality of our close relationships are examples of nonfinancial factors in our lives that require vigilant awareness.

Having become clear about your own vision, purpose, and goals, you know what you seek. You are in a position to begin learning what you need to know and keep abreast of in order to meet specific goals. It is vital to build such knowledge and awareness. Then when someone mentions reading that interest rates may tumble because of such and such, your ears will pick up. You will tune in simply because you now recognize where this piece of information fits. Or, sensing a drifting away from a close friendship, you can repair the connection. This sort of multilevel awareness links the tangible with the intangible. It connects our inner and outer selves.

DISCIPLINE

Without real intention and the will to proceed, we cannot use any other tool optimally. It's like buying a computer without wanting to learn how to operate it. Alone, it is just another piece of electronics hardware. Add the intention to learn and the discipline to follow through, and we make the computer's utility available to us.

Whole books have been written about discipline. They define it and suggest techniques for nurturing it. My purpose here is only to draw attention to discipline as an essential nonfinancial tool so that you can consciously elect to use it.

INFORMATION—THE MODERN POWER TOOL

Information is a money equivalent, and it is also wealth. That is, it can be financial or nonfinancial. Either way, it has remarkable—and often unrecognized—power. For example, having data to support an intuition about a possible stock market movement can be worth a great deal. Not everyone got caught in the October 1987 market "correction." A very few saw selective signs—both financial and intangible—and sold out before the huge drop in the Dow.

I recall talking with a man who had been concerned for a long time about both the financial and the nonfinancial trends he was seeing. On the financial side, he saw a Congress unwilling to address the federal deficit, a growing individual debt level, and a widening trade deficit. Nonfinancially, he sensed a growing hysteria around stock purchases and real estate buys. All of these facts and observations together seemed to support his intuition of disaster, and he decided to sell out almost completely in August of 1987, just two months before the crash. As a result, all of his bull market gains were preserved.

His financial moves followed from using a number of investment tools in synergy, including the discipline to be attentive to changes, the awareness of information that was timely and appropriate, a network of economic cohorts, and the ability to listen to his own hunches (intuition).

Was he so smart? Certainly not. He simply used several tools in appropriate combination. We all do this at some level anyway, though often unconsciously. My point is to make this process a fully conscious one.

LEARNING

Our competitive and fast-moving world presents the opportunity for nonstop education. Learning is a tool of great importance for both financial and nonfinancial progress because it is enabling. It increases value.

Never give up the chance to learn. Read books and periodicals. Formal courses are available, as are less formal ones through university extension and community college night schools. Look over the various financial newsletters and subscribe to those that seem to be especially relevant to your goals. Use libraries. Network. Use your expanded self-awareness to choose the learning that is appropriate to your purpose.

ADVISORS

Advisors, the subject of chapter 7, can be seen as both tools and resources. Use them with care and only as appropriate to your purpose and need. They can be most powerful tools when used in this way.

FUN

Fun is a tool in that it helps us get things done. If we can approach a task with the idea that it might be fun, we can avoid the feeling of heaviness that often accompanies doing something solely to fulfill an obligation. With this lighter attitude, we experience less energy drain and tension.

The whole investment process can be seen as

THE IMPORTANCE OF PUTTING ALL YOUR TOOLS IN ONE TOOLBOX

Although I have artificially divided tools into financial and nonfinancial categories, in practice they are often joined. For example, compounding (a financial tool) can be used to save for education (a nonfinancial tool), which can have a financial impact when focused on a well-paying career. Or an advisor (a nonfinancial tool) can be used to financial advantage, as in the case of investment advice, or for a nonfinancial purpose, as in the case of a counselor helping with conflict resolution.

In other words, don't put the financial and nonfinancial tools in separate toolboxes. Put them in the same one! That way you can "mix them up" and get the benefit of their full synergy.

an adventure—as a way to stretch. In fact, there ought to be an element of fun in almost everything we do. The "Am I having fun yet?" test is important. If you are not having fun because of fear of something new, get over the fear by building familiarity, and then enjoy the confidence that comes with familiarity. If fun is not there because the subject and activity do not hold interest, then consider delegation—bring in advisors—but do not abdicate the function. As we have seen, abdicating responsibility simply does not work.

A Life Plan— The Ultimate Tool

A plan is perhaps the most important tool you can have. Like a map, it will guide you as you drive through unfamiliar territory. You will have a sense of where you are relative to where you have been and where you are going. The whole purpose of the True Wealth process is to provide the means for you to create a life plan that is based on clarity of goals flowing from a sound under-standing of your vision and purpose. The plan is the ultimate tool—the place where it all comes together and you see the whole cloth. The threads have been connected in ways that give strength.

Writing a life plan is the subject of the final chapter. At that point you will sketch out how you intend to achieve the financial and nonfinancial goals you have set for yourself. Writing always creates resistance, forces thought, and helps to develop clarity. It will help you to bring together all the aspects of the True Wealth process in relation to your own vision and purpose. You will want to consider, for example, how much risk you are willing to take and to balance that with strategies to cover core family needs for shelter, food, living costs, and the like. You will look at diversification, the need for cash reserves, budgets, the use of debt, and so on.

Only a couple more areas need to be addressed to prepare you to make this synthesis— the financial and nonfinancial environments in which you will be making and implementing your decisions, and the spectrum of investment possibilities open to you. These are the subjects of the next two chapters.

We act separately together despite
all the boundaries we create.

9

FINANCIAL & NONFINANCIAL ENVIRONMENTS

Thanks to technology, we operate in a truly global arena. Transportation and communications technologies have so shrunk distances that economies and cultures everywhere have become interdependent. A U.S. car maker is affected by competitive pay scales in other countries. Pesticides sold to the Third World come back to haunt us in the form of tainted imported vegetables. Changes in superpower relationships have far-reaching economic and political influence. At the same time, trading in some financial markets goes on for twenty-four hours a day, and currencies are constantly seeking balance in response to constantly changing values and trade balance positions.

We know everything that is happening elsewhere in the world. On our TVs we see pictures of distant wars and food shortages. Disease originating in one place quickly spreads across borders. Despite our war on drugs, the problem seems to worsen, thereby joining highly industrialized user nations with Third World producer nations. In short, national borders can no longer keep out ideas, information, or disease.

We influence the events and peoples that influence us. As experimenters, we are a part of the experiment. The stock market, for example, is really a complex composite of worldwide human behavior expressed in economic terms. **In watching others, we are also watching ourselves.**

The purpose of this chapter is to create awareness of our financial and nonfinancial environments as an important tool in managing resources and expressing our vision and purpose. As we make this effort, we come to appreciate more and more how deeply interconnected we are in complex and ever-changing ways.

There is no perfect way to plan. Complete predictability is impossible, which is why economists vary so widely in their forecasts and advice. Our aim is to work toward becoming aware, not of all possible forces, but of the primary ones affecting us. These forces may be beyond our direct control, but we must be prepared for their

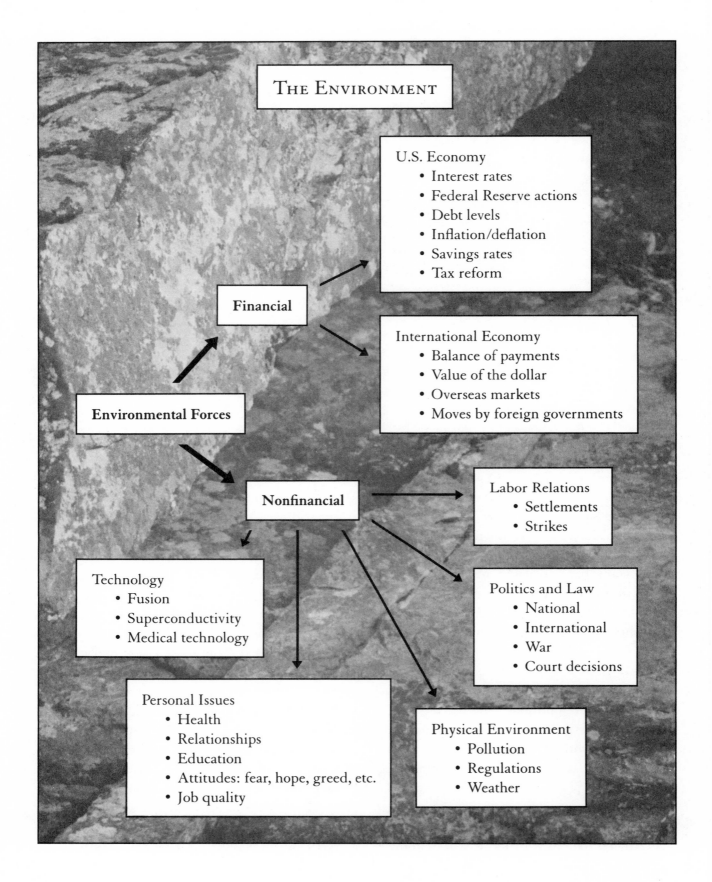

THE ENVIRONMENT

Financial

U.S. Economy
- Interest rates
- Federal Reserve actions
- Debt levels
- Inflation/deflation
- Savings rates
- Tax reform

International Economy
- Balance of payments
- Value of the dollar
- Overseas markets
- Moves by foreign governments

Environmental Forces

Nonfinancial

Labor Relations
- Settlements
- Strikes

Politics and Law
- National
- International
- War
- Court decisions

Technology
- Fusion
- Superconductivity
- Medical technology

Personal Issues
- Health
- Relationships
- Education
- Attitudes: fear, hope, greed, etc.
- Job quality

Physical Environment
- Pollution
- Regulations
- Weather

unpredictability and learn to work with them in order to reach our goals.

The Environment diagram suggests broad areas that make up our increasingly interdependent world. It is not meant to be inclusive, but merely to give an overall picture, to indicate a few of the specific changeable elements that can affect us even from afar, and to activate thinking.

What Is Our Responsibility in This Complex Picture?

We are fully responsible for whatever happens to us. As rampant change gives rise to occasions for both gain and loss, we must keep abreast of the financial and nonfinancial forces that shape these events and realize that we are a part of them. To ignore them is to invite danger or miss opportunities. There is no way to sidestep this issue. Yet keeping tabs on an unpredictable economy is not easy even for the experts who spend all their time at it.

How, then, can we cope?

Instead of fearing this responsibility, we need to become aware of the environmental elements that seem to influence us the most, and then to act in ways that best reflect who we are within the scope of our total resources. In the financial realm, for example, our local and global economies play an enormous role. In fact, their influence seems so all-encompassing at times that we tend consciously to ignore nonfinancial factors, thinking they can have little importance. Yet their influence is equally pervasive.

Nonfinancially, for example, we face a rapidly changing physical environment, stressful work places that can impair our mental and physical health, and the effects of our own general behavior on our relationships. We are influenced by Supreme Court decisions, weather changes, earthquakes, floods, fires, political change, war and peace, the march of technology. We also experience the warmth of close relationships, the beauty of the world around us, and the vitality of breath and hope for the future. With a growing appreciation of the flux in these nonfinancial areas as well as in the financial realm, we can start to connect with changes that are appropriate to us. In so doing, we learn that we actually do have a way to work with otherwise seemingly "uncontrollable" environments.

We can fight ignorance with education; substitute hope, vision, and courage for fear; reach for balance to overcome greed. As Roosevelt so aptly put it, "The only thing we have to fear is fear itself." He used his courage and vision of who he was to lift the country out of the Depression.

In sum, it takes building an awareness of *all* of the interconnected forces to be able to intuit the actions and responses that are appropriate to our vision, purpose, and goals.

Chaos—The Overall Context

Both financial and nonfinancial systems are organic; they are not artificial structures. Being consciously and unconsciously formed and used by people, they are living systems. As we shall see, business cycles are therefore "natural" in that they are expressions of how we act separately together. In collectively expressing our independent individual actions, they often appear disconnected, uncontrollable, and incomprehensible. They work within a greater context, which we have come to call chaos.

Chaos theory teaches that life is random and thus unpredictable. Sit by a mountain stream. Throw a stick of wood in the water flowing smoothly by, and watch it float downstream. By calculating the rate of the evenly flowing water, you can predict when the stick will reach a certain point downstream—unless it hits turbulence caused by submerged rocks. With this one random event, all bets are off, for the flow rate is now unpredictable. In fact, the stick may now get caught in an eddy and float no farther.

Financial markets experience similar random turbulence. Early in 1990, the currency markets were doing just beautifully when a rumor started that President Gorbachev was going to resign. Immediately everyone scurried to buy dollars as a safe haven. Then, a few days later, when Gorbachev announced that he favored the reunification of the two Germanies, German financial markets reflected the good news by going up. Both events were unforeseeable, nonfinancial, and random, and they had an immediate impact on an organic financial system.

The OPEC move to raise the price of crude oil in the early 1970s is another example of a random event that caused immediate turmoil in our lives as well as in our pocketbooks.

The principle works nonfinancially, too. Someone sitting in a wheelchair as a result of a freak diving accident has experienced an unpredictable but radically life-changing event.

As involved investors, we must move in ways to be successful amid non-linear events that just suddenly pop up. In the long term, the stream of life is unpredictable.

Now, how can we possibly cope with such randomness in our lives? Chaos theory provides at least a partial answer to this question. It teaches, and our own experience bears out, that predictability is possible in the

short term. It is mainly in the longer term that unpredictability is the norm. For example, we often laugh at the inaccuracy of weather forecasters, who seem always to be in error. In the short run, however, they do very well. By monitoring pressure areas and watching their movements by satellite, they are able to make very presentable short-term predictions. But ask them to forecast precipitation a year from now, and they can be laughingly far off because of random events they can't possibly know about. Consider the often-noted example of two butterflies flapping their wings in Japan, thus initiating a series of random events that could end up causing a tornado in Kansas. Small changes in initial conditions can bring about vastly different outcomes. One random, destabilizing event can create any number of surprises, especially in the long term.

Yet within all of this chaos, there is order. Cycles exist that we can observe and rely on. Our solar system has highly predictable elements within its unpredictability. The sun rises and sets as if run by a clock. Every living thing has a natural life cycle: A bristlecone pine can live six thousand years. A human can squeeze out ninety to a hundred years. The life cycle of an adult butterfly may be days. Whatever the organism, there is a natural span, even though random events may alter a specific life. Every year goes through seasons, although the seasons vary in length from year to year. All living things begin, grow, mature, and die.

In short, there is predictability within the overall context of randomness, and often what appears to be artificial (such as financial markets) is in fact organic. Awareness of this context is important for the perspective it offers on both financial and nonfinancial changes and trends.

The Role of Perception

In becoming aware of the changing world around us, we must understand that what we see has a very personal twist. We call this view a perception. In other words, we all see events differently. What one person sees as a danger, another sees as an opportunity. In the midst of any stock market crash there are always opportunities for gain. Out of a severe illness, great healing can come.

The reality of something is really a function of how we perceive it, as opposed to how it may really be. How we feel about someone often depends on how we characterize something that he or she did. In fact, what we perceived may not bear any resemblance to what really happened. We have all had the experience of waking up one morning and feeling glum, and waking up the next morning and looking forward to the day with joy. Yet nothing has materially changed from one day to the next *except* our perception.

The economy, too, is basically shaped by perception. I recall reading the predictions of two economists. One saw a steadily growing economy and new highs for the stock market, while the other, perceiving the shadow side of events, predicted an inflationary depression. These were individual perceptions, but when such perceptions become collective, they create movement. For example, when enough people independently perceive fear or deep uncertainty in the economy, their behavior as a result of that perception (say, massive selling in the stock market) precipitates change.

Nonetheless, we tend to see the economy as a structure existing apart from ourselves, run by others, and beyond our control or participation. This is completely untrue. Economies are organic structures whose working—or not working—we all contribute to. Like living creatures, economies change constantly as we change and cause them to take new forms.

Arthur Deikman, in his piece entitled "The Meaning of Everything,"* teaches that we live in a world of form and structure and that these structures, which we often consider permanent and static, are really in a constant process of change over long periods of time. The chair we sit on may seem like a firm support right now, but it is actually in the process of disintegrating. Similarly, we think of our bodies as more or less permanent structures, and yet they are also constantly in change, with cells wearing out and being replaced daily. In a year, our bodies will be different because of what we and the environment do to them.

The economy is no less mysterious. It too is in motion, and to understand it we must be aware of it as process, for that implies development or change. The economy is the sum total of the inputs of our composite behavior based on our collective perception of what is going to happen and how the new circumstance will affect us. These group behavior patterns affect us individually. **We remain both individuals and members of the group; we act separately together.** Although the group effect creates forces we may or may not like, we are free to respond as individuals quite apart from what the economy is up to. If our timing is right and we know how to take advantage of our perceptions, we will be fine. Perception born of awareness brings that sense of rightness because the inner response is connected with the outer happenings.

In recent years, for example, we have collec-

*In *The Nature of Human Consciousness*, edited by Robert E. Ornstein. Copyright © 1973 by Robert E. Ornstein, published by W. H. Freeman and Company.

tively been a nation of buyers. We have bought TVs, VCRs, houses, stocks and bonds, cars, travel, etc. To do this, we have created a lot of personal debt, to the point where many of us have zero or negative net worths (that is, we owe more than the value of what we own). As individuals, we are like Third World countries! As corporations, we have also taken on frightening debt loads in order to purchase one another's often overvalued stock in leveraged buy-outs. Corporate cash flows have been poured into financing this debt instead of being invested in research, production, or market development. As a nation, we spent heavily on a military buildup during most of the eighties, thus diverting much of our engineering talent from commercial applications.

By contrast, the Japanese have been savers and long-term investors. They have bet on the commercial long haul and been less concerned with short-term purchases at the personal level or military spending at the national level. They have achieved prominence in TVs, electronics, cars, and steel. In the future, they will probably be focusing on banking, insurance, and computers. While their trade balance is favorable, ours is negative. Where their debt is low, ours is high. We borrow from them.

The two economies are different because individuals within the collective behaved in a different way financially, based on a different way of being. How we are creates an environment that affects our well-being as individuals and as a nation.

To understand the underlying causes of economic change, therefore, we need to see the economy in human terms. Economic slowdowns or upturns are the result of humans acting out their roles in ways that create either fear (as in a depression) or confidence (as in a period of expansion). Similarly, inflation and its impact stem from human activity.

Whenever we buy something, or don't buy it, we contribute to the economic environment. A long-term buying spree can create jobs—and accompanying growth and investment opportunities—on the one hand, and high debt levels and bankruptcies on the other. We need to be aware of this kind of economic polarity in the actions we take.

Our perception of the course of events governs what we do. We all see the same picture but perceive it differently. Two photographers looking at the same scene will produce very different images because their focus, based on who they are, is different. The point is to be open to all the important factors and then to bring the focus of our goals to bear on what we see as a way to create options.

Economies as Self-Correcting Systems

Any economic system works best when it is balanced. Like any natural living organism, it strives to right itself. Our task is to realize that a serious state of imbalance is being reached in time to do something about it. For instance, when debt levels become excessive or asset values become inflated, history tells us that we can expect the economy to enter a new phase.

What happens when indebtedness reaches a worrisome level in any nation? Depression may result—as in Europe in 1873 or the United States in the 1930s—or inflation may soar, as in Germany in the 1920s. (Hitler came to power as a result of that hyperinflation.) Twenty years ago, Argentina was seventh in world productivity. Today, with a crippling amount of foreign debt, it is fiftieth.

During the late 1600s everyone thought England would rule the economic world forever. As a result, securities of the Hudson Bay Company and the East India Company, among others, were seriously overvalued. When the distortion was realized (a group perception), the great South Sea bubble burst, and everything crashed. A seventy-year bear market followed.

What will happen in present-day Japan? Their stock prices are the highest ever seen. Although our own markets seem to offer better values, investor purchases keep pushing the Japanese shares higher. Does the fact that a crash has not occurred ensure that it never will? Historically, when enough people decide that values are too high, they sell out. What impact would a crash have on us over here?

In the United States, what really happened on October 19, 1987, when the Dow-Jones average fell over 500 points in a single day? What happened when the bond markets crashed the preceding April? (In a way, the earlier crash was more serious, because it hurt people who thought that bonds were secure.)

In asking these questions, I am trying to point to the underlying forces that bring about change. My aim is not to offer a forecast, but to start you thinking about the almost purposeful way in which the economy sometimes seems to operate. When you are sensitive to the key financial and nonfinancial forces in the external environment, you can move with the changes in order to achieve goals.

THE ECONOMY AS A LIVING PROCESS

To assess what is happening in the world and how it will affect us, we need to step back and get a sense of process. It is a bit like being in an airplane and looking down at all the activity below, detached from it and connected at the same time. In the economy, things go on that seem far beyond our reach, and yet we are a part of it.

As a living process, the economy has both an economic and a noneconomic component. Unless we see both parts, we miss its wholeness, fail to learn, and are probably destined to repeat mistakes until we do learn.

Let's look at the financial environment first. Like any other living system, the economy seeks balance. As it gets farther away from center, it starts to self-correct—despite anything we may do to encourage or discourage it in the short run. If we take a long view of tinkering with the economy, almost any move by the Federal Reserve Bank, or Fed, is somewhat akin to rearranging the deck chairs on the Titanic. No Fed boss can possibly be held responsible for the forces put in motion by years of low savings and high debt. Nor can he or she avert the effect upon inflation of such events as an unpredictable Arab oil embargo, a savings and loan crisis, the leveraged buyout craze, or the current deficit situation.

I don't mean to say that the Fed is not useful, or that in the current situation a depression is imminent, but only to point out the limitations of any federal system. After excessive abuse, there is a point when the economy will react to heal itself through a recession, depression, correction, soft landing, or whatever else you want to call what it takes to restore balance. However, no one really knows precisely when this "healing" will start.

When, for example, a healthy stock market cycle starts to heat up because of investor frenzy—as with super speculation in a bull market—the system corrects itself by crashing. It nonselectively wipes out the speculators who departed, for the moment, from a realistic sense of value. Thus a new balance is achieved.

In 1929, some people thought that the upward spiral of stock prices would never end. To get more money to invest, they borrowed against the stocks that they wanted to purchase. As they, and their lenders, would come to see, the security for these loans (the stocks themselves) was anything but secure. The borrowing generated more funds, which drove up prices further. "Suddenly," or so it seemed, there was a group change in perception—a nonfinancial insight with financial consequences. When enough people saw the folly, it was too late.

The awareness always starts with a few individuals placing the first few sell orders. Others follow, and for a while the analysts call the activity normal "profit taking." Then everyone wants to sell, few want to buy, and the self-correcting aspect of the living system manifests itself without any assistance from government or individuals. The imbalance that may have taken years to cre-

ate is corrected in hours. The system is back to rights as far as it is concerned. The excess has vanished, the "cleansing" has been completed, and we are left to absorb the learning.

A new cycle has begun.

CYCLES WITHIN CYCLES— A HISTORICAL PERSPECTIVE

This process is not new. In the 1920s, the Russian economist Kondratieff plotted broad cycles as far back as the 1780s. As you can see from the graph,

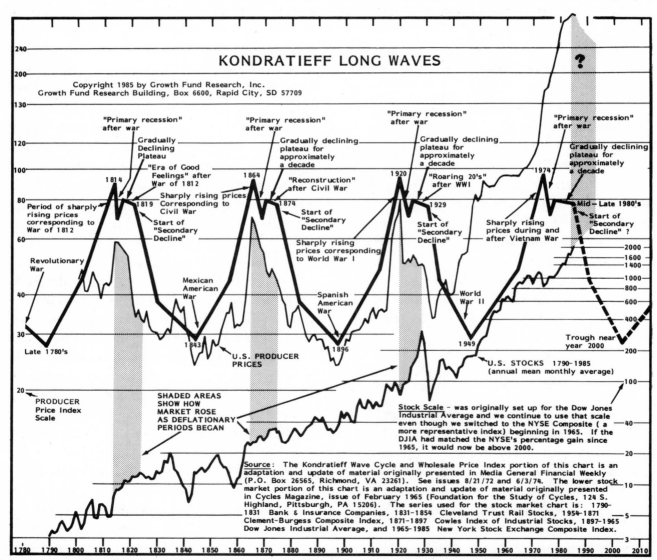

Source: Reprinted from *Growth Fund Guide*, Box 6600, Rapid City, SD 57709.

his long wave cycle lasted from forty to sixty years. Shorter business cycles moved within the longer ones. An extrapolation of the Kondratieff theory into the present time has striking accuracy. Note that the stock market average has been plotted below that of the primary wave. The similarity in peaks and troughs is remarkable.

Kondratieff's waves are just one, very controversial, example of cycle theory. Other theorists have plotted ten- or hundred-year cycles that are equally interesting. None can be said to predict developments with absolute accuracy, but they are useful in postulating the presence of cycles in a world of seemingly random events.

Although cycle theory would indicate that we are in for a major depression, there is really nothing to fear, for several reasons:

- Cycles refer to general trends; they do not forecast dates. Cycle changes are simply an observable part of living.
- As we have seen, life is often random or nonlinear, and what seems to be a "scheduled event" in a cycle can become something quite different. Randomness can change things, as can our perceptions.
- Cycle change is corrective and thus healing. It may look destructive, but like a raging forest fire, it is not. Fires are restorative. They clear out dead underbrush, kill scrub that inhibits the growth of new plant life, and provide the heat for seeds to open and germinate. The blackened landscape soon heals and comes back stronger than ever. In the same way, major changes in the economic system bring it back to a sustainable balance from which one can again move ahead.

The leveraged buy-out craze of recent years is a financial case in point. Greed led to insider trading and the resulting gross overvaluations conspired to create high corporate debt. As the economy slows, the debt service cannot be met and corporate failures occur. As the holders of junk bonds lose, the system self-corrects, eliminating over-inflated values.

HOW INSIGHTS CAN LEAD TO CHANGE

Changes in the economic system don't happen all of a sudden. Long before a crippling debt level becomes unsustainable, for example, there emerges the perception, among a few, that too much debt has been taken on. These few look behind the debt and see the overvaluation of assets that has gotten out of hand. This nonfinancial insight, when finally seen by many, can eventually bring about a financial correction or crash.

Greed, fear, and ignorance, three nonfinancial forces, are often the precipitators of bull-market endings and the recessions that follow them. When the investment community acts *separately together* out of these emotions, the consequences can be disastrous. Conversely, hope, vision, leadership, and hard, purposeful work will lead to periods of great economic growth, technical breakthroughs, and other very positive economic activity. We got to the moon in just under a decade because we had a president who dared to have a vision and set a national goal. Churchill's extraordinary leadership and courage brought Britain through the dark days of 1940.

Financial events, then, frequently turn on nonfinancial factors, sometimes negative, sometimes positive. As we have seen, the dark and the light are two sides of the whole. Each of us has elements of light and shadow within us.

Economies follow broad human patterns. They reflect living forces coming together in often random and unpredictable ways to create change—often chaos. Out of it all eventually comes order.

Economic Signs to Watch for and Typical Actions to Consider Taking

If you are not used to monitoring the financial environment for signs of change, it may help to know some of the characteristics of different stages in a typical economic cycle. The following map presents a purposely oversimplified and hypothetical view of a four-part economic cycle as mature growth slows to stagflation, to recession, to stabilization, and then healthy growth begins again.

This representation is not a definitive or complete economic statement. It is only a simple means of expressing the economy as process—one in which we are all intimately involved. I hope it will serve as a starting point for creating an awareness of the environment relative to your goals.

Remember that an economy is not artificial. It has a pulse and is a reflection of what you and I think, feel, and do. Sophisticated mathematical models of the economy are not ends in themselves; they are a way of expressing human interactions in statistical form. To the extent that any forecast is able to account for human or nonfinancial elements, it will be more accurate and more in touch with actual historical developments.

Although there isn't room for the map to show the full impact of nonfinancial factors, they are critical to successful predictions. The map does show the classic historical relationships of different events in the cycle, thus providing a context in which you can judge various phenomena. Notice the classic behavior of inflation as one stage gives way to another. Interest rate movement is also represented. Historically these two elements have behaved in certain identifiable ways, which is why so much attention is placed on them in economic news. Random events can, and do, alter such behavior, but an awareness of the historical patterns is a good starting point.

The actions noted on the map as typical of a particular stage do not reflect individual needs. For example, a retired couple may never invest in higher-yield instruments, regardless of the economic stage, because of their need for capital preservation and steady income. An unmarried and aggressive younger person, on the other hand, may adopt risks well beyond what is typical. Use the map to get a sense of the classic changes, but act in financial and nonfinancial ways that are appropriate to who you are and your goals.

In short, when we can see a context for the data to which we are constantly exposed, the data becomes informative. By applying our experience to this information, we gain insights with which to make better investments.

One cautionary note: Forecasts based on such insights are inherently limited because no one has all the data on current events and no one can take the unpredictable into account. Moreover, each of us brings our predispositions and individual perceptions to the process. This explains the wide variations even among economists. One thinks it's summer and all is well, while another, feeling a chill in the air, suspects it's fall and worries about winter. Still another agrees that it's fall but forecasts an Indian summer and relaxes all caution. And another, having been frozen during a previous winter, always wears long underwear! Thus, one key to interpreting data is to network with others in order to get different points of view and a critical audience for our own narrow judgments. Being tested in this way is a means of developing critical thought.

The impossibility of full predictability does not lessen the need for study. Ignorance is a common reason for failure. Nevertheless, just as you think you have it all figured out, a savings and

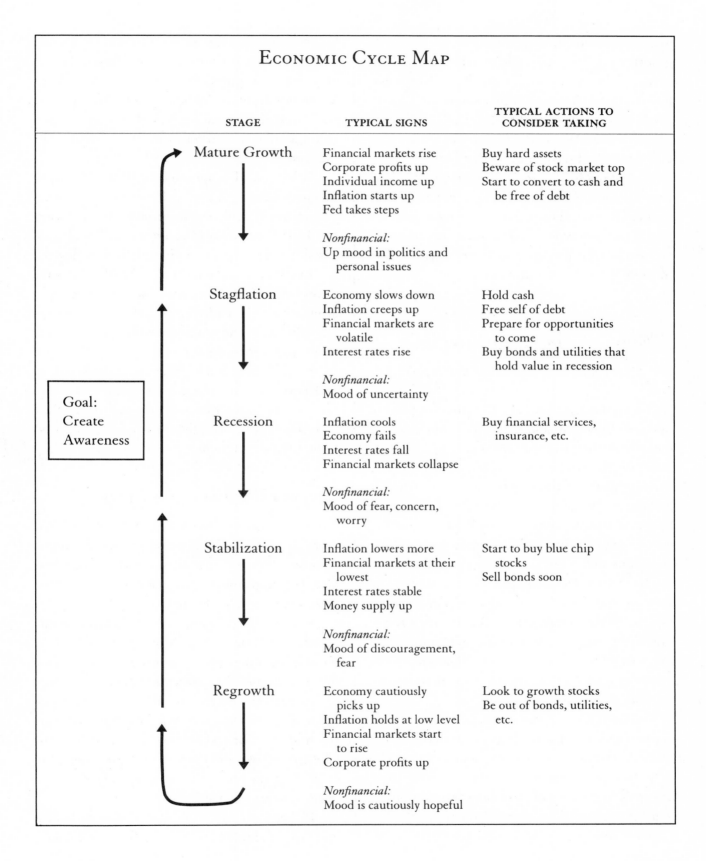

ECONOMIC CYCLE MAP

STAGE	TYPICAL SIGNS	TYPICAL ACTIONS TO CONSIDER TAKING
Mature Growth	Financial markets rise Corporate profits up Individual income up Inflation starts up Fed takes steps *Nonfinancial:* Up mood in politics and personal issues	Buy hard assets Beware of stock market top Start to convert to cash and be free of debt
Stagflation	Economy slows down Inflation creeps up Financial markets are volatile Interest rates rise *Nonfinancial:* Mood of uncertainty	Hold cash Free self of debt Prepare for opportunities to come Buy bonds and utilities that hold value in recession
Recession	Inflation cools Economy fails Interest rates fall Financial markets collapse *Nonfinancial:* Mood of fear, concern, worry	Buy financial services, insurance, etc.
Stabilization	Inflation lowers more Financial markets at their lowest Interest rates stable Money supply up *Nonfinancial:* Mood of discouragement, fear	Start to buy blue chip stocks Sell bonds soon
Regrowth	Economy cautiously picks up Inflation holds at low level Financial markets start to rise Corporate profits up *Nonfinancial:* Mood is cautiously hopeful	Look to growth stocks Be out of bonds, utilities, etc.

Goal:
Create
Awareness

loan crisis crops up, a war breaks out, a foreign government collapses—and there goes what little predictability you thought you had. Who could have foreseen the extraordinary events in Eastern Europe as people moved to throw off their Communist yokes? Where did Gorbachev come from, and who could have guessed that he would provide the impetus for the forces now in motion? Because these events will have an impact on our military budget, they will alter our economic picture. The point is that when random events occur, we need to be prepared to accept them and to move in ways to accommodate them.

The Nonfinancial Environment— The Other Half of the Picture

As we are seeing, to get the full story we need to integrate the nonfinancial aspects of our environment with the financial. What is happening politically? Are there major positive or negative changes in the natural environment that are affecting our world? Have there been important Supreme Court rulings that will have a bearing on our lives? What is going on in our personal environment?

It is already clear that a nonfinancial factor such as fear, greed, or ignorance can leave an imprint on financial markets. Fear during a recession often triggers a run toward gold. Greed can drive us to bid up investment valuations to the breaking point. These are just two among many possible reactions.

What of the impact of a turnabout in political orientation? We all saw a big change in the switch from President Carter to President Reagan. The political mood of any country can have a big effect on one's environment. Consider war or peace. The current trend toward democratization in Eastern Europe, as well as within the Soviet

Union, is astounding. Should this trend continue, and should we get important treaties on the use of atomic weapons, we might well be able to lower our military budget, reduce our deficits, and boost the educational level throughout the nation so that we can compete more effectively in the world.

What of demographics? With the baby boomers turning forty, will we become savers again? What will be the impact of a growing Hispanic population in some states? The list of variables affecting our environment is endless.

Everything is connected. The distinction I draw between the financial and nonfinancial is arbitrary and is made for purposes of discussion only. Financial and nonfinancial factors can influence each other because, as process, they are united and inseparable. At issue is building an awareness of your total environment so that you can tune in to the forces at play that most affect you. Then, and only then, can you elect to do something about them.

CYCLES IN OUR PERSONAL LIVES

Our environment is nonfinancial in very personal ways as well. I call these other aspects "mini-environments" because they are closer to home and thus seem more manageable. Their impact, however, is far from being minimal.

For example, consider a young adult who enters the work place after finishing school. He is at the start of a new cycle. On his own for the first time, he has health, youth, and hope.

At first, the long hours at work are energizing. He marries someone who also has a job that she finds fulfilling. The next few years float by. Children arrive, and to make room for them, the couple buys a home and assumes a large mortgage. A new cycle has begun.

Perhaps because of long hours at the office and lack of time to exercise regularly, our young man puts on weight. Work that he had once found invigorating he now finds stressful. Tension, like inflation, takes its toll, silently. There is no awareness yet to break the silence. The job offers economic opportunity (a useful goal), and it takes on importance as his family reaches for the material things that growing families need.

Eventually health responds to stress. His lower back goes out now and again, the flu bug bites more often than before, and he begins to suffer headaches.

The pace stiffens even more as he wins job advancements and as personal debt increases to meet the family's needs. As Churchill once said, "Bet more than you can afford to lose, and you will learn how to play the game." The young man is learning how to play the game.

As changes are occurring in the work place, his relationship with his wife becomes strained. They seem to have less time to be together than before, and the children demand most of their attention. The difference, like the effect of creeping inflation, isn't noticeable at first. As with glaucoma, there is no immediate pain and the damage is done over time.

Then one day the distance between them reaches a certain point and they ask, "What happened?" This is the point at which awareness kicks in and we "see" the mini-environment. Much of it—the work place, for example—looks well beyond our control, yet we created it. We chose our spouse and our job, and we agreed to have children. We also chose to react to the various parts of our life in the ways that we did. Events that we liked to blame on our boss were really our own doing. Suddenly we realize that we created this nonfinancial mini-environment. When this happens, we have begun a new cycle—one of awareness development. With awareness comes the possibility of making changes. We must simply pay attention to the evidence that something in our life is trying to right itself—just

as a recession is evidence of an economy attempting to right itself.

How we relate to one another, our work, and our state of health are just three aspects of our personal environment that we know from experience can affect our goals. How do these aspects influence *your* nonfinancial environment? To what extent are you driven by fear, hope, greed, joy?

RESPONDING TO SIGNS OF CHANGE IN OUR PERSONAL LIVES

The task is to sharpen awareness. This is what we did in the chapter on vision and purpose when we sought life qualities. The same process applies here. We must be aware of the tea leaves before we can read them.

A bad back, chest pains, or headaches are examples of body signals that something is out of balance. Before popping a pill, ask what the pain is attempting to teach. If we can understand the pain in relation to who we are, then the steps that we take to restore balance will be born of this new awareness. They will be customized—appropriate to us as individuals.

I do not represent that reading the signs is easy. How often do we hear of people who go through several minor heart attacks without being conscious of them? They may recall a small chest pain, but they never gave it a thought. Yet the body was screaming for help. Some of the tea leaves that present themselves are as large as oak leaves and we still do not see them.

Sometimes others can see us better than we can see ourselves. If you believe this to be the case, and if you have built up trust in a spouse or close friend, then ask him or her for feedback. Counselors are available for this purpose as well. Being total strangers to you and your life, they are often effectives guides in the quest for awareness. The route you take doesn't matter. The point is simply to develop nonfinancial awareness so that you can keep track of your whole self constantly reaching for balance and in this way continue to be who you are. This is the ultimate intervention.

Influences from Abroad

Beyond our domestic economy and nonfinancial concerns are the international events whose consequences touch us daily in direct or indirect ways. Because we live in a truly global environment, we cannot escape—or afford to ignore—these distant forces.

In April 1989, the Federal Republic of Germany's Central Bank raised its short-term interest rates and wiped out any hope that U.S. short-term rates would quickly ease. In fact, the West German action had repercussions in our own financial markets: the dollar fell, and bond and stock prices dropped. Although stocks recovered shortly afterwards, investors in the United States were quick to see how an overseas reaction to fear of inflation can have an impact here.

A car worker in Detroit is tied to one in Asia. Goods are now built wherever the costs are lowest and the quality acceptable. Long ago the United States lost out in steel, shipbuilding, TV manufacturing, and small electronics. We failed to remain competitive as the world became smaller. As the industrial revolution spreads along the Pacific Rim, competition heats up even more. Korea, Thailand, and Malaysia are starting to become world-class players, for example.

The range of overseas influences applies nonfinancially, too. As rain forests are systematically destroyed in Brazil, the weather and the amount of oxygen the planet generates are affected. Some pesticides used to produce more food now appear to be a health threat. Our drug dependency is tearing at the very fabric of our society. What began on a poppy farm in Burma ends in gang murders in New York.

Technological advances—a nonfinancial factor—are linked to and can drive the financial worldwide. If fusion at room temperature were actually achieved, the economic and political war over oil would just go away, and the environment would quickly become a cleaner place. Current oil-oriented investments would be threatened, and whole new businesses would emerge. Changes of similar magnitude came about with the invention of the transistor, which ended the life of the vacuum tube, created whole new businesses, and changed our lives in many ways.

Extending awareness to take in international happenings need not be overwhelming. You must simply be alert to any information you read or hear that could potentially have a major impact on your goals.

The context for judging new developments—whether domestic or global, financial or nonfinancial—is your goal structure. If you are a monk living in a cave in Nepal and have vowed to spend your life in meditation, the raising of interest rates in Germany will not be of much concern. It is only necessary to be aware of events that affect *you* and *your* goals. This greatly narrows the field and helps you relate events to your purpose.

Given So Much Data, How Can an Ordinary Person Cope?

The secret to coping with the environment is not being alone.

Network with others. Realize, too, that the task is not as big as it sounds. Once you have recognized the importance of developing awareness, you will find that reading a newspaper or

watching the news takes on new meaning. You pick up on data that previously passed by unnoticed. Without writing anything down, you automatically integrate data into a context where it becomes usable information. If you form a group to help, you expand your reading universe, get valuable confirming and opposing views of data, and get a test bed for your insights. Members of your group may all look at the same organized data and draw different conclusions. A glass that is half full to some is half empty to others. The point is that each person supports the others in achieving an awareness of meaningful trends.

For example, when you read that interest rates are climbing, you take note and look for confirmation in other places. You place this development within a context so that when you talk with a friend or a professional planner, you have a reference point. When you are listening to the news and hear a comment about inflation, you tuck away this information, too, as indicative of how the economy is behaving. If you hear of a trend that you do not understand, you have a network from which to learn or with whom to discuss how any emerging factor may affect your goals.

Life's unpredictability can make this task look trying. If even the experts can't make forecasts with absolute accuracy, and if sudden unforeseen events like an oil embargo, the dramatic changes in Eastern Europe, or (more personally) a serious illness can drastically alter your environment, why should you try?

You try because you are a part of your environment, and only when you work with awareness will you *feel* a part of it and thus be able to cope. Recall that ignorance is one reason for failing at investments, whether financial or nonfinancial. If you become sensitive to the fact that serious illness can indeed alter your life, you may be more attentive to health issues and to activities that promote health. If you know what defensive investing is, then you can use it to protect yourself in down markets. Although the doom you anticipate may not happen exactly on schedule, you will be armed with a knowledge of what to do if it does occur.

In all of this, I may seem to be saying that if you are aware, you will be able to predict the short-term swings in markets and therefore prosper by these perceptions. Although becoming aware can better the odds, chaos theory teaches that random events can cause us to miss market timing completely, even in the shorter term. Add to this any unbalanced perceptions you may bring to the process, and it is easy to see that any forecast you develop should be presented with a lot of humility.

Fortunately, instead of betting everything on one well-thought-out scenario, you have the option of investing both in safe places (should the world tumble) and in higher-risk places (where you can prosper should more positive events occur). Such a move, made within the context of who you are and your goals, is simple diversification, which we will deal with in the next chapter.

Remember, though, that being "safe" at all times is not necessarily preferable. When the stick in the stream hits turbulence, when our world gets shaken up financially or nonfinancially, we can become creative, feeling the full energy within us, drawing closer to people around us, experiencing more fully who we already are—in other words, becoming completely alive.

Continue to work with the development of your awareness, but be conscious, too, that in the midst of life's uncertainty, something better may be trying to happen. I know a young man who lost all of his money when his investment advisor bet it on a wrong market projection. In the crisis period that followed, he discovered who he was and began truly to live.

The most important point is this: whenever faced with a financial or a nonfinancial decision, return to who you are and connect your vision with the decision that seems most in line with it. Reconnect, remembering that it is connections that are the conduits for True Wealth. Reexperience the qualities you represent and act from that place.

Then when a stock market crashes, an illness strikes, an untimely death in the family occurs, or you get fired from a job, you are still yourself, representing the qualities you bring to living. Knowing who you are, you can act in keeping with your goals, using all of the financial and nonfinancial resources available to you.

In the end, we must all act in an unpredictable world. If it were fully predictable, it would be boring and without opportunity. By acting in connective ways, by always returning to who we are, we stay linked with what we do. Our search for connection will always bring us back into balance, just as our outer environment is always finding ways to right itself.

Managing True Wealth means making choices
in line with who we are.

10

A WEALTH
OF POSSIBILITIES

The time to *act* has arrived. Everything that has come before has been leading to this point, when we will start making financial and nonfinancial investment decisions in line with who we are and with the support of our total resource base.

This is the point at which we will link our dreams and visions with such everyday concerns as paying bills, raising children, working with relationships, investing, and relating to a changing world over which we have no direct control. Intentions are no longer enough; we must begin choosing specific options from among the many possibilities.

Although this may seem like the hard part, it isn't really. We are more than ready to act because:

- We know who we are and where we want to go. We have clear goals.
- We have identified the total resources we have available for support.
- We understand the levels of risk we are willing to undertake.

- We are familiar with advisors who can help us, tools at our disposal, and environmental factors that can affect us.

The possibilities are legion. Deregulation in financial markets has spawned many new products. Years ago, only the banks and savings and loan associations, by and large, offered accounts where liquid funds could be parked. Today banks and S&Ls not only compete head-on rate for rate, but many other institutions also offer places for investors to deposit funds at interest. The brokerage community (both full service and discount) has entered the field with money market accounts that rival bank products. Sears has joined the game with its acquisition of Dean Witter, and American Express has moved into similar financial areas. The mutual fund industry has more than doubled its offerings since 1982 and now provides yet another place for investors to park money at interest when they are "between funds." And beyond all of these possibilities is the maze of limited partnership opportunities, collectibles, options, unlisted securities, and metals available to investors.

Another cause of burgeoning choices is the twenty-four-hour trading that instant communication has made possible in some parts of the world. As a result, we can not only trade without delay at home, we can also buy financial products in Japan, London, and Europe. Add to this capability the offerings from the international fund industry, designed to make trading in international equities even more convenient, and the possibilities seem endless.

The good news is that with all the solicitations, you and I get more choices, competitive rates, and convenience. The bad news is that the marketplace seems cluttered and confusing. However, look at it this way: such complexity results from the competitive product offerings of a new financial industry trying to get your business by meeting your needs better than the competitor down the street.

What about the nonfinancial choices?

The nonfinancial choices are, if anything, even more numerous than the financial ones. They include how we use our time, the work we select, the education we seek, the steps we take to maintain or improve health, the friends we choose, and the enemies we create. How can we select among all the options? How do we judge the risk of each? Where can we find the time to follow up all the possibilities? In both the financial and the nonfinancial realms, how can we even begin to think about choosing among the familiar options, let alone uncover those that are less obvious?

Fortunately, thanks to our homework on vision, purpose, and goals, we are in the enviable position of being able to quickly weed out a large number of options as just not in line with our clear objectives. Moreover, it is possible to simplify the whole investment process by categorizing the options and applying a set of selection

criteria that will allow us to narrow the field even further. Before we turn to this approach, let's be sure we understand what investing is all about and why it is a good step to take.

What Does "Investment" Really Mean?

Committing financial and nonfinancial portions of our net worth to the investing process means entrusting to it our money, time, health, energy, relationships, education, and skills, to mention just a few. It means letting go of these resources temporarily with the expectation that they will later contribute more to our goals and sense of well-being. Such "letting go" is not easy; the very notion calls up uncertainty.

The *American Heritage Dictionary* defines an investment as a "possession acquired for future income or benefit," thus limiting it primarily to a financial activity. In the True Wealth process, the definition is much broader, for it includes nonfinancial investments as well. This inclusion acknowledges that what we have is linked to who we are and that this connection is one of the sources of well-being.

Our investment process is therefore different from the traditional one. It is deeper and much farther-reaching. Because it is connective, it touches people as well as things. In fact it is the people aspect that makes the things valuable.

We will be involving our whole selves in the process, not just our money. Seen in this way, **investments are simply extensions of who we are, put into a process that extends to what we do.** They are a part of the whole, not apart from it. As we saw earlier, all the different aspects of our lives are like the threads that form woven cloth. A tug on any one part of the cloth affects all the rest. The strength of the cloth is in the matrix, or connection, of threads. Woven, they are strong;

separately, they are weak. Our aim is to achieve strong connective selves and individual empowerment, enabling us to become who we are.

Another important point about the building of wealth through investments is that **wealth is "unlimited."** That is, in reaching for it, we do not need to take anything away from others. This applies to both financial and nonfinancial resources. Take money, for example. We can create it through investments without robbing others. By starting a company, we create value. By inventing a new product or service, we create money. By offering our work in service, say as an architect or attorney, we earn fees. Any time we invest a part of ourselves, we create wealth at no expense to others. To the extent that we offer one another competition, we sharpen both ourselves and those with whom we compete. In making investments, we gain and at the same time contribute to others—especially when what we are doing is congruent with who we are. Investing is building, and building is constructive.

Simplifying the Investment Process

Options abound, it is true. At times you may feel as though you would just as soon find someone else to act in your behalf. It is not your field, I hear you say. You are overextended just trying to be good at what you do.

But the process doesn't have to be as arduous as you might think. The steps that follow will simplify it. They will be carried out within *your* context because the criteria for choosing will be based on who you are and the resources you have available to pursue your goals. The same link that ties your financial and nonfinancial goals to your vision and purpose will connect you with the investments you select. Simplification and connection, therefore, are basic to the method you will use to choose investments.

The following few steps are all you will need. They are summarized in the accompanying map.

Step 1. Review your vision and purpose—the connection between who you are and what you do. This will center you as you begin the process.

Step 2. Review the selection criteria: your goals; propensity for risk taking; resources; age and stage in life's process; the investment quality of the asset group and the specific asset you are considering; any special knowledge you may have; diversification; and the financial and nonfinancial environment. All of these criteria will be discussed in detail in the next section.

Step 3. Divide all the investment possibilities into broad categories of like investments. Then apply the selection criteria to decide which of the categories is appropriate to your needs. This initial selection will simplify the task of choosing individual investments.

Step 4. Apply the same selection criteria to each category of choice.

Step 5. Choose specific investments.

Step 6. Up to this point, the selections made represent only intentions. Now act on these intentions. As you make the investments, record them in a log, and be sure you understand how they relate to your goals.

Step 7. Monitor progress. In a chaotic world subject to random events, everything is in constant and rapid change. It is therefore important to check periodically whether the results of choices made earlier are still appropriate to current goals.

Step 8. Because this process, like life itself, is continuous, it can be represented as a circle. Replanning may be necessary if monitoring reveals a need for change. To effect change, follow the same process over again.

Steps 7 and 8 include a bonus. In addition to helping you attain your goals, they can help you *learn*. When you act on your decisions, be sure to take note of your thinking at the time of investing so that, when you see some results, you can look back and evaluate what you thought then, given the outcome now. In this way you will learn. The same goes for monitoring, which entails following your investments to see if they are meeting your goals. By linking choice with performance, monitoring is an indispensable learning tool. This learning theme will be developed further in the final chapter.

Selection Criteria to Help Narrow the Choices

This is the starting point—the place where we will decide, for example, to buy a high-quality bond for secure income, as a means of achieving the quality of freedom, or to swim as the exercise of choice for promoting health. In other words, we will act on goals that reflect our most important qualities. Within this context, choosing among the various financial and nonfinancial categories will be made easier by applying several criteria.

The Selection Criteria diagram on page 146 summarizes the process we are about to begin. We will look at each criterion in turn.

GOALS

Do not consider any investment unless it accords with a goal you have written down earlier. If you are vague about your goals, return to the goals chapter and become clear about them. This is a case of being true to yourself.

Recall that your goals are an outer expression of the inner vision you identified at the outset of the True Wealth process. They complete the link. Put them out before you. Look at each one and acknowledge its appropriateness to your purpose.

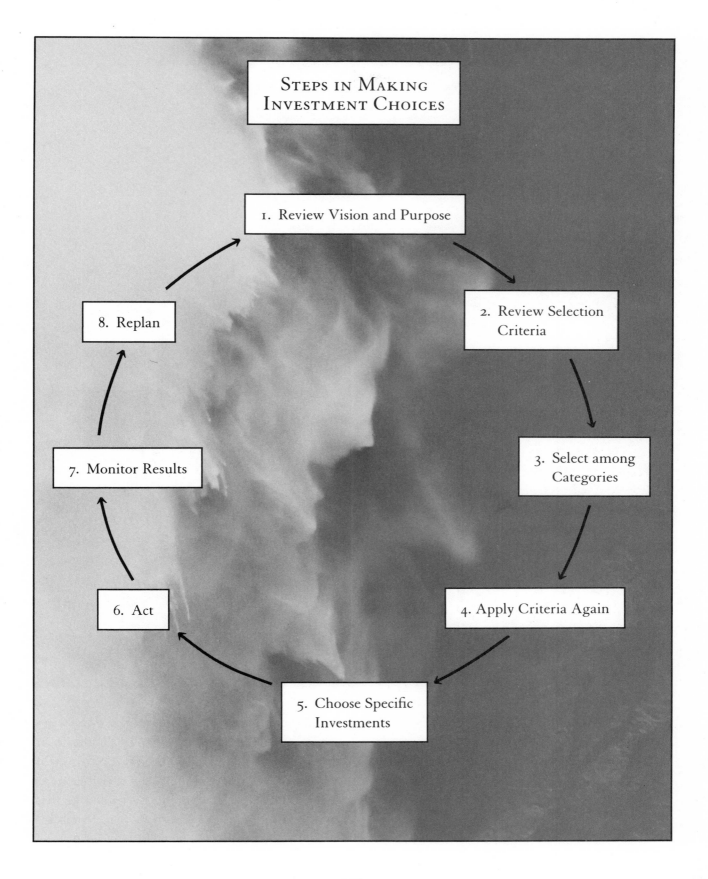

Steps in Making
Investment Choices

1. Review Vision and Purpose

2. Review Selection Criteria

3. Select among Categories

4. Apply Criteria Again

5. Choose Specific Investments

6. Act

7. Monitor Results

8. Replan

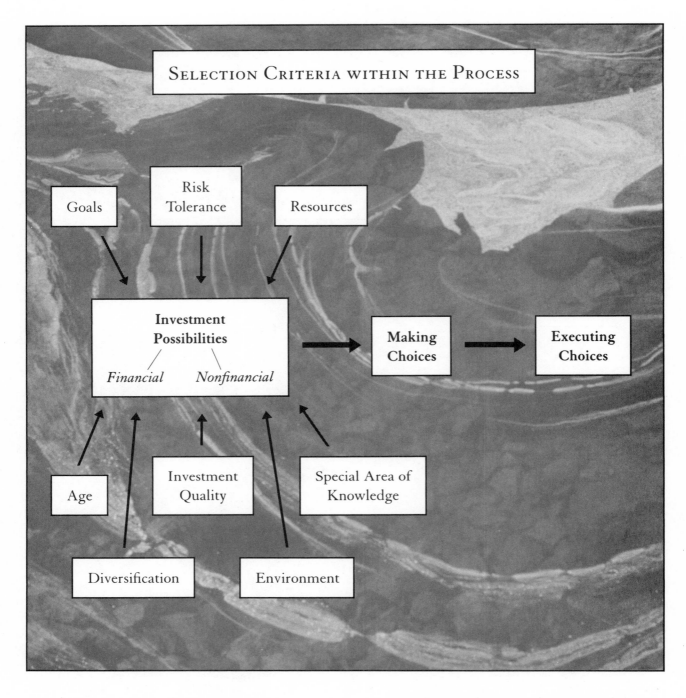

SELECTION CRITERIA WITHIN THE PROCESS

Goals

Risk
Tolerance

Resources

Investment
Possibilities

Financial   *Nonfinancial*

Making
Choices

Executing
Choices

Age

Investment
Quality

Special Area of
Knowledge

Diversification

Environment

See if you can taste, smell, hear, and touch each one. Use every sense to visualize its completion. You have heard the expression, "He wants that car so badly he can taste it." From this multisensory place we can make the goal real and specific.

If you want a home, see it in your mind's eye. Smell the flowers planted outside. Hear the wind coming through the windows. Touch the front door handle and go in. Hold the dream in as real a form as you can. Making the goal conscious in this way will trigger awareness of resources that can be brought forward to support it. It will remind you of people who can help.

What are some ways in which your goals can influence your choices? Consider the case of a person who feels that she is locked into a job with little future. After working on her vision, she discovers that freedom is an essential quality in her life. In fact it is a lack of freedom that makes her job unsatisfying. An aside: it is never the job that is at fault; at issue is how we bring ourselves to it. In this case there is clearly a mismatch. Since one of this person's goals is work that brings freedom, she decides to take the time to explore other possibilities, both within the company and outside. She knows the risks: Asking her employer for a change may result in her being laid off. Or she may have to leave the firm and start her own business. On the other hand, she may be able to find another spot within the same company. In any case, she decides to keep her financial assets safe and liquid so that they will be available to support her goal of finding freedom in a new job. She is using the financial to support the nonfinancial.

Or consider the engineer who also wants more freedom in his life. He seeks a more flexible work schedule in order to realize this goal. He is a runner and wants to start his workday an hour later so that he can run in the morning. Because he is a top achiever, his employer elects to meet his needs. He achieves his goal. Did he take a risk in making the request? Perhaps. But he was clear about a goal connected to a life quality that meant a lot to him. It all ties together.

RISK TOLERANCE

Review the chapter on risks, keeping in mind that risking is an art of creating opportunity. In a general way, you have already given some thought to the level of risk you would be comfortable entertaining. Refresh your thinking, and be willing to see each specific possibility as both risk and opportunity.

Do not risk beyond your nature. You are who you are and that is perfect. This process implies no judgments, since its overall goal is for you to become who you already are. The only task is to appreciate once again that risking has an up- as well as a downside and then to apply this balanced perspective in acting to meet your goals.

Risking is an inner game. To play the game, you will want to explore your inner response to each risk that is presented and then decide whether to make the investment. If you decline the risk, you may choose to work on your feelings about it to a point where the risk, relative to the opportunity, becomes acceptable. For instance, someone having difficulty with his boss might not want to risk a confrontation. After months of grief, however, he might seek advice from friends or go to a workshop on conflict resolution, because the risk of not speaking up has become greater than the risk of being forthright.

When you ask yourself what level of risk you are willing to take to reach for the opportunity offered by a given investment, the answer is, of course, "It depends." This response is reasonable because, as you learned earlier, people are able to take large risks in some areas and none at all in others. To assess your risk tolerance in a concrete way, give yourself some examples of investments you would be willing to make and some you would not. For instance, would you be willing to hold cash in a certificate of deposit but not to buy commodities? Would you risk 2 percent of available assets in an aggressive mutual fund but nothing in a nonpublic start-up company? As long as certain financial bases were already covered, would you consider investing in a more aggressive vehicle such as real estate, where the money would be tied up for years? (With this last move, you would be hedging risks in one area by investments made in another. This is one aspect of diversification—another of the selection criteria.)

With such "practice runs" you can zero in on

the level of risk you will entertain. This knowledge will be especially important if you decide to use an advisor, in that you will be able to be quite specific about your needs.

Look at your tolerance for risking in the nonfinancial realm as well. What won't you do and what will you do? Be honest with yourself. If relationship issues are a problem that is keeping you from meeting goals, it may be worth the risk of facing the issues in order to take advantage of opportunities that may flow from your initiative.

Play the game. For example, I will not sky dive, but I will ski. I won't race cars, but I will snorkel. These distinctions may seem silly at the outset, but you will soon get a feeling for where the line is for you. This is important knowledge. The line may move, depending on the area of risk. In any case, apply what you learn as one of the criteria for selecting investments.

RESOURCES

The extent of available resources has a lot to do with any investment program. As you start to review the assets you have available for investing, recall the need to withhold some, both financial and nonfinancial, for emergency purposes. We need to be as jealous of our time, health, or energy as we tend to be of our money.

The timing of available funds, or cash flow, is also important. For example, funds coming in from the liquidation of an asset sale may not be disposable for six months. Some funds may be available for the long term and some for the short term. The same may be true of nonfinancial assets. You may have time to invest in two months but not now.

In addition to money you may have, be aware that another source of investable funds is borrowing. If your goal is to buy a home, you will prob-

ably make the down payment in cash and borrow the rest. It is also common to borrow to start a company, often by securing the loan with other assets. This way of funding financial investments is linked to risk taking, as the following examples indicate. They also illustrate how connected all these criteria are.

A young single man I know had few financial assets, but his engineering job paid $70,000 a year and in general he had a good earnings history. He thought that he could borrow on this income stream to start an investment program and use his earnings to service the loan. However, other criteria came into play. How did he feel about the risk of borrowing, and how much risk was he willing to assume in the investment that was the reason for the borrowing? After consulting with an investment advisor, he did decide to borrow, and within a year had done well with the mutual fund the advisor had recommended.

I also recall a young woman who had good equity in her home, which a financial planner urged her to borrow against in order to have funds for investment purposes. As a single parent, however, she saw her home as a refuge for her children, and she could not even consider the thought. It was as if her home were sacred. The risk factor for borrowed funds using this source was too great; her decision was no. On the other hand, she might well have been open to borrowing on stocks, assuming she had any.

Although debt may be a way to obtain funds for investments, it can be a problem or a boon depending on the situation. Most Americans already borrow heavily without ever going to a bank or seeing a loan officer. They simply use the credit cards sent to them in the mail. The problem is that most of what they buy consists of luxuries that have no value as investments, so they end up with debt and no offsetting asset.

Nonfinancial resources are just as important as financial ones. As we saw earlier, they often drive financial resources. Recall the story of SyberVision, in which Steve DeVore used a non-financial liability—his childhood polio—to create a thriving business. In another case we studied, I worked with a person fired from his job as vice president of a small company to compile a list of contacts—nonfinancial assets—who could help him start a new career. He succeeded with very little money because he invested *himself*—his knowledge—and he leveraged his contacts once he was able to see them in this light.

Thus, be attentive to nonfinancial resources because they have great power. When you look at your nonfinancial balance sheet to find resources for investment, you may find some that will also further financial goals.

AGE

Age is a criterion because it can affect your willingness and your ability to manage your investments. Younger people generally have more energy and can squeeze in more projects than older people. They also tend to have more sustained health. These factors can have an impact on some types of investments, such as starting a company. On the other hand, some older people are tremendously excited about life and have boundless energy. If you are making a real estate investment that requires active management on your part, do you have the energy (if older) or the know-how (if younger) to make it work?

Young people can entertain higher risks because they have time to recoup after a financial failure. They can also optimize compounding. Time is both a financial and nonfinancial advantage of youth. Two other nonfinancial advantages are health and energy. Older people have the nonfinancial advantages of knowledge, wisdom born of experience, and long-term relationships.

The age factor is entirely individual. It could be neutral, or it could be pivotal. As you consider various investments, just be aware of any impact it could possibly have.

INVESTMENT QUALITY

Judging quality can be tricky. Because people determine quality and success, attention to management is critical to any inquiry into investment quality. That is why, for example, many of the more successful mutual fund managers make periodic on-site visits to their investments. They seek insights into people as well as their output. Although quarterly financial data represent how people are doing in financial terms, statements of this kind are no substitute for knowing something about those who produce the results.

How can you apply this advice? By being open to what is said in the news about how the successful managers work; by calling a fund and asking for any articles about the managers; and by discussing management in your network group. In short, just stretch your awareness to include this sort of information, because people are always at the core of quality.

In the case of bonds, assessing quality is easier because bonds are given individual quality ratings that are readily available. Newspapers list the ratings for some bonds; if you can't find the ones that you're interested in, call a broker for the information.

The people factor is also important when you are considering nonfinancial investments. Before you went in for heart surgery, wouldn't a second opinion be in order? Wouldn't you want to check out the surgeon who was going to do the job? After all, your health and life are at stake. In the field of education, diligence is equally important. What is a school's reputation? If you are just starting out, you will be investing at least four years in undergraduate work and that is a sizable commitment of time and money. Investment quality is vital in the intangible area as well.

DIVERSIFICATION

Risk is inherent in life; without risk there would be no opportunity. Since you cannot avoid some risk if you wish to gain, it is best to spread the risk among many categories of investment. In this way you can hedge. You will be following the popular wisdom of "not putting all of your eggs in one basket."

Spreading the risk—called diversification or asset allocation—is a standard procedure backed by considerable experience. Put positively, diversification is as much a way to benefit from up markets as it is a way to protect yourself in down ones.

Some people diversify in the face of a specific market risk. For example, if uncertain times arrive—say, the transition period between a boom and a bust—they have stakes in defensive investments (for instance gold) in anticipation of a decline, as well as in equities in case the market goes up significantly instead. In such cases, perception of the market drives a change in investments.

SPECIAL AREA OF KNOWLEDGE

Diversification is not the thing for everyone, and this other point of view is valid too. On the theory that it is best to invest in what you know best, those who have an investment specialty tend to stay within that area. This is often true of real estate specialists. They are knowledgeable in specific geographic areas and they understand trends. Using classic financial leverage, they do well. Their personal assets are often all in real estate.

Corporations sometimes restrict themselves to one area as well. Founders of successful companies often do not diversify all that much after obtaining liquidity because they have developed a deep knowledge about their products, markets, and successful management style. As a result, they feel they can be most effective and confident about their continued success and financial future by holding stock in their own companies rather than diversifying.

For most investors, though, diversification is one of the key criteria to consider in making any new investment or adding to an existing one. How well are *you* diversified? How will the need for diversification affect your choices?

THE ENVIRONMENT

As we learned in the chapter on this subject, we are all a part of the world around us and are influenced by that world. Everything we touch is changing. Change affects us daily. The final criterion, therefore, requires you to examine your financial and nonfinancial environment for signs that are conducive or counter to the accomplishment of your goals.

I remember a group of three who started a company with a very advanced software product. They had written a competent business plan after completing the software development using their own money. Their future looked good. Then, as if out of the blue, came the downturn in 1969. The economy was on the skids, and the lead prospective investor reneged on a verbal commitment for venture funds. The three had used up their own funds. With no new money to finance a marketing campaign, the company went under. Management had not

taken the economic environment into account. If they had, they could have delayed their start-up or stretched out their own funds to help them weather the storm.

In a smaller way we, too, face this issue when we contemplate a major investment in a house, education, or a new car. Those whose incomes are subject to market fluctuations (which is most of us to varying degrees) need to be attentive to economic forces over which we can have no direct control. Even if we continue to perform well, will our jobs always be there? In this rapidly changing and competitive world, the answer may well be, probably not. Some economists anticipate that on average, we will change jobs at least six times before we retire. The United States has lost much of its steel, consumer electronics, and auto business to foreign competition. Technology has made the world smaller. We communicate instantly, shifting money around with the pressing of a few computer keys. We trade in commodities worldwide. Everything is connected to everything else. The changing environment, therefore, is a crucial factor to consider in selecting investments.

The nonfinancial environment is equally important. When we select a job, for instance, we take on a whole new environment—new people, established relationships with which we must reckon, the corporate culture, stress levels that can affect our health, and competitive pressures, as well as the opportunity to grow, the option to win, and many other positive factors that may have persuaded us to take the job in the first place. In most cases, we consider all of these elements without realizing it. When we become conscious of them, we are in a better position to act.

The purpose of all of these selection criteria is to put us in a better position to act in concert with our goals.

Financial Categories

Lumping like investments together enables us to look at the overall picture more easily. Such categorizing is useful because all the assets in a given category tend to behave in a similar fashion. As a result, their appropriateness as a function of risk/reward, diversification, or liquidity can be judged more easily. Also, by applying the criteria we just discussed, you can discard whole categories right at the outset, thus eliminating hundreds of individual options—a significant advantage in the weeding-out process!

With regard to financial options, we can gather all the stocks in one bin, bonds in a different bin, real estate in another, cash and cash equivalents in another, and commodities in still another. Oil wells and natural resources can be stashed in a category called tangible assets. These groups can be further condensed into just four categories:

- **Cash and cash equivalents.** Typically viewed as holding areas, these options include bank accounts, money market funds, certificates of deposit, commercial paper, Treasury bills, and brokerage accounts that enable clients to park funds in these kinds of places.
- **Fixed income and debt instruments.** These investments offer relative safety because they represent the "fixed liability" of the federal government, state or local authorities, or corporations. Examples are U.S. government bonds, state or municipality

and high-grade corporate notes, and the preferred stock of utility companies. This category would also include funds that manage bonds, notes, or preferred stocks.
- **Equities.** These investments include the stocks of corporations (representing ownership in the corporations) and mutual funds that manage stocks. Clearly, the risk level varies widely, as do the funds themselves. Some are purposely speculative while others have quite conservative goals. In other words, the buyer has a choice.
- **Tangible assets.** This final group consists of assets such as real estate, futures, metals, and natural resources like oil and gas. Investments may take the form of limited partnerships, corporations, or mutual funds, to name only three possibilities.

This particular breakdown is arbitrary but has been widely used for years. You may choose a different set of categories. Whichever you select, the purpose should be the same—to simplify. You will be enhancing the effectiveness of this approach by also bringing a sense of who you are to the selection process.

The advantage of these particular "lumps" is that they address broad needs. Income, a frequent investment goal, is addressed by the category of fixed income instruments. The goal of capital appreciation is met by equities and tangible assets, though these categories have different risk levels and levels of liquidity. People use cash and cash equivalents for parking uninvested funds on their way to investment in other places or as a safe place to wait out a perceived storm on the horizon.

DECIDING ON PERCENTAGES TO ALLOCATE PER CATEGORY

After you choose among categories, and *before* you decide on specific investments, you need to figure out what percentage of your resources you want to allocate to any given category. One person might decide, as a first cut, to put 20 percent in cash, 50 percent in fixed income, and 30 percent in equities. Making such a calculation allows you to think and "feel" your way through allocating your funds before you get muddled in evaluating a specific stock, bond, or money market fund. You can then apply the selection criteria in the light of how you will be allocating your funds.

Next, look at the amount to be put into a given group, say 30 percent in equities (in a $10,000 resource pool, this would amount to $3,000), and begin to consider specific investment

in this category, with or without an advisor. The example at the end of this chapter will elaborate on this process. My purpose here is simply to show that these decisions are nothing to be feared.

ASSESSING THE CATEGORIES BASED ON RISK/REWARD AND LIQUIDITY

Two popular measures of the appropriateness of a prospective investment are risk/reward and liquidity. The following table is a brief comparison of the categories based on these factors. While it

RISK/REWARD AND LIQUIDITY RATINGS

	RISK	REWARD	LIQUIDITY	ADVANTAGES	DISADVANTAGES
Cash and cash equivalents	Low	Low	High	Safety—some insured; modest return; most are predictable	Mostly taxable; return fluctuates; inflation risks
Fixed income and debt: notes; discrete bonds; preferred and convertible preferred stocks; fixed income funds	Moderate*	Moderate*	Moderate* to high	Liquid; constant return; deflation hedge; some tax-exempt	Inflation risk; interest-rate and market sensitive
Equities: stocks; mutual stock funds; restricted stocks	Moderate to high	Moderate to high	Moderate to high	Higher return potential; often inflation hedge	Little deflation hedge; cycle sensitive; more risk
Tangible assets: natural resources (oil, gas, etc.); real estate; futures	High	Moderate to high	Low	Leverageable; inflation hedge	Some are tax sensitive; requires special knowledge

Note: This table represents typical conditions. In special conditions, departures do occur. For example, although savings in an S&L are insured, depositors might have to wait years for a payout in a crash situation.

*Bonds can be high risk under certain conditions. However, losses are usually momentary because all bonds that mature do so, unlike stocks, at face or par value.

doesn't cover all the criteria, it is generally informative. Note, too, that these characteristics can change in certain economic environments—witness the bond crashes in 1987 and 1989. People who had regarded bonds as "safe" because they were debt instruments, as opposed to equity, suffered losses if they sold out.

Each assessment has exceptions at one time or another. For example, although bonds are typically considered safe as an instrument, the so-called junk bonds may not be worth much during periods of economic contraction when the issuing company cannot service the debt. Municipal bonds are also considered safe, but during New York City's solvency crisis, the city had difficulty honoring its debt.

For the most part, however, the table gives an accurate overview. The important thing is to remember that when we invest financially, we are a part of something bigger—like the economy—and that external influences can either aid or hurt our investments. Becoming first aware, and then informed, is the only defense. This applies nonfinancially also. At any specific time when a purchase or sale is contemplated, it is helpful to consult an advisor for the current, detailed picture.

Now, with regard to the task of putting all this on paper, you hopefully will have formed a network. You have possibly decided on an advisor or advisors and have begun to integrate the financial news into your life planning process. Here is what you may be facing: One investment house, based on their economic research, suggests that interest rates will drop 1 percent during the next five months, a scenario in which municipal bonds should prosper. Another prominent house, forecasting steady growth and no recession, promotes stocks. Still another group, not altogether sure how events will unfold, advises hedging your bets by buying both stocks and bonds, so that you can respond to either a recession or near-term growth. What do you do? While attempting to perceive how near-term markets will behave, you also bring your very personal goals and other criteria to bear. In this way you align your choices with who you are instead of using the economic environment as the only criterion. You earn money to live life rather than live to earn money. Be conscious that this is what you are doing when you connect your investment choices with who you are.

For example, after discovering that service was a core quality, a man I know chose to retire to spend time with a nonprofit group. Consequently, he now focuses on investments that provide steady income rather than on those that offer less predictable gains at higher risk. An example of a completely different but equally valid kind is offered by a young engineer who wants to express his creativity and freedom by starting his own company. He therefore invests everything in a new start-up company, an investment representing high risk in an illiquid asset (the stock of his own firm). Because both men see the link between what they are doing and the way in which they invest, they have a deep sense of rightness about their activities. It is this sense of rightness that you will be seeking as you make investment choices.

MOVING FROM CATEGORIES TO SPECIFIC CHOICES

Categories are useful for simplifying the selection process; they bring us closer to making specific choices. But no one invests in categories. The next task is to select specific investments within each category of choice. To be sure that we find suitable investments, we will again apply the selection criteria.

Suppose, for example, that you have chosen the categories of cash equivalents, conservative fixed income and debt instruments, and lower-risk equities. You can totally ignore all tangible asset options as well as all the stock and bond possibilities that represent higher risk. This greatly narrows the field and makes any conversation with an advisor much more to the point, because you can demonstrate that you know where you are and where you are going and how your choices are tied to who you are. This ability represents self-empowerment. **Own that power.**

Whether you use advisors or not, look to invest in quality. Be sure to express your goals. Mind the admonitions about diversification, and keep in mind any particular needs or advantages of your age group. Be open to the current and possible future behavior of the economy, be true to your feelings about risking, and live within your resources. If you have special investment knowledge in a given area, count it as a nonfinancial resource and be open to ways of using it profitably in line with your goals. Remember that knowledge and familiarity lower risk and heighten the odds for success.

Nonfinancial Categories

The difficulty in defining nonfinancial investment categories is that we are all so individual. Each of us needs to become who we really are and doing so can take many different paths. Nonetheless, I offer some of the more popular categories as an aid to creating your own. The procedure is much the same as for financial investments. You first select the categories in which you want to invest, then choose a working area within each category, and then a specific action to achieve your goal. If health is the category, for example, exercise might be the working area, and swimming the specific intervention.

As with financial investments, you can use the eight selection criteria to help you choose among categories and to make specific choices within categories. In the nonfinancial realm, however, there is one additional criterion that is crucial—the degree of excitement or interest any particular investment awakens in you. Think of how differently we approach activities that interest us than those we feel apathetic about—the difference is in how alive we feel. So always apply that test as a most telling measure of an investment's appropriateness.

HEALTH

Typically we don't pay much attention to health until we become ill. Then we devote large amounts of money, time, and energy to it. Illness captures our attention because it gets in our way. When we have health, we tend not to honor it. When we lose health, we are reminded of how important it is.

What is *your* relationship to health? Is it on your list of goals in some form?

Investing in health can take many forms: exercise for general physical well-being, weight control, and stress reduction; diet for weight control as well as self-confidence; meditation for quieting the mind, stress reduction and giving up smoking; yoga as both exercise and meditation. Increasingly we see the link between mental and physical health—for example in the way that diet and weight loss can build self-esteem.

RELATIONSHIPS

This is a big category because we all forge ties to people who mean a lot to us. Close relationships are different from the contacts we make in the course of everyday life. Our relationships include friends, spouses, partners—anyone we would define as "someone who would listen to us without judgment." We also have a particular relationship with ourselves.

There are many, many ways of investing in this category. They may include deciding to get to know someone better, following up on a friend in need, or investing in extended counseling or therapy for ourselves.

EDUCATION

Education is a central nonfinancial asset for many of us. When younger, we tend not to value it. When we get older, we acknowledge its importance. Those who lack education tend to envy those who have it.

As with the other categories, education can be attained in many ways. Formally, it can be gained by full-time or part-time attendance at the high school, college, or postgraduate level. On the informal side, education is represented by travel, reading, educational audio- and videotapes, correspondence courses, night school, learning on the job, etc.

If you choose education as one of your categories, how might you invest in it? Suppose you were interested in languages; learning a new language would be your working area within the category of education. Then take the choice one step further. Your learning options include listening to language tapes in the car on the way to work every day, enrolling in classes, hiring a tutor, exchanging lessons with someone who wants to learn English, or even spending some time in another country. Once you choose a specific plan, you are ready to act.

"SELF" ISSUES

Many people choose this category and for any number of different reasons. You might want to work on self-image, on power issues (or on a lack of power), on disposition, ability to be flexible, or self-discipline. The list of options is long. If an improved self-image was your goal, you might select counseling as the working area and an appointment with a counselor as the specific action

taken within this category. If physical flexibility was an issue, you might choose to address it in a yoga group. Finding one and signing up would be specific actions to start your investment working for you.

AGE

Many issues come up around age and aging, probably as many for the young as for the old. For some, financial concerns are troublesome. In these cases, since financial assets are basically nonfinancially driven, the nonfinancial balance sheet is the place to start.

At some level all of these categories and issues are connected, as we know. For instance, concern with age may manifest itself in a self-image problem, tying this category to the previous one dealing with self issues. A working area of health might also include an intervention noted under this category.

LIFE QUALITIES

We worked on life qualities in the chapter on vision and purpose. As a result of that work or from working with your nonfinancial balance sheet, you may have developed an interest in deepening a specific quality (for instance, peace) in your life. Peace would be the working area, and anything from learning to meditate to walking in the woods might qualify as an action toward reaching that goal.

The action choices are completely individual. Make a note of the ones that connect most closely with the qualities you seek.

CONTACTS

Meeting and becoming involved with people is a goal that most of us have at some level. For most of us, loneliness is a nonfinancial liability. People are essential for almost anything we want to do. We make contacts at work for business reasons; we do it at home for social reasons. As we saw in the chapter on tools, networking is one way of making contacts, and networks are important to True Wealth.

Examples of typical working areas in this category are the office, a church group, or a network. The specific action you take to further contacts might be joining a church or forming a network of friends.

ℵEXERCISE
COMPLETING THE FINANCIAL AND NONFINANCIAL INVESTMENT WORKSHEETS

In this exercise you will actually select financial and nonfinancial investments. Start with either worksheet and begin to note the categories of importance to the goals you have developed. Complete both financial and nonfinancial categories before proceeding to the next level.

FINANCIAL OPTIONS WORKSHEET

Date _____

Categories		Choosing		
		Category	Percentage	Specific Choice
Cash and Cash Equivalents				
• Treasury bills		_____	___	_____
• Commercial paper				
• Money market funds				_____
• Savings accounts				_____
Fixed Income and Debt Instruments	Selection Criteria:	_____	___	_____
• Bonds and Treasury notes	Goals			_____
• Income stocks	Risk tolerance			_____
• Fixed income funds	Resources			_____
	Age			
	Investment quality			
Equities	Diversification	_____	___	_____
• Listed stocks	Special knowledge			_____
• Stock mutual funds	Environment			_____
• Restricted stocks				_____
Tangible Assets		_____	___	_____
• Real estate				
• Natural resources				_____
• Gold and metals				_____
• Futures				_____

Nonfinancial Options Worksheet

Date _____

Categories of Choice   Specific Selections

                                           Working Area   **Specific Choice**

_____   _____   _____

_____   _____   _____

_____   ➜ | The eight selection criteria; level of excitement or interest | ➜   _____   _____

_____   _____   _____

_____   _____   _____

_____   _____   _____

The next level may require the counsel of your advisors. For example, you may want advice regarding which mutual fund is best for a given need. There are many choices, and you may not be comfortable making the final selection on your own. Moreover, the final selection within a category may require research, so completing the worksheets will probably not be something you can do at a single sitting. To help you, I have included an example (in the next section) of how a husband and wife made their selections based on the guidelines in the forms.

A reminder: The selection process works best when we connect who we are and how we feel with what we choose. This is a connective process. Being really clear about our goals (and how we chose them) will guide us to make the right choices.

Financial goals are often nonfinancially driven. Our investable financial and nonfinancial net worth is the result of past choices. Our future finances and sense of well-being will emerge from how we invest in the present. We are in control and we are fully responsible.

The Steps That One Couple Took to Make Their Investment Decisions

Brian and Anne are in their late forties. Brian has a well-paying job with a stable company in a sound industry. He is highly regarded at work. Anne has a college degree with a major in art. She has been a housewife and mother during their entire marriage. They have one child who is now out of college and earning on his own. They are buying their own home, and want to become financially independent in fifteen years. Both have chosen the qualities of freedom and peace. Anne selected the quality of beauty as well.

Goals

To achieve financial freedom, they want to accumulate $500,000 beyond the value of their home, in addition to their current net worth of $109,000. Their home will be paid off within fifteen years.

They both value health and have decided to exercise and watch their diets. Brian has had some lower-back pain over the years. He is a weekend exerciser. Anne swims now and then. They want to be more purposeful about exercise and to learn about foods in order to stay healthy.

Anne's major goal is to become an architect. She plans to attend graduate school and wants to start straightaway.

Both Anne and Brian want to increase their level of intimacy with each other as a route to feeling more at peace. For each of their goals, they have set a time frame that will help them measure progress.

Risk Tolerance

Neither Brian nor Anne has a propensity for taking major risks. Brian's father frequently spoke about the Depression, and the memory of his father's suffering has caused Brian to be financially very cautious. In sports and other aspects of their lives, neither Anne nor Brian has taken up activities that could be considered remotely dangerous. Their relationship has been their biggest risk to date, and Anne has been more willing than Brian to risk in this regard. It was she who first called for greater intimacy.

Resources

Brian and Anne worked hard to compile their financial and nonfinancial statements, which follow on pages 160 and 161.

Discussion and Decisions

Brian and Anne have looked at their joint goals and reviewed the qualities they both seek. They agree that Anne's graduate work and career are of primary importance. Because they do not have a high tolerance for risk, they decide to remain in fairly conservative financial investments. They are still young enough to take advantage of compounding. To learn about the current economic environment, they decide to build a network for discussing financial issues and opportunities. They also intend to seek out an advisor whom they can consult before making any new investments.

Reviewing their financial balance sheet, they decide that their conservative investment in bonds represents a good safety net. Their bonds have staggered maturity dates, making it possible to sell them when funds are needed, and they carry little risk in normal times. Only the couple's stocks are at risk. Anne and Brian agree, therefore, that their bonds and stocks are the resources they have available for investment. (Because their assets are conservative and they have a low debt-to-asset ratio, they don't need to diversify at this time.)

In looking at their liabilities, they realize that the balance due on their credit cards is costing them 18 percent per year. Their car loan and other miscellaneous loans (for the TV, etc.) are above their comfort level. They therefore agree to pay off most of these high-interest loans.

The couple estimate that it will take Anne two years to prepare for her new career and that it will cost $20,000 in all:

- $15,000 for graduate school
- $3,000 to complete the prerequisites at a local college
- $2,000 for commuting, books, computer, supplies, etc.

They see Anne's further education as a nonfinancial investment that will have financial as well as intangible benefits. They believe that both will benefit from it. They decide to earmark the needed funds and put them in a safe investment haven. This leads them to their first financial move: they sell $10,000 worth of the $15,000 they have in individual stocks and put $5,000 into high-quality bonds having short maturities. In this way they lower their risk and have a total of $30,000 in high-grade, liquid bonds available to pay for Anne's education when the funds are needed. They use the remaining $5,000 to pay off their car and most of their miscellaneous loans. Later they plan to sell the remaining $5,000 in individual stocks and to purchase shares in a stock mutual fund recommended by their advisor.

They do not have any retirement plan yet. However, after learning about the benefits of a tax-deferred plan and the advantages of tax-deferred compounding, they decide to join the 401(K) plan offered by Brian's company. Their contributions will come from earnings. They will also continue to save money in a savings account or money market fund.

When Anne finishes her degree in three years, the family will have two incomes. They already enjoy health and life insurance benefits from Brian's employer. They decide, therefore, that since they have already provided for Anne's education through their funded reserve, they will feel comfortable putting a bit more capital into higher-risk, higher-return investments, rather

Anne and Brian's Financial Balance Sheet as of 1/5/90

ASSETS		LIABILITIES AND NET WORTH	
Cash	$1,500	Home Loan	$30,000
Savings	1,000	Credit Card Balance	1,500
		Car Loan	4,000
Stocks	15,000	Misc. Loans	2,000
Bonds	25,000		
Paintings	7,000	Total Liabilities	37,500
Home	85,000		
Cars and Miscellaneous	12,000	Net Worth	109,000
Total Assets	**$146,500**	**Total Liabilities and Net Worth**	**$146,500**

Note: The statement shows that Anne and Brian have not been very adventurous. They have never been in commodities (but who has?). Anne would like to have more paintings, but their budget will not allow it. They have been a saving couple. Early on they paid off their college bills, and they are not interested in having new cars or in using their credit cards to buy luxuries. They have a minimum cash reserve for emergencies and are building net worth by paying down their mortgage. Their house has appreciated at a handsome rate in the past; they hope it will continue to do so.

Anne and Brian's Nonfinancial Balance Sheet as of 1/5/90

ASSETS	LIABILITIES AND NET WORTH
Education: College degrees	
Health: Generally good	Brian is overweight; neither exercises regularly
Relationship: Generally excellent	Would like more intimacy
Family: Good ties with their daughter and in-laws	
Friends: Each has good ones	Perhaps a few "enemies"
Contacts: They have started a network to aid them in financial planning.	
Hobbies: Anne paints and designs dresses and furniture; Brian has built some furniture that Anne designed. Both enjoy music, dancing, and going out to dinner.	
Personal:	
Do not hold grudges	Impatient
Average physical strength	Tend to be gullible
Creative	Not self-motivated
Good public speakers	Need lots of sleep
Average energy	Poor with foreign languages
Can carry a tune	
Good writers	

Note: Although for simplicity's sake I combined Brian's and Anne's balance sheets, it is best not to do this so that you can see who is who. Also, this example is a very abbreviated one.

than trying to manage a stock portfolio themselves. They will make these investments as savings permit. They investigate a real estate option but hesitate because of its lack of liquidity and the "all-in-one-basket consequence." REITs are ruled out because they do not have a reputation for consistent performance. Moreover, Anne and Brian are not knowledgeable in this area and are unable to find an advisor who knows much either. Collectibles, high-risk ventures (such as an offer of stock from a friend who is starting a company), and commodities are all far too risky. They seek an investment that will provide the liquidity they may need and that will offer the potential for appreciation.

By applying the selection criteria, Anne and Brian have been able to focus on the three categories of cash equivalents, fixed-income and debt instruments, and equities, and then to make specific moves within these categories. All this planning has taken a lot of time, but they now feel as though they have a grasp of their world and of the connection between the investment process and who they are. They have become actively involved in shaping their own financial future.

Regarding retirement, Brian and Anne estimate that by investing in Brian's retirement plan each year and by saving after Anne is earning, they will be able to meet their long-term financial investment goals. There will be sacrifices—no new cars every two years, no luxuries. Someone in their network suggests that this conservative approach seems foolish because it does not fully optimize their assets. Although this is true, they have chosen to fund Anne's education because in this way Brian can honor her goal. The point is that each of us must do what feels right. Brian's action is a nonfinancial expression of support that holds meaning within the relationship. If Anne didn't work, she would not become all she may choose to be. The money they will spend on her education, or the money she will eventually earn, is less important than her expressing creativity in her field.

Nonfinancially, Brian and Anne decide to begin exercising regularly—she by swimming at a neighborhood pool and he by running. They will also invest in their health by eating more carefully. Because long work hours and stress have created distance in their relationship, they agree to make time to be together each week, and decide to sign up for a couples workshop at their church.

FINANCIAL OPTIONS WORKSHEET

Date 6/15/90

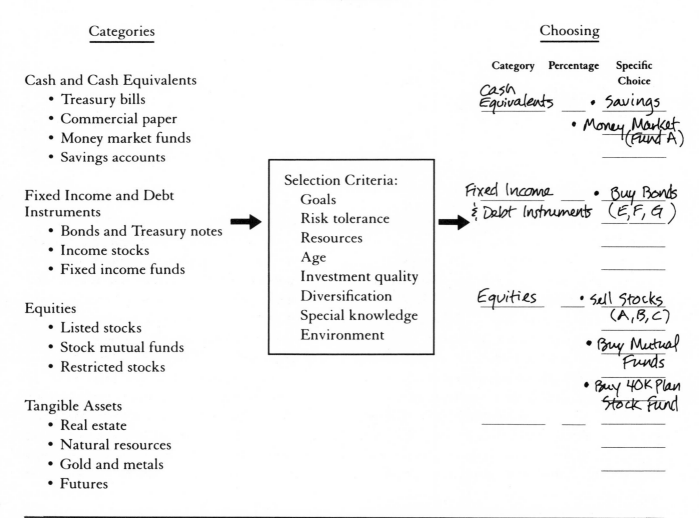

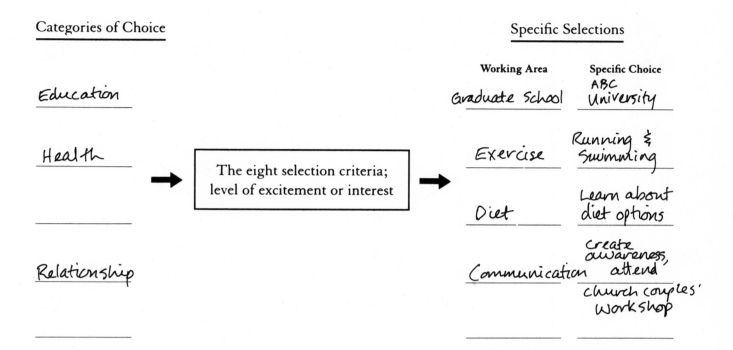

Nonfinancial Options Worksheet

Date 6/15/90

Categories of Choice

Specific Selections

	Working Area	Specific Choice
Education	Graduate School	ABC University
Health	Exercise	Running & Swimming
	Diet	Learn about diet options
Relationship	Communication	Create awareness, attend church couples' workshop

The eight selection criteria; level of excitement or interest

---

Their financial and nonfinancial plans are shown in the accompanying worksheets.

We want to do what we do because it reflects who we really are. That is what brings a sense of rightness to our lives. That is why there are no sure answers about investment policy. All of us may be climbing the same mountain, but we are on different paths.

For example, another couple with assets similar to Brian and Anne's might take a more aggressive approach, borrowing on all their assets (including their home) and putting it all at higher risk to earn a higher return. Still another couple, desiring freedom in their life, might put all of their assets into starting a company.

There is no right way to invest. There is only *your* way, which relates to the goals that form a bridge between who you are and what you do. Becoming aware of this connection is at the core of the True Wealth investment process because it is the way to relate the more philosophical aspects of vision with the nuts and bolts of everyday living.

Take time to explore your choices. If you come up against a wall, look at what is standing in the way. It may be fear, the need to stop and network, or the need to work something out with a spouse. Or you may simply be unclear about the qualities you are pursuing and how they connect. Just discovering the source of the blockage is partway to the solution.

A life plan is a formal connection between
you and others regarding your intention
to manage your own wealth.

11

YOUR LIFE PLAN

You have done a lot of work to get to this point. In becoming aware of your **vision and purpose**, you wrote notes and a statement about them. You know the qualities you want to express because they are the ones that link who you are with what you do every day.

Working from your purpose, you developed specific **goals** that describe how you intend to go about doing what you do. These are divided into financial and nonfinancial categories.

You took an inventory of your financial and nonfinancial **resources** to see what was available to support the accomplishment of your goals. This exercise made you aware of the ties between who you are and what you have.

Exploring **risk taking** was the next input. You noted financial and nonfinancial risks you had taken in the past, risks you are taking now, and risks you would—or would not—take in the future. You began to see risk as opportunity rather

than just as danger. Out of this came a sense of how you will use risk as a financial and nonfinancial means of completing your goals.

You then looked at all the **possibilities** and began to make selections with the help of **advisors, investment tools,** and an awareness about the economy and your nonfinancial **environment.** This is where it all came together. You chose financial and nonfinancial categories in line with your goals, risk-taking tolerance, and resources. Then you narrowed the field to specific choices.

The final steps in the True Wealth process involve writing up a plan, implementing it, and following up to test whether its assumptions are sound. Monitoring results has another reason— to see if a sense of well-being develops. After all, a sense of True Wealth is what we are after, and the plan is a tool for achieving that sense. The plan-writing steps are represented graphically in the following diagram.

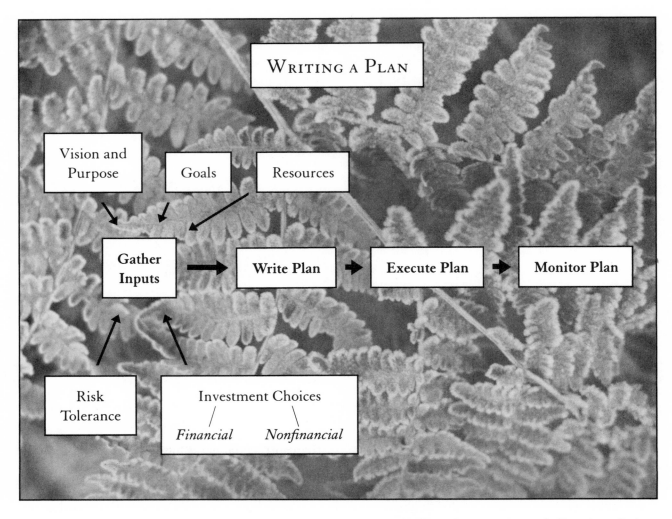

WRITING A PLAN

Vision and Purpose

Goals

Resources

Gather Inputs → Write Plan → Execute Plan → Monitor Plan

Risk Tolerance

Investment Choices

Financial   *Nonfinancial*

Why Put the Plan into Writing?

Besides being a principle tool with which to obtain goals, a written plan is well worth doing for several other reasons.

1. A written plan fosters accurate communication with an advisor or a spouse. It is so easy to talk and so difficult to write. Writing forces you to focus. Communication is a form of connection that you have worked with during this entire True Wealth effort. The nonfinancial process of communication is probably more important than the financial content. A plan ties many of the pieces together, thus creating options.

2. A plan gives a sense of direction. It is a written document that reaffirms your heading. It expresses intention. When you know where you are and where you want to go, you are already most of the way to your destination. Too many people have no idea where they are in the world, much less where they would like to journey. As a result, life buffets them about and they end up, like fall leaves, where the wind blows them.

3. A plan provides a way for you to reach a consensus with someone with whom you share life. Its execution may reveal conflicts that can then be resolved. As we have seen, one spouse may defer the use of a resource

toward his or her goal in favor of the other's objective. This sort of give-and-take is a part of relationship and underscores the element of connection that is at the heart of the whole process.

4. Because the plan is written, you can compare results with assumptions. Nothing stands still; everything is in a state of constant change. This means that your plan, too, must change if it is to reflect reality. For instance, change is suggested when something you thought would happen does not. Monitoring outcome enables you to take corrective action when it is needed.

5. Finally, **writing is the first step of action**. Until now, you have planned. From now on, you will act and follow up on that action.

Note that writing the plan is not such a large task as it may sound, since you have already completed a lot of it in doing exercises along the way. Use a looseleaf binder or notebook so that you can easily amend and update the plan.

A Table of Contents for Your Plan

The following table of contents is meant as a basic structure on which you can build your plan. Add to it to suit your needs. You will want to insert all the important aspects that will shape your future as you continue to become who you already are. It is like trimming a Christmas tree. Hang whatever ornaments will express "Christmas" for you.

VISION AND PURPOSE

Use your notes to write a short summary of your vision and purpose. If you are preparing the plan as a couple, each of you should express your own individuality in this section. Write individual summaries of life qualities and how these quali-

ties relate to what you have chosen (or will choose) to do.

The very process of writing reinforces the awareness of connection between the inner self and the outer world.

GOALS

Return to your notes and worksheets from this section. It was here that you linked the world of your hopes and dreams to the one where you pay bills, go to work, tolerate traffic jams, and otherwise deal with all the little things that can rattle you throughout a day.

Add your goals to the plan. Be sure that they are specific, measurable, and time-based actions that, when complete, will reflect your vision. These are the tasks that will edge you toward well-being.

If you are part of a couple, some of your goals will be joint ones (such as buying a home) and others will be individual (such as swimming for health). Write all of these goals down. You might put the joint goals on one page and the individual ones on separate pages under the name of the person whose task it will be. Be sure to do one set for the financial category and one for the nonfinancial. Because each goal has a specific completion date, you will refer to the plan often to see whether you are on schedule—and hopefully you will find out why if you are not.

RESOURCES

This section, too, is really already written. You have already listed financial and nonfinancial resources to which you can turn for support in accomplishing goals. Pull these together for insertion in this part of the plan. Remember that your balance sheets are statements as of a given date. As time passes, they become obsolete and you will need to do new ones.

Keep reviewing and adding to your lists of resources. Since financial assets are basically non-financially derived, the list of intangible resources is particularly important to maintain.

Also, look at the liability side to find opportunities. Illness can be re-addressed as encouragement toward health. Heavy financial debt can cause you to refocus on liquidity by lowering debt. Insights here can spawn new goals to be achieved with the support of your resources. It is all linked. Almost anything can be changed, provided you are aware of it.

RISK TAKING

As there is no safe path to anywhere, we face risk as a matter of living. The issue is how we see and handle risk.

Review the exercises you did to explore your tolerance for risking. Stay within your comfort zone while remaining open to stretching a bit to see the opportunity end of the risk/reward polarity. Remember, though, that there are no judgments. Just be who you are. If you connect with yourself, you will act appropriately.

For those of you in a couple, be aware that goals almost always involve risk and that the two of you will see the risk differently. Compromises are an inevitable part of living, anyway. What is new is the greater awareness you now bring to the negotiating process. Resolution in this area will result in a closer relationship because the process demands communication, which opens all sorts of opportunity in and of itself.

Although in the past you may have taken risks unknowingly, today you will be more alert. That change is powerful. You will see the results of your power in the actions you choose to take.

ASSUMPTIONS

We act on information and feelings. Sometimes our assumptions are right and at other times wrong. A factor we thought was critical (such as falling interest rates) may not be what drove a given investment after all. Our belief about a medical intervention helping a particular illness may have been unfounded. The expectations we held for a financial investment (the purchase of a stock, for instance) or for a nonfinancial effort (learning a language) may not have been met.

We live in a changing world. Since everything is linked at some level, we are bound occasionally to miss being aware of a force that influences our

financial or nonfinancial investments either up or down.

The important thing is to learn from the results. We do this best by recording the assumptions made at the time an action is taken.

I am a general partner in a real estate venture—a large plot of raw land on which we built a building to a tenant's specifications. We missed. The investment is going "sideways." Cash flow from the tenant pays the bills, but the town has fallen on hard times (the result of a random event in the real estate industry) and no one wants to buy the property from us as an investment. We made assumptions about future growth that turned out not to be valid. But we learned from the experience by reflecting back on the assumptions we made when we bought into the project.

To complete this part of your life plan, look over the financial and nonfinancial investment selections you have made and search for the assumptions underlying each one. Some will be nonfinancial, for example the feeling of risk you think you will experience in taking a particular action. Others will be purely financial, for instance those relating to interest rate movements, inflation levels, corporate profits, and the like.

Write down your assumptions for each investment you intend to make. You can look back and see whether they were in line with what actually happened. You can judge how economic events, as they unfolded, affected your financial investments so that you can learn from them. Remember that you can learn as much from what goes astray as from what you do correctly.

ADVISORS

Who are they? Why did you select them? What part have they played in the past, and what role will they continue to play? List your advisors by specialty. Include "unpaid" advisors like friends.

Since you acted on their counsel, they form a part of your assumption base.

Be sure to list the nonfinancial advisors as well as the financial ones. As we have seen, the intangible aspects of life planning are powerful.

Current advisors will sometimes lead to new ones; keep an eye out for those whose energies can be helpful to you. By the same token, you will want to be alert to how *you* can be supportive to others. You both engage advisors and are an advisor. This is an important aspect of the nonfinancial side of this coin.

SPECIFIC INVESTMENT MOVES

Since the plan has not been implemented yet, your list of investments will represent only intentions at this point. Incorporate the data from the financial and nonfinancial options worksheets that you completed in the chapter on possibilities. Amplify them if need be. For example, you may have noted an intention to make a real estate investment but did not have a particular one in mind at the time. Update your plan as you have more information and make specific choices. Changes are easy because of the looseleaf format.

In any case, be as specific as you can. The whole purpose of the possibilities chapter was to center on a choice. Therefore, note the exact moves. For instance, sell stock A at 32 or better and buy fund B at market price. Apply to the following three graduate schools by October first (name the schools).

ODDS AND ENDS

For ease of reference, and because this is a *life* plan, you will want to note where important documents are stored—wills, stock certificates, passports, certificates of ownership, title to your home, marriage license, birth certificates, notes receivable, tax support documents, and the like.

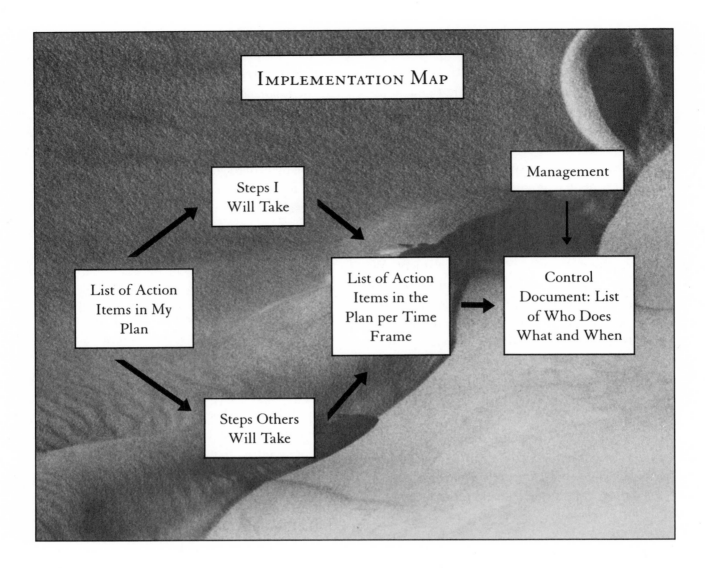

IMPLEMENTATION MAP

Such items are often kept in a safe deposit box, but many people also store them at home in a fireproof file. Wherever you keep them, maintain a current inventory in your plan book.

Implementation—Intention Moves Toward Action

As the accompanying map shows, implementation is really a management issue. You will have to decide how much of the implementation process you will do and how much others will carry out per your instructions. Because your plan in-

cludes specific action steps with due dates and assignments of responsibility, it is an efficient control document. It shows the financial and non-financial assignments you gave yourself and others for each of the investment selections you have made. Writing everything down makes for a clean approach. Nothing is left to speculation. Each player knows his or her role and the time frame for carrying it out. As advisors report to you, you can track the completion of action steps assigned to them, just as you note your own progress with the steps you chose to carry out yourself. The plan enables you to determine where you are at any given time.

For example, your financial list might look like this:

1. Call broker and place a sell order for stock A @ 32.
2. Upon sale, invest proceeds plus $4,000 in mutual fund B.
3. Follow up on confirmations of these sales.
4. Place order for Treasury bonds in amount of $10,000.

Your nonfinancial list might look like this:

1. Apply for graduate school.
2. Call attorney for appointment re will.
3. Schedule time for hobby—contact others who enjoy the same interest.
4. Call X to get advice on diet.
5. Start a running program.

These lists do not yet assign responsibility for action, though for many of the tasks the agent is obvious. To be clear, however, you would write the assignments beside the tasks, along with completion dates. Your expanded list might look like this:

ACTION ITEM	DUE DATE	PERSON RESPONSIBLE
Financial Tasks:		
(1) Sell stock A @ 32	4/5/90	Broker
(2) Put proceeds in fund B	4/10/90	Broker
Etc.		
Nonfinancial Tasks:		
(1) Apply to graduate school	7/3/90	Me
(2) Draw up will	5/5/90	Attorney
Etc.		

With this document, you are in control. You also have an overview of what is going on. For a graphic view of this, you might want to return to the chapter on goals and refer to the Mind Map (page 50), which shows another way of exhibiting the tasks that are to be done at any one time. This is useful for those who, like me, are visual and hate lists.

Monitor and Feedback Loop

You have done a lot in developing a written plan and implementing it. However, it is not enough.

Change brought about by random events can alter any plan. Our world was far different on October 20, 1988, than on October 20, 1987, after the Dow had plummeted over 500 points in a single day. A car accident—a nonfinancial event—can change a life in an instant, as can the loss of a job or the challenge of a new job, a divorce or a marriage, retirement, or a high cholesterol count or a heart attack.

Life is always changing, and we need to be nimble enough to change with it. Consequently, we will need to monitor both the actions we take and changing environmental influences. Early feedback on our progress will enable us to remain on our course of following our goals.

How do we go about the monitoring process?

Like implementation, monitoring is a management function. Some things we will monitor ourselves; others we will want to delegate. We ourselves are probably in the best position to judge personal matters, such as how we are doing in a relationship or at school. Others can possibly do better at commenting on the status of the economy and its likely impact on us.

Follow-up is really a loop. It brings us back full circle to our vision and purpose, as the Investment Process map indicated. If you decide to change your goals because of a shift in direction (retirement, a major career change, divorce or marriage, etc.), then many of your action items will change. If, at the other end of the process, conditions —such as a stock downturn—alter the output from an investment, you might want to take corrective action at the investment level but would have no need to alter a basic goal.

The aspect that never changes is the expression of who you are in terms of life qualities. The issue, as always, is to relate who you are to what you do through goals that outline how the doing will get done.

Look again at the sample control document on page 171. By expanding it a bit, you can also use it as an efficient monitoring tool. The person responsible for follow-up is noted in a separate column, and how often the item should be monitored is noted in another column. The final column provides space for noting any changes you may deem necessary. In this way, outcome is measured against expectations. Any differences are noted and remedial actions can be taken. Your complete control document might look like the one below.

MONITORING TO KEEP IN TOUCH WITH ENVIRONMENTAL CHANGES

Monitoring events over which we have no control is a substantial part of the task. Within the financial area, for example, it is important to watch the economy. A newspaper or TV report may comment on unemployment figures, a move by the Federal Reserve Board, an international crisis, a retail sales trend. You touch base with your network, which periodically discusses such events. Sensing a change that may affect one of your investments, you elect to act on the insight by selling a stock or bond. Trade imbalances, which may not have set you to thinking before, are suddenly tied to unemployment rates at home. In other words, you begin to see relationships between news items and your investment world.

It isn't necessary to spend a lot of time keeping track of changes. The trick is to sharpen your awareness in a new direction. Chains of events happen all the time, and you react as a matter of course. Now, however, you see events in a connected way that was not available to you earlier. You are able to act with a focus born of seeing the events in the light of goals that might be affected by them.

Nonfinancially, the same thing applies. You keep up with health issues: an article on heart disease triggers diet changes; when someone mentions that a computer screen can affect your eyes, you listen because you use a computer. A TV program on parenting catches your attention because it touches on family issues that you listed among your nonfinancial goals.

MONITORING AS A MEANS OF CONTINUED LEARNING

Another key benefit of monitoring is that it provides an opportunity to learn. Learning, or education, is many things; it is a tool, a resource, a

ACTION ITEM	DUE DATE	PERSON RESPONSIBLE	FOLLOW-UP	HOW OFTEN?	PROPOSED CHANGE
Financial Tasks: (1) Sell stock A @ 32 Etc.	4/5/90	Broker	Me	Monthly	
Nonfinancial Tasks: (1) Apply to graduate school Etc.	7/3/90	Me	Me	Report card dates	

goal to be pursued. Always continue to learn, both experientially and intellectually. Network and remain aware. Keep searching for people who can advise you. Next to yourself, other people are your most important asset. Consider family, friends, and even enemies as sources of support. (You can learn a lot about yourself from enemies.)

Mistakes are a way of learning, too. Without them, there would be no change, and change is what keeps us alive. If you do not make many mistakes, perhaps you are not risking enough.

Monitoring and feedback loops always highlight error and help us spot change. We all make mistakes, so why worry? The issue is how we react to them, not whether we ever make any. When you make a mistake, therefore, ask yourself, what can I learn from this? How does this affect a goal? But refrain from judgments about yourself or others.

The aim of the True Wealth process is to pursue who you are. When things turn sour, it may well be time to review your goals to see whether they are still appropriate for expressing your purpose right now. Since life qualities can be realized in many different forms, there is no reason to get stuck in any one or two. The issue is often resolved just by changing the form. Sometimes an investment fails not because it was inappropriate, but because of some nonfinancial behavioral issue. Careers can change for the good when people change job functions. I recall one person who was fired for doing a poor job, when the real issue was that he was not in a job that allowed him to use his strengths.

Mistakes contain important messages. They are opportunities for learning.

A Final Personal Word

I have given all sorts of advice from an outside perch, but I have really asked you to ignore it all and to go within to experience who you already are. I have written about money, but I have really been dealing with human values and life qualities. By connecting with who you are, you make the invisible visible. Your nonfinancial balance sheet reveals your real wealth and creates options—and that is empowering. Achieving wealth is, very simply, a never-ending process of continuing awareness that leads to self-knowledge and self-empowerment. Keep in touch with who you are, join the nonfinancial with the financial, be clear about your goals, explore your environment, and use time appropriately.

Namaste.

Glossary

ASSET

A tangible or intangible property that is owned but not necessarily paid for. A home, on which there may be a mortgage, is an example of a tangible property; it is the asset of the person holding the title. A traditional example of an intangible asset would be a patent. However, in this book, nonfinancial aspects of our lives are considered to be assets also. Examples are health, education, relationships, contacts, attitude, travel, and age.

BEAR MARKET

The stock market in a downward trend.

BLUE CHIP STOCK

The listed stock of a large, stable, well-run corporation that has a long history of profits and dividend payouts.

BOND

A debt instrument. When someone buys a bond, he or she is loaning money at a specified rate of interest for a fixed term of time. Most bonds are issued by the U.S. government, municipalities, and corporations. They generally are in amounts of $1,000 or more and are traded (bought and sold) in financial markets. Because they are loans, bonds, unlike stocks, do not represent ownership. Bondholders are therefore creditors and get preference in the event of liquidation.

BULL MARKET

The stock market in an upward trend.

CASH EQUIVALENT

An investment vehicle that offers a high degree of safety and liquidity. Examples are Treasury bills, certificates of deposit, commercial paper, money market funds, and savings accounts.

CERTIFICATE OF DEPOSIT (CD)

An obligation of banks or savings and loan associations at a specific interest rate and for a set period of time, usually three months to a year but sometimes several years.

COLLECTIBLES

Special properties such as fine art, antiques, and stamps that have value because people collect them for one reason or another.

COMMERCIAL PAPER

A short-term promissory note issued by a major corporation and stating a specific interest rate and time period.

COMMODITIES

Tangible items like metals and grains that are traded in large quantities on commodity exchanges. Such investments are specialized, involve large amounts of money, and are extremely risky.

COMMON STOCK

A security of a corporation that represents equity or ownership in the corporation.

COMPOUND INTEREST

Interest earned on interest. When interest has been earned, and when it remains on deposit in the same account in which it was earned, it behaves like capital on which future interest will be calculated. The interest simply gets added to the original principal, and new interest is calculated on an ever larger capital base.

DEFENSIVE INVESTING

Any investment choice that is made in anticipation of difficult times ahead.

DIVERSIFICATION

A way of spreading investment risk by including many different investments in a single investment pool. A mutual fund is a good example. Instead of buying a given stock, an investor can, through a mutual fund, buy an interest in a pool of stocks. In this way the investor is not tied to the fortune—or misfortune—of any given security. Other ways of diversifying include investing in several categories (stocks, bonds, real estate, etc.) and, for real estate investors, buying properties all over the U.S. rather than in just one location.

DIVIDEND

An income payment approved by a corporation's board of directors and made to holders of common or preferred stock.

DOW-JONES INDUSTRIAL AVERAGE

An index representing some thirty of the large blue chip companies traded on the New York Stock Exchange. The Dow-Jones average is based on each company's total capitalization as indicated by its stock price when the average is calculated. The Dow is calculated daily to reflect the trend of common stock prices.

FACE VALUE

See PAR VALUE.

HEDGING

Taking an offsetting position to reduce risk. For example, a farmer may elect to sell an entire corn crop at a negotiated price now for delivery in the future as a means of protection against uncertain market conditions later on.

INDICATOR

A statistic covering business or financial events. Indicators are issued periodically (daily, weekly, monthly) and are generated as an aid to tracking the different elements of the economy. They are a way of keeping abreast of the economic environment and are very helpful for decision making. Some of the more common indicators track trends in interest rates, stock prices, money supply, retail sales, new housing starts, and federal deficits.

INDIVIDUAL RETIREMENT ACCOUNT (IRA)

A retirement plan open to any individuals who have earned income, even if they are covered by some other plan. Each participant's contribution is currently limited to $2,000 a year. Earnings are tax-deferred until retirement age (59½), after which they are taxed when withdrawn at rates current at that time. Tax-law changes now in process may affect the deductibility of IRA contributions.

KEOGH PLAN

A pension plan for self-employed people allowing them to invest a given percentage of their earned income for eventual retirement on a tax-deferred basis. Earnings are not taxed until withdrawal after retirement age (59½), at the rates that apply then.

LEVERAGE

A way of controlling, usually through borrowing, a large asset with a small amount of capital. For example, someone who buys a house with a loan owns (controls) the home with only the down payment, as opposed to owning the home by paying for the whole thing with cash. Because leverage "magnifies," allowing the user to control a larger amount of capital with a smaller amount, it works to emphasize both profits and losses.

LIABILITY

In financial terms, a debt owed to a creditor. A current liability is a debt that must be repaid within one year. A long-term liability is that portion of a debt that is due beyond one year. Thus a home mortgage will typically have a current and a long-term portion to it. As with leveraging, a financial liability can magnify the profit potential of an investment if all goes well. If it does not, it can amplify loss.

A nonfinancial liability, as used in this book, exists when, for example, a person "borrows" from health by neglecting diet and exercise and becomes ill. When someone misuses or fails to nurture a relationship, he or she starts to incur a relationship liability that can end in rupturing the relationship. Other nonfinancial liabilities include procrastination, lack of discipline, enemies, a poor disposition, and anything else that is an obstacle to achieving goals.

LIQUIDITY

The ease and speed with which an asset can be converted into cash with a minimum risk of loss. Taking money out of a savings account can be done in an instant and without loss. By contrast, selling a piece of real estate can take a year or more and the price realized may be less than the original cost. Similarly, although listed stocks can be sold quickly, the price obtained is not always equal to or better than the cost. These examples show different degrees of liquidity.

MONEY MARKET FUND

A mutual fund that has safety and income as its goal. Such a fund typically invests in such short-term investments as CDs, government securities, and commercial paper. It is professionally managed.

MUTUAL FUND

A managed portfolio of selected stocks and bonds that is divided into shares and sold to the public. Mutual funds are popular because they are professionally managed and because shares can be sold at the net asset value (net assets less net liabilities divided by the number of outstanding shares) on short notice. This value is calculated daily and is available in the newspaper or at the offices of the fund by phone.

NAMASTE

A greeting common among Buddhists and Hindus by which one person, speaking from the inner divine part of himself or herself, greets a similar place in the other person.

PAR VALUE

The value of a bond at maturity. Also called *face value*.

PORTFOLIO

The aggregate of securities owned by an individual, a company, or an institution; the whole investment package. A portfolio can consist of stocks, bonds, venture capital stocks, real estate properties, etc., or combinations of investments.

An individual also possesses a nonfinancial portfolio of assets, which can include health, age, education, friends and contacts, belief structures, attitudes, and so on.

PREFERRED STOCK

A class of stock that a corporation may issue that has a prior claim on earnings, and usually on distribution of assets, over common stock.

QUICK RATIO

The relationship of short-term assets to short-term liabilities. Short-term assets are assets that can be converted into cash within thirty days; short-term liabilities must be repaid within one year. The quick ratio is used as a test of liquidity.

RETURN

See YIELD.

RICHES

As used in this book, the material, financial part of True Wealth. Compare WEALTH.

SECURITY

A general term for stocks and bonds.

STOCK, LISTED AND UNLISTED

A listed stock is one for which a quote is readily available, so that it can be traded on a market. An unlisted stock has no readily available quote and can only be bought and sold through private agreements. A typical example of unlisted stock is that of young emerging companies being privately supported by high-risk investors. Sometimes, a large, well-established firm can also have unlisted stocks if the company is privately held. An example is Ford Motor Company before it went public.

TREASURY BILL, BOND, AND NOTE

Obligations of the U.S. government that differ according to the length of time for which they are issued. Treasury bills have maturities of three, six, or twelve months. Treasury bonds mature in from ten to thirty years. Treasury notes mature in from two to seven years.

WEALTH

From the Middle English word *welthe*, meaning well-being, and *weal*, meaning welfare or faring well. Wealth has come to mean a great quantity of material or an abundance of goods. In this book, it is used to include the intangible as well as the material because the nonfinancial aspects of life are central to promoting well-being.

YIELD

The income received from an investment. Also called *return*.